Death and Deliverance

Robert Mason Lee

The Haunting
True Story of the
Hercules Crash at
the North Pole

Macfarlane Walter & Ross
Toronto

Macfarlane Walter & Ross
37 A Hazelton Avenue
Toronto, Canada M5R 2E3

CANADIAN CATALOGUING IN PUBLICATION DATA

Lee, Robert Mason, 1956-
Death and deliverance

ISBN 0-921912-34-X Cloth
ISBN 0-921912-49-8 Paperback

1. Aeronautics — Northwest Territories — Ellesmere
Island — Accidents — 1991.   2. Aeronautics, Military —
Northwest Territories — Ellesmere Island.   3. Survival
after airplane accidents, shipwrecks, etc.   I. Title.

TL 553.5.L43 1992   363.12′492   C92-094265-2

Printed and bound in Canada

In memory of those who did not return
to tell the tale:

Captain John Couch
Captain Judy Trépanier
Master Warrant Officer Tom Jardine
Warrant Officer Robert Grimsley
Master Corporal Roland Pitre

Died in the service of their country
October 30–31, 1991

Contents

Acknowledgments

THIS ACCOUNT would not have been possible without the help of the Canadian Forces. Many of the people I interviewed are mentioned in the text and appendix. The motivations of those who cooperated were refreshing. I was never pressured, directly or indirectly, to give the book a particular slant; those who helped simply expressed the desire that this incredible story be told with vigour and fullness. I hope this rendition is their reward.

I'm grateful to the many survivors, who shared their stories with me. These stories were painful, and I recall more than once interviewing through tears. I hope I have treated them with respect.

The commander of the Canadian Forces Air Transport Group, Brigadier-General Gordon Diamond, provided his own knowledge and opened many doors. His staff, notably executive assistant Captain Jamie van Gelder, made arrangements swiftly and efficiently.

I was given much valuable assistance of a specialized nature. Pilot instructors gave me generous hours of flight time on the CC-130 Hercules simulator in Trenton, Ontario, to experience firsthand many of the manoeuvres described in this book. In Edmonton, I was provided a course in the night vision trainer at the Canadian Forces School of Aeromedical Training, and with instructors at the Canadian Forces Survival Training School. I had the use of Canadian Forces library material and aeromedical research, primarily dealing with visual illusion in flight. I was given aircraft operating instructions, search and rescue manuals, mission logs, and officer training texts. Staff at all these institutions were open and helpful, and their support is gratefully acknowledged. Any factual errors are the result of my own carelessness.

I was pretty much given the run of Canadian Forces bases in Edmonton, Trenton, and Greenwood, Nova Scotia. Arrangements were also made for me at bases in Kingston and Ottawa. Thanks are due to the base commanders and their personnel. I was most demanding of CFB Edmonton commander Colonel Mike Wansink and his executive assistant, Captain Norm Bonikowsky. Their contributions are greatly appreciated.

Staff at the Search and Rescue Headquarters in Trenton opened their files and their memories to me. Thanks are due to Master Warrant Officer Pete Howard and Master Warrant Officer Roy Jackson. The files were also opened at the Edmonton Rescue Coordination Centre, whose principals are mentioned in the text.

Individual squadrons should be singled out for providing assistance. In Greenwood, these were 413 Squadron, 405 Squadron, and 415 Squadron; in Trenton, 424 Squadron, 436 Squadron, and 429 Squadron; and in Edmonton, 435 Squadron and 408 Squadron. Thanks are due to their commanding officers and personnel.

Major Simon MacDowall, senior public affairs officer in Edmonton, was an invaluable guide through the military. In his absence, Captain Rod Gray admirably filled the breach. In Ottawa, Major Don Marsh filled the same role at National Defence Headquarters, as Bob Russ did at Canadian Forces Communications Command.

I got to know many Hercules pilots and flight crew, all of whom were helpful guides to the characteristics of this gutsy and versatile aircraft. Major Paul Baldasero, Major Marvin Macauley, and Major Jim Burger were three of the best teachers.

The SARtechs are a world unto themselves. We took a while to size each other up, but I came to admire them greatly. The names of the SARtechs I interviewed are all mentioned in the appendix, and I thank them. They are a boisterous, generous, kind, and competent group. They are humble in their actions. I hope this account helps to increase awareness of their contribution to the country, in daily acts of salvation that go unrecorded.

Special thanks to Pam Ritchie and Darlene Macauley for opening their homes. I grew fond of Jan and Dawn Macauley, and of their beagle, Star.

The *Ottawa Citizen,* where I while away my working life, provided swift approval of a leave of absence. Jim Travers, the editor, extended it several times without complaint and with good cheer. I was encouraged to write the book by my friends and colleagues, notably Roy MacGregor, Charles Rusnell, Graham Parley, Greg Weston, and Chris Hall. The *Edmonton Journal* was generous with its offices, and I thank publisher Linda Hughes, editor Murdoch Davis, and their staff.

I thank Ron Cohen of Montreal and Paul Edwards of Los Angeles. Both acted with integrity, discretion, and a genuine interest in the story.

Neil McNeil provided tangible and moral support, merely adding to my large storehouse of appreciation.

This book is one of the growing number of titles brought to life by the remarkable publishing house of Macfarlane Walter & Ross. John Macfarlane, Jan Walter, and Gary Ross possess sterling character, single-minded dedication to quality, and a collaborative approach that have endeared them to many authors. I am blessed to find myself in their stable.

Thanks are due to my copy editor Barbara Czarnecki for her careful attention to the manuscript.

I am happy for the abiding presence of Marni, and for the measureless love of Jacqueline.

I am also indebted to the three blue herons, the green heron, the two pairs of Canada geese, the bald eagle, the mink, the pair of sea otter, the two pairs of mallards, the four pairs and two spare of wood ducks, the two pileated woodpeckers, the hummingbird who dances in the waterfall, the white-tailed doe and her bashful fawn, the golden carp that rise each day to be fed, as are we all, by hands unseen. These are the visible presences of Garyland, where this book was written. Garyland healed me and taught me. Gary Ross, its guardian and my editor, taught me even more.

Finally, my gratitude to Nicole Bourget, for her loveliness, and for having enriched my life.

The book is dedicated to those who did not return, whose names are recorded on a separate page. My personal inscription is to my father: William Alexander Lee, Sergeant (RCMP, retired), regimental number 14848. In a tattered envelope in the back of a desk drawer, my father keeps a souvenir of his days in the Mounted Police. It is a collection of yellowed newspaper clippings. They are accounts of the time he coordinated a search for a lost three-year-old boy in Bragg Creek, Alberta. The parents are pictured holding the boy, who was found dirty but hungry after many days. The mother is quoted as saying she was very happy to have her son returned.

I once wondered why those clippings meant so much to him; now I know. For the many times your love has rescued your son, Dad, this book is for you.

White Rock, British Columbia
April 1992

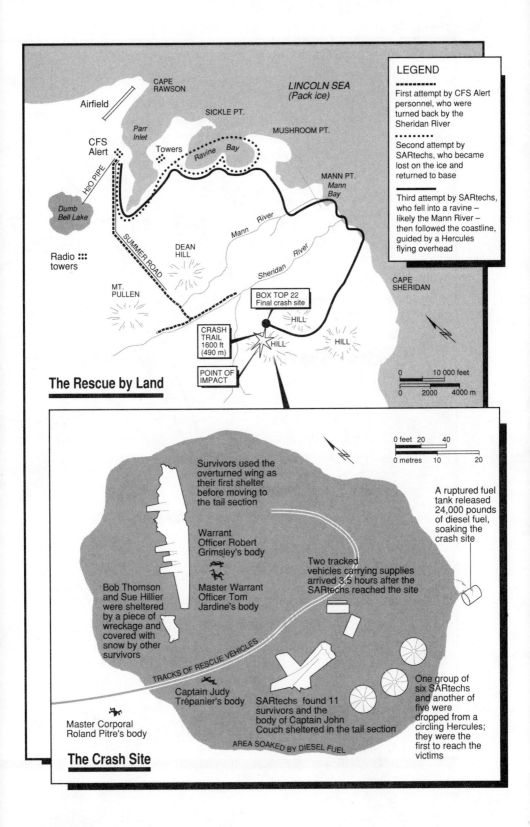

LEGEND

----------- First attempt by CFS Alert personnel, who were turned back by the Sheridan River

··········· Second attempt by SARtechs, who became lost on the ice and returned to base

—— Third attempt by SARtechs, who fell into a ravine – likely the Mann River – then followed the coastline, guided by a Hercules flying overhead

CAPE RAWSON

Airfield

LINCOLN SEA (Pack ice)

SICKLE PT.

MUSHROOM PT.

Parr Inlet

CFS Alert

Towers

Ravine Bay

MANN PT.
Mann Bay

H2O PIPE

Dumb Bell Lake

Radio ::: towers

SUMMER ROAD

DEAN HILL

Mann River

Sheridan River

CAPE SHERIDAN

MT. PULLEN

BOX TOP 22 Final crash site

HILL

CRASH TRAIL 1600 ft (490 m)

HILL

HILL

HILL

POINT OF IMPACT

The Rescue by Land

0   10 000 feet

0   2000   4000 m

Survivors used the overturned wing as their first shelter before moving to the tail section

0 feet 20   40

0 metres 10   20

A ruptured fuel tank released 24,000 pounds of diesel fuel, soaking the crash site

Warrant Officer Robert Grimsley's body

Two tracked vehicles carrying supplies arrived 3.5 hours after the SARtechs reached the site

Bob Thomson and Sue Hillier were sheltered by a piece of wreckage and covered with snow by other survivors

Master Warrant Officer Tom Jardine's body

TRACKS OF RESCUE VEHICLES

Captain Judy Trépanier's body

Master Corporal Roland Pitre's body

SARtechs found 11 survivors and the body of Captain John Couch sheltered in the tail section

One group of six SARtechs and another of five were dropped from a circling Hercules; they were the first to reach the victims

AREA SOAKED BY DIESEL FUEL

The Crash Site

The Rescue of Box Top 22

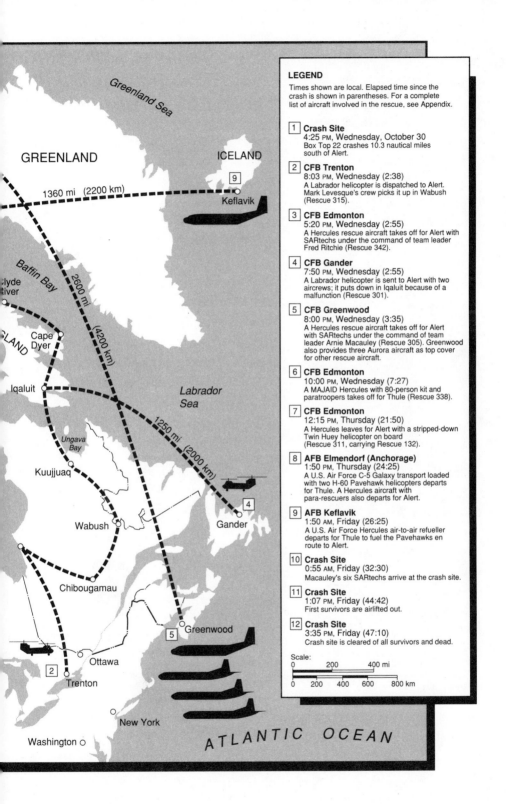

GREENLAND

ICELAND

9

Keflavik

Greenland Sea

1360 mi   (2200 km)

Baffin Bay

2600 mi

(4200 km)

Clyde River

Cape Dyer

LAND

Iqaluit

Labrador Sea

1250 mi   (2000 km)

Ungava Bay

Kuujjuaq

Wabush

Gander

4

Chibougamau

Greenwood

5

Ottawa

2

Trenton

New York

Washington

ATLANTIC OCEAN

LEGEND

Times shown are local. Elapsed time since the crash is shown in parentheses. For a complete list of aircraft involved in the rescue, see Appendix.

1 **Crash Site**
4:25 PM, Wednesday, October 30
Box Top 22 crashes 10.3 nautical miles south of Alert.

2 **CFB Trenton**
8:03 PM, Wednesday (2:38)
A Labrador helicopter is dispatched to Alert. Mark Levesque's crew picks it up in Wabush (Rescue 315).

3 **CFB Edmonton**
5:20 PM, Wednesday (2:55)
A Hercules rescue aircraft takes off for Alert with SARtechs under the command of team leader Fred Ritchie (Rescue 342).

4 **CFB Gander**
7:50 PM, Wednesday (2:55)
A Labrador helicopter is sent to Alert with two aircrews; it puts down in Iqaluit because of a malfunction (Rescue 301).

5 **CFB Greenwood**
8:00 PM, Wednesday (3:35)
A Hercules rescue aircraft takes off for Alert with SARtechs under the command of team leader Arnie Macauley (Rescue 305). Greenwood also provides three Aurora aircraft as top cover for other rescue aircraft.

6 **CFB Edmonton**
10:00 PM, Wednesday (7:27)
A MAJAID Hercules with 80-person kit and paratroopers takes off for Thule (Rescue 338).

7 **CFB Edmonton**
12:15 PM, Thursday (21:50)
A Hercules leaves for Alert with a stripped-down Twin Huey helicopter on board (Rescue 311, carrying Rescue 132).

8 **AFB Elmendorf (Anchorage)**
1:50 PM, Thursday (24:25)
A U.S. Air Force C-5 Galaxy transport loaded with two H-60 Pavehawk helicopters departs for Thule. A Hercules aircraft with para-rescuers also departs for Alert.

9 **AFB Keflavik**
1:50 AM, Friday (26:25)
A U.S. Air Force Hercules air-to-air refueller departs for Thule to fuel the Pavehawks en route to Alert.

10 **Crash Site**
0:55 AM, Friday (32:30)
Macauley's six SARtechs arrive at the crash site.

11 **Crash Site**
1:07 PM, Friday (44:42)
First survivors are airlifted out.

12 **Crash Site**
3:35 PM, Friday (47:10)
Crash site is cleared of all survivors and dead.

Scale:
0   200   400 mi

0   200   400   600   800 km

CHAPTER ONE

Wolf Dreaming

THERE IS, at the very top of the earth's land mass, a small outpost dedicated to the gathering of signals intelligence. Located near the northern extent of Ellesmere Island, 500 miles from the North Pole and just across Robeson Channel from the tip of Greenland, the Alert listening post is the most northerly permanent settlement in the world. Those responsible for the station do their best to discourage any notoriety from attaching itself to this distinction. The Canadian Cabinet's authorization for the establishment of the intelligence post is sealed. The Alert operations are classified. The post cannot be visited without the approval of the commanders of both the Air Force and the Communications Command, two of the five elements that make up the Canadian Armed Forces.

Although a good deal of general information about the polar station can be gathered from overt sources, the finer details of its operations are closely held. Simply put, it's a spy station. The intelligence it gathers is distributed within the Communications Security Establishment in Ottawa and the National Security Agency in Washington. Neither organization is known for its public disclosure.

One particular detail of the Alert operation preoccupied Bob Thomson on the night of October 29, 1991. An outgoing, athletic man of thirty-eight, Thomson lay in bed at his home in Foxborough, near Trenton in southern Ontario, trying to concentrate on a copy of Pierre Berton's book *The Great Depression*. But the problem at Alert kept distracting him.

Thomson would be rising early, to catch the Armed Forces service flight to the polar station. It would be a long journey but an interesting one; he liked to bring back tales of life near the Pole. His mission on this voyage was to take responsibility for a military supply problem. For the life of him, he could not figure out what to do with all those teddy bears.

Thomson was regional manager of CANEX, Canadian Forces Exchange, the company that provides shopping to all of the Canadian Forces postings around the world. Its outlets range from large supermarkets to tiny canteens. CANEX maintains a store for the 200 or so Canadian Forces personnel at the Alert station.

Five hundred teddy bears. Somebody must have had rocks in his head when he sent that many teddy bears up to Alert. The CANEX store at Alert is a small one, with very limited space for inventory, and now Thomson had to find a way to get those teddy bears out of there. He could pull, at best, a Priority Seven on the weekly supply flight, "space granted if space available." On that normally scheduled service – one military airlift a week – it might be months before he got the bears out of Alert and reallocated to another CANEX store. By then it would be past Christmas, and the bears would be homeless.

Thomson had managed to squeeze some cartons of audio equipment on board the pending flight north. These were mainly floor-model stereo systems from the CANEX store at the Canadian Forces base in Trenton, and he thought the station's personnel might be feeling the need for music. People in isolation have a use for Walkmans and compact disc players.

Thomson saw some promise in the fact that, on this trip, the weekly supply run coincided with an Operation Box Top. Twice a year, Air Command dedicates three c-130 Hercules medium-sized transport aircraft to a supply mission to Alert. Goods are shipped by sea from Montreal the 2,175 miles north to the massive U.S. air base at Thule, Greenland, and flown from there by Hercules the 420 miles to Alert. The Box Top flights from Thule to Alert – three planes going twenty-four hours a day for ten days – ferry virtually all the station's needs for the ensuing six months: 800,000 gallons of diesel fuel, for the power generators and heating system; 100,000 gallons of aviation fuel, for the weekly service; hinds of beef, sides of pork, sacks of flour, cases of soft drinks, and tons of staples to prepare some 120,000 meals for the station's personnel; strapped cords of lumber, stacks of drywall, paint and nails and caulking and screws for the construction crews; engine parts, lubricants, and fuels for the station's vehicles; sensitive electronics components, in sealed and padded boxes; computers; clothes; medical supplies; films; soap.

Some of the Box Top flights to Alert came back empty. Maybe one of the returning Hercules flights would have room for 500 teddy bears.

By his side, Thomson's wife, Elaine, struggled with a problem of her own. She felt strangled by guilt. She and Bob had met while he was attached to the Canadian Forces in Borden, Manitoba. They married and had moved frequently since: to Cold Lake, in northern Alberta; then to the extended honeymoon of a posting in Germany; and finally back here to southern Ontario. Elaine had always surprised him with her independence. On his first day on the job in Germany, she had walked six miles to join him for lunch, unbothered by the foreign language or the incomprehensible street names. It was Elaine who had ferreted out the Alpine ski clubs and organized their summer bicycle tours through Provence, embracing life in their new communities and making them home.

3

The alarm clock-radio was on her side of the bed, and Bob had asked her to set it for three o'clock. She had "forgotten." On this particular night, she felt vulnerable and dependent and did not want him to leave. She was being selfish, she knew, but she was bothered by the thought of spending a solitary week in their new house. It was bigger than the places she was accustomed to – a sign of Bob's rising fortunes within CANEX – and it was still strange to her. It did not yet feel like home. She did not relish the prospect of spending her nights alone.

She kissed Bob. He put his book aside and returned the kiss. Theirs was a good marriage, loving and companionable. Later, after Bob had turned off the light and said goodnight, Elaine had a change of heart. She would only make his life more complicated if he missed the flight. She told herself she was being foolish. Quietly, without disturbing him, she reached over and set the alarm.

That evening was a flurry of activity at the Hillier family home in Trenton, where Sue, a vibrant woman of thirty and the bright light of the house, was making her final preparations for the same early-morning trip.

Sue had been making lists for weeks, ever since Bob Thomson had phoned her boss, Aldo, at the Lauraldo Hair Connection in Trenton. Aldo couldn't take the hairdressing job Thomson offered because his wife, Laura, was expecting. Laura and Aldo owned Lauraldo; Sue Hillier was an independent who worked at their beauty salon.

So Aldo had told Sue about the job, and Sue had jumped with excitement. Fantastic! The North Pole! This is hilarious, right, but I've just been reading about the Arctic in *National Geographic.* This is great!

4

Sue did some fast mental calculations. At Lauraldo, she paid a 50-per-cent commission to the house. The commissions were worth it, because being freelance gave her the freedom and the opportunity to travel. In one week at Alert, she could push through an awful lot of colours and cuts and perms. She'd pocket all of it – there was no house take. And she figured to do a fast trade in hair-care products as well. "What women really need," she told her boyfriend, "they don't have at CANEX. I mean, CANEX has Head & Shoulders, and that's about it. And Christmas is coming up, so what would the men want to send to their wives? Well, the suppliers are coming out with their Christmas boxed sets, and they're a good deal. I mean, Joico shampoo and leave-on conditioner, and a gel, for nineteen ninety-five?"

So she added boxed sets to her list, which already included hair dryers, curling irons, scissors, clippers, conditioners, shampoo, perms, and colours: four boxes, each the size of a card table. And clothes, which were important to her trade. Sue once wore blue jeans to work and the clientele, let me tell you, they couldn't believe it. "Sue," they said, "that just isn't you." And it wasn't. Sue never again wore denim to the job.

When Sue Hillier went to work, she had to be immaculate. "Being a woman," she said, "I'm very picky." Hair and nails perfect, dress slacks and a sweater, which had to be angora or mohair. The sweaters cost a fortune, but they were warm. Stand by that door, get a gust of cold air every time a client entered or left, and warmth was all the more important.

As it would be in the North. "Take extra things," her mom had suggested. "You never know if an Arctic storm will come up. You could be stuck there an extra week."

Adrian was out running errands around town, getting the last-minute things. He was a good boyfriend. They were talking about buying a house and moving in together, which made the extra income all the more worthwhile. He had told her to take extra cash for the American base exchange at Thule, where they sold Greenland woollens. Mittens and socks and U.S. currency were on her list. Good, reliable Adrian: if there was one problem with their relationship, it was his job. He was a bomb disposal expert with the Armed Forces, and sometimes she worried. Such a dangerous line of work, especially in contrast to the bland predictability of her own.

As her final act of preparation, Sue broke her great-grandmother's cape out of mothballs. She had thought long and hard about whether to take the cape to the Pole. It was a stunning creation in black velvet. She'd been giving one young woman a trim – the woman was stationed at the Trenton air base, and her hair had to be just so: no longer than the bottom of the collar, no pins showing under the beret – and the young woman had urged her to take some fun things, too. Plus, Hallowe'en was coming, Sue's favourite time of year. So she unpacked the cape to admire it. It was dramatic, with shoulders out to here, and white satin lining without even a trace of yellow. She packed it among her Alert things, along with a black wig. Darn right, she told herself. Come Friday night at the North Pole, I'll look really scary.

———————

Across town, at the Yukon Lodge in Trenton, some of the radio operators due to take the same flight north had decided to forgo sleep entirely. They were heading up to Alert for the full tour, six months in isolation, and they regarded short-timers such as Sue Hillier and Bob Thomson with something between envy and disdain.

For Master Corporal Mario Ellefsen, it was his third tour to Alert. His trade was known as "communications research"; in laymen's terms, he was a radio operator who spoke French, English, and Russian. His wife, Tammy Ellefsen, was a radio technician.

They'd met on the job. This meant it was possible for Ellefsen to talk to his wife about his work, something he wasn't able to do with many people.

The reason for the Alert station's existence is threefold. It conducts studies of Arctic weather; some official publications would have you believe that this is its primary, indeed its only, role. It asserts Canada's claim to sovereignty as far north as the Pole, a function it fulfils by its mere presence. And it conducts "communications research," a euphemism more tellingly expressed by the official admission that it "monitors foreign country communications." The principal role of the station has always been to sniff the Arctic winds for voices speaking in Russian. Some of those voices it detected in inter-city telephone calls in Moscow; some were snatched from satellites; some were intercepted between aircraft and the ground.

Established in 1958, Alert was a product of the Cold War. Its location was chosen because it lay roughly halfway between the capitals of the communist and capitalist worlds. Being so near the Pole, it was about the same distance to anywhere on the same latitude. Geographical concepts become distorted as the lines of longitude converge: Alert is 2,160 miles from Edmonton, the nearest Canadian city. But it is closer to Stockholm, which is about 2,000 miles distant. It is closer to the Latvian port of Riga, a metropolis of Cold War intrigue, than to its own supply base of Trenton.

Ellefsen had pulled his first tour of the station just after his marriage. He and Tammy had taken a three-week honeymoon and visited her family in Nova Scotia. She took the first separation hard. By the time his second tour rolled around, they had a newborn daughter, and Tammy had taken his six-month absence even harder. For this third tour, he would be leaving behind two daughters, aged four and two. Tammy had cried every night for the past week. Ellefsen had arranged for another radio operator,

Private Bill Vance, to share a ride with him to the Ottawa bus terminal. Tammy would cry all the way home if she drove him, and that wouldn't be safe. Sure enough, when he walked out the door, Tammy had started crying; then the girls, who couldn't understand, had started crying; and then Ellefsen had started bawling, too. He waved goodbye and stepped into the cab with Vance, who himself had recently become engaged. It was a custom among those going to Alert to have recently become engaged, married, or imminent parents, as it is before enforced absences in wartime.

Ellefsen planned to spend the months of Arctic darkness working out at the gym; his goal was three hours of exercise a day. At least he would return fit. Leisure pastimes are not in shortage at Alert. The station has two five-pin bowling lanes with an automatic pin-setter. It has a curling rink with two sheets of, paradoxically, artificial ice. There is a rock club and a camera club, a library, a closed-circuit television station, and a radio station where anyone can be a disc jockey for a day. There is a recording studio, and a theatre with 150 seats. There is plenty of wholesome activity, precisely because the personnel, Ellefsen included, regard the posting as a desolate, bleak interlude in their Armed Forces careers.

No amount of entertainment, however, could distract him from his fears that he was losing his daughters forever, and that their faith in him would be irreparably shaken. For the next six months, he would be able to call his wife and children for only twenty minutes every five days on the radio-telephone. Relationships tended to suffer when the conversations began, "I love you. Over." As a result, perhaps, Alert amounts to a school for problem drinkers. Much of the social life revolves around the alcohol found in each barracks common room and at the mess.

There are three messes. Commissioned officers drink at the "bridal suite," the sergeants and warrant officers at the "old folks' home," and the junior ranks at "Club 180" – named for the number of days in a tour. Discipline is not rigidly enforced. The chief warrant officer, responsible for enforcement of rules and a feared figure in the South, is invariably named "Valentine" at Alert. The mess steward doesn't wear a shirt, so Club 180 can boast of having the Arctic's only topless bar.

At Alert, the men and women pass the time and wait for the Hercules transport that will take them home – their "Herkie bird," they call it. There are two tours at Alert. The May-to-November tour is better, because the sun, once risen, never sets. For outings, there is a single road from the base to Crystal Mountain, so called because of the natural ice cave that forms in the winter months and opens, like a melting cathedral, in the summer. The November-to-May tour, on the other hand, requires stoic endurance. It is spent in near-complete darkness; the road is closed, and storms lash the station with little warning. It is during this tour that the order to "button up" is regularly given, each time a storm front moves in from the Pole. Vehicles are driven to shelter, furnace fuels are topped up, stray personnel are gathered indoors. Then a detail, known as "the hangmen," strings ropes between the buildings. Visibility during Arctic storms is often reduced to zero. For three hours or three days, until the storm blows itself out, the staff are imprisoned by the elements. They have little with which to bide their time but hard drink and Herkie-bird dreams.

Ellefsen and Vance were joined at the Ottawa bus terminal by Master Seaman Douglas Montgomery, known as Monty, another radio specialist. They travelled together to the lodge in Trenton and debated whether to sleep. They had brought beer and ordered pizza, and at about one o'clock in the morning they drifted off, despite their intention to stay awake through their last night in "the world." Then a friend of Ellefsen's hammered on the door, and the two men sat talking until two o'clock. Two hours later, the three radio operators dragged themselves to the base air terminal.

It was four-thirty in the morning when they arrived; their orders had instructed them to show up no later than four. When they got there, the doors were locked. The terminal wouldn't open for another half-hour. The men shoved hands into pockets and stamped their feet to keep warm. Wasn't it frigging typical of the frigging military?

———————

While her fellow passengers shivered in the cold, Sue Hillier was waking up. She hated waiting and had set her alarm for four-thirty, giving herself just enough time to shower and dress before Adrian picked her up and drove her to the air terminal.

Sue was in the kitchen, waiting, when her mother padded in, dressed in her nightgown and slippers. Marg made coffee while they chatted. Around the Hillier household, Sue was the morning songbird, and this morning she had plenty to sing about. Did she have everything on her list? Would Adrian arrive on time? She began to worry about missing the flight.

They sat across from each other, with their cups of coffee. Her mother provided the reassuring backbeat. I shouldn't think so, dear. Oh, of course he will, don't worry. Sue and her mother enjoyed each other's company, especially at this hour, when everyone else was asleep. At one point Marg caught herself staring oddly at her daughter.

"What is it, Mom?"

Oh nothing, Marg said. She never had been a morning person, that's all, and look, there's Adrian now, time to run.

They kissed goodbye, Marg wished her a safe trip, and Sue bundled out the door with her many bags and boxes. Then the kitchen was still again, and Marg finished her coffee in troubled silence.

She'd dreamed that she had seen herself die. They had put her in a coffin, placed the coffin in the earth, and shovelled dirt on top of her. It was cold, and utterly black, and the earth spilled onto her face. Sipping her coffee, Marg shivered at the recollection of trying to push the cold black dirt away with her hands.

Adrian's lights swept across the kitchen wall. Sue had known something was wrong, Marg thought, but it was better that I didn't tell her. Buried alive, yet! No sense worrying her with an old woman's silly dreams.

———————

There were thirteen passengers on the service flight from Trenton to Thule, a trip of almost eight hours. At Thule they would change planes before continuing up to Alert. Two of the passengers – Sue Hillier and Bob Thomson – were civilians. Others were supply specialists, going up to sort out a new computer link meant to ease the formidable logistics of supplying such a remote installation. The rest, with one exception, were radio technicians and operators, in for the full six-month tour.

The exception was a fresh-faced young captain named Wilma de Groot, recently graduated from medical school. She was being sent to Alert for a week of routine examinations and treatment. The station has two medical aides but no qualified doctor on permanent staff. De Groot, just out of training and on the low end of the pecking order, was given the assignment.

Elaine Thomson pulled up at the terminal to drop off Bob – she had not only set the alarm but driven him to the base to see him off. Thomson noticed de Groot for the first time as he approached the check-in counter. She was arguing with the junior rank on duty. De Groot had packed the Arctic clothing assigned to her into a duffel bag, and she wanted it checked onto the aircraft as baggage. The junior rank told her she would have

11

to unpack the kit and carry it on board as hand luggage. Those were the rules. No exceptions. The baggage clerk stood on regulation where he could not stand on rank.

"Oh, all right," de Groot snapped. She grabbed her bag and walked off.

"First-timer," Thomson told the baggage clerk as he took de Groot's place at the counter.

The clerk shrugged. "First-timer, old-timer, don't matter. Rules is rules."

Thomson walked over to her after checking his own things. "Saw you getting a hard time."

De Groot mumbled something.

"I know the rules sound arbitrary," Thomson said. "But you really do need your Arctic gear up there. You never know. A storm could come in and we'd be stuck in Thule for a week."

De Groot gave him a dismissive smile. She had other things on her mind, which had made her snippy at the baggage counter. She didn't like carrying the bag of Arctic kit. The kit contained a knee-length parka with hood, felt-lined Arctic mitts, and mukluks. It was bulky. But more troubling was the thought of leaving George. It was hard enough being newlywed and separated, living in Trenton while George finished his internship at St. Michael's Hospital in Toronto. The last thing she needed was to lose one of their precious shared weekends, especially since they had planned to celebrate her twenty-sixth birthday. But then, George had a way of keeping in touch.

Are you listening, George? She never knew, could never tell whether George was tuned to her frequency. She would find out later, when they saw each other again. It was like that, being married to a psychic when you had no such powers of your own. It seemed that all her primary relationships were with people who were, at the least, empaths and, at the most, like George, virtual mind-readers. De Groot considered herself about as

psychic as a tongue depressor. But she accepted her special connection with George even though she could not claim to understand it.

I love you, George. Maybe he'd pick that up. I love you and I
have to carry all this stupid Arctic gear on board. It's heavy and
it's awkward. That's why I was upset. She had to explain her emotions to him. That, too, was part of being married to a psychic.
You had responsibility for two emotional lives, your partner's as
well as your own.

The embarkation announcement came over the public
address system, and the thirteen passengers bundled their gear,
headed out into the darkness, and boarded the plane. The Hercules is not a comfortable way to fly. It is loud, it vibrates, and the
seats are nothing more than hard nylon webbing arranged in
bench rows. There are rows along each side of the aircraft, and a
central row with seats placed back-to-back. The passengers sit
facing the sides or the middle of the aircraft, not the front as in
commercial aviation. They must wear hearing protectors, and
conversation is next to impossible. It is dim in the cabin, and
cool.

The long flight to the U.S. base at Thule was uneventful. The
passengers read when they could or nestled among the cargo and
tried to catch some sleep. As they headed north up the coast of
Greenland, Sue Hillier was thrilled to see her first iceberg
through the porthole. It was a gloriously shimmering greenish-
white presence, a resplendent cathedral of ice.

The passengers had expected to spend the night in Thule, but
there was no room in the transient quarters. Instead, they were
told, space would be made available for them on the next Box
Top flight to Alert. The three Hercules craft were shuttling back
and forth continuously, so there wouldn't be much delay. They
were loaded into a waiting area, devoid of furniture save for a
few hard chairs and a coffee machine. Coffee was twenty-five

cents, and the machine didn't take Canadian quarters.

This was as close as Sue would get to U.S. shopping, as she learned when she checked the notice board and found that the base store would not be open until four o'clock in the afternoon. They were scheduled to leave on their Box Top flight at three.

"Great," she said, to no one in particular. "Here I am with American dollars up to the ying-yang, and I can't even get a cup of coffee."

"You must be a civilian," said Wilma de Groot.

Pleased to share the company of another woman, Sue began chatting – about hair, which she always found a convenient opener. You really should think about doing something, you know. Just because you're in the military is no reason not to do something with your hair. Most of my clients are from the military. You'd be surprised what you can do and still stay within the restrictions....

Their chat was interrupted by the public address system, announcing that Box Top 22 was loaded with fuel, baggage, Bob's stereos, and Sue's many boxes of hair-care products, and was ready for departure.

Sue was surprised to learn she would be on a "wet lift," a transport carrying a cargo of diesel fuel. She had heard these flights were awful, smelling of diesel that clung to the clothing for days afterwards. But she was pleasantly surprised when she stepped inside. This Hercules was older than the one they'd taken from Trenton, but the fuel tank inside was new. It was also airtight, for the cabin smelled fresh and cold.

Sue took her seat and began to read a novel in preparation for takeoff. She had grabbed the book from Adrian's extensive collection of science-fiction paperbacks. This one was about time travel. She liked such stories, because they filled your mind with fanciful possibilities. Like, if the plane passed through a time warp and Sue had spent the rest of her life in some distant past, she never would have got on this airplane, in which case she couldn't have gone back in time in the first place....

———————

In Emergency at St. Michael's Hospital, George Iwanchyshyn looked up at the clock. They'll be leaving Thule soon, he thought. He'd been married to Wilma six weeks and liked to stay in close touch. He began to reach out to her in his mind, but then Emergency was inundated with trauma cases and he put thoughts of her aside, bending to his grisly work.

George had not had a chance to tell Wilma about his parents' dream. On the eve of her departure, somewhere in the hours between Elaine Thomson's decision to set the alarm clock and the arrival of the radio operators at the air terminal, George's parents had woken at the same time from a troubled sleep.

"What is the matter, dear?" asked Mr. Iwanchyshyn.

"I had a dream," said Mrs. Iwanchyshyn.

"About a dog?"

"Yes, a big one."

"I had the same dream. Let's look it up."

The elderly couple drew on their dressing gowns and consulted an old and valued family text. It was a compendium of dreams and omens, brought from Ukraine. As they read, they realized that all the dream symbols, and the combination of those symbols, pointed in the same direction.

"What do we do?" she asked.

"There is nothing to do now, except wait."

They had both dreamed of a giant dog, so big it must have been a wolf. Yes, it was definitely a wolf. It had been running across the snow in pursuit of some people. Just who the people were, neither could say. But they both remembered the beast clearly: its snapping jaws, its red tongue, its angry snarl, and the saliva dripping from its teeth.

Wilma de Groot's in-laws looked at each other in wonderment and horror. For they had both, at the end of the dream, in the moment just before waking, seen blood upon the snow.

CHAPTER TWO

Clockwork

THULE IS LOCATED on the west coast of Greenland near the 76th parallel, at about the same latitude as Grise Fjord on the southern tip of Ellesmere Island. It is surrounded by the largest ice sheet in the northern hemisphere, which covers four-fifths of the country to an average depth of about a mile.

Greenland may be a desolate place, but the United States recognized its strategic importance after World War II, when it administered the Danish island as a protectorate. Under a NATO agreement, the U.S. in 1951 began construction of a mammoth air and radar base. By 1960, the Americans had even installed the first nuclear reactors on the ancient ice cap. These were built a prudent 140 miles inland at Camp Century, which has supplied the base at Thule with abundant heat and light ever since.

That same year, the Canadian Forces at Alert resisted the temptation to litter the Arctic with nuclear waste. They were hauling their water by stoneboat from a well and warming it one pot at a time on Coleman heaters. They warmed their huts with a diesel-fired furnace and read old paperbacks by the light provided by a diesel generator. For runway lights, they stuffed gasoline-soaked newspaper into barrels and set them on fire.

Avionics have improved significantly since, of course, and at the Thule air base they are as advanced as anywhere else. But

Thule is a difficult airfield. The Greenland ice cap to the south and east is an area of such severe air turbulence that a loud warning is printed on United States Air Force approach plates and air navigation charts. When the wind is coming off the ice cap, the turbulence extends to the approach and departure flight paths, which run east to west.

This happens often. Thule is a place of such violent weather patterns that aircraft left outside overnight, even large transports, are parked with their noses pointed into the prevailing wind. Otherwise they run the risk of being flipped over. Hercules pilots are not allowed to park their aircraft outside when the wind springs up at Thule. They have to head south.

The airfield is also surrounded by high terrain and obstacles. The runway is at an elevation of 167 feet above sea level on the west end, rising to 251 feet on the east. About two miles east of the runway there is an obstacle 1,800 feet high. A few miles to the south, the terrain rises to nearly 3,000 feet. This presents an obstacle that aircraft on a missed approach must climb and bank sharply to avoid. Thule is an airfield that demands experience and skill of its aircrews, which is why Hercules commanders preferred a seasoned crew on this run.

Captain John Couch had been making the run for three days now. He did not have a seasoned crew. Two of its members were "pipeliners," graduates on their first tour of duty. This had concerned Couch at first, though it was not his style to make a fuss. He'd just kept a close eye on them. This was their third run between Thule and Alert, and with each flight his confidence in them had grown.

The two flight officers in the Hercules sit beside each other, with the aircraft commander in the left seat and the first officer in the right. Taking his seat, Couch nodded to his first officer. Lieutenant Joe Bales smiled back, a broad, toothsome beam. Bales had the rangy frame, big hands, and ingenuous face of a farm boy. When Couch looked at Bales, however, what he saw was 500 hours' experience, only half of them on the Hercules. Couch himself had 3,500 hours.

Bales was an enthusiastic pilot who had gained flying experience before attending the Canadian Forces flight training school in Moose Jaw. In pilot training, though, the largest propeller-driven aircraft that recruits learn to fly is the single-engine, two-seat Musketeer. It has an engine generating 180 horsepower, which puts it in the rubber-band category of aircraft power plants. After that, recruits can move directly into the four-engine Hercules. The training system makes them knowledgeable about the aircraft and capable of flying it from one point to another, but there's no teaching experience.

This policy of putting pipeliners into the first officer's seat of the Hercules had led to a growing unease among the more seasoned aircraft commanders. The simple fact was that a kid could be walking down the streets of Moose Jaw one day and occupying the co-pilot's seat of a Hercules one year later. Within another eighteen months, he could be aircraft commander. There have been Hercules aircraft commanders of twenty-two years of age and eighteen months on the Hercules; as one experienced pilot said: "No civvy operation in their right mind would do that."

That young man or woman might know the book on the Hercules. But he or she would have had no time to acquire air sense. The policy had been compounded by a high attrition rate and a designated three-year tour of duty. It meant that one-third of the flying officers every year were new on the job. Those aircraft commanders who elected to stay on the flight deck felt themselves prematurely aged. They also worried about becoming prematurely embalmed.

If John Couch had been unsure of his first officer, he had amplified the sentiment for the navigator in the back. When the navigator spoke over the intercom, Couch heard a voice that trembled like a sprig. Although Lieutenant Michael Moore had more than 1,100 hours on the Hercules, he was a youth of twenty-five summers. He looked as though he would be more comfortable using a compass to guide a Boy Scout trek through the woods than steering a medium-sized transport across the High Arctic. Still, he was performing capably on the Box Top runs, gaining composure with every flight.

At least the engineer was experienced. Sergeant Paul West, just over Couch's shoulder, was an immeasurable relief to the pilot. West was an old hand, and a steady one. A little on the touchy side, maybe, being damn near a perfectionist; but he was as reliable as Old Paint. West had spent more than five years as engineer in a search and rescue squadron; Couch also had search and rescue experience. Both men believed there were no more demanding flight conditions than those encountered in search and rescue, and they gave each other credit for the experience.

"Flight engineer's pre-start check complete," said West.

The lengthy list of pre-flight checks began. Couch, with his right hand, edged the four condition levers from "ground stop" to "first forward." The aircraft hummed to life as energy ran through the circuits.

"ATM's on. Move external power."

"Check."

Joe Bales monitored and confirmed the checks. At thirty-three, he was a year older than Couch but appeared much younger. In part, it was a physical distinction: Couch was balding and had a mature set to his brow and mouth; Bales had a thick patch of dark hair and a boyish eye. But it was also a difference in bearing. Couch's thousands of hours in the left seat of the Hercules showed in the smooth way he moved through the pre-flight routine. Bales was eager to demonstrate his competence, eager for not the slightest mistake.

"Is three clear?" West asked into the microphone.

"Number three engine clear," came the reply from the ground crew, confirming there was nothing in the way of the propellers.

"Turning three," said Couch. He turned off the fuel enrichment – the engines would still be warm, and there was no sense in beefing up the enrichment and risking a stall or torching the engine, the equivalent of a flaming backfire. He engaged the starter motor, and it cranked the turbine of the inboard engine until it reached about 20 per cent of its available revolutions per minute. The engine ignited with a mighty roar and raced on its own as it rapidly gained acceleration.

"Ignition. Oil pressure. Hydraulic pressure," called West, reading the vital signs of the engine. It climbed to ground idle speed, allowing the aircraft's generator to turn the other engines.

"Is number four clear?"

"Four engine clear."

"Bleeds on four."

"Turning four."

Both the right-hand engines were now turning. The ground crew on the runway below, exhaling great white drafts of breath, hauled away the external power generator. The two left-hand engines were started in sequence. The flight deck rumbled more loudly but somewhat more evenly, as engines took hold on either side. The Hercules is a noisy aircraft even on the ground, and normal conversation was now impossible in the cockpit.

"Pre-taxi check," Couch called. "Compass systems."

"In gyro," said Moore. "Number one at two five seven, number two at two five eight."

This sequence was pleasing to Couch. The procedure had been scripted long before, by design and experience, and everyone had only to follow the script with religious technicality. All pilots are aware of the thinness of the parchment, woven of physics and mechanical engineering, that keeps their heavy metal afloat in a sea of ether. They have different ways of coping with the surreal dream of flight. Some thrive on adversity, believing that challenge hones individual judgment, and that judgment provides a sort of surface tension under the machine. Others need regularity and routine; they believe the system will work and the machine will not break if the proper steps are followed. All pilots, of course, have a place for both their own air sense and their respect for procedure; but all fall more on one side of the balance than on the other. Couch was a systems man.

"Radio. Radio altimeter. Navaids. IFF."

"On stand-by pilot."

Over the headset, air traffic control at Thule provided takeoff clearance, departure frequencies, headings, and altitudes. The controller described a precise flight plan that would be rigidly followed. The Hercules would not plunge blindly into space but would follow a track as clearly as if wagons had plowed ahead, carving ruts through the sky. After two runs to Alert in the past three days, Couch could have done it in his sleep.

West turned the dials above his head, applying forward and aft anti-skid. Couch checked his weight load – 24,000 pounds of diesel fuel and thirteen passengers. Passengers, of course. This was the flight that was transporting personnel as well as cargo. He called for a taxi check. The aircraft's landing lights were illuminated, sending bright daggers onto the reflective tarmac. The Hercules inched ahead.

"Brake check."

The transport lurched to a halt; the flight deck nosed down, then rocked back up.

"Brakes normal."

They edged ahead once more. Couch made his final calls for instrument checks. He turned the Hercules to the left and right and gently moved the control surfaces: rudder, elevators, and ailerons. Often, in cold weather, they need a little extra persuasion before takeoff. The viscosity of the hydraulic fluids increases in the cold, and the controls have to be coaxed before they agree to full travel. The Herc lumbered away from the terminal and past the base operations hangar as Couch recited the routine confirmation of the departure flight plan. The flight deck of the Hercules takes a lot of movement during taxi; it clumps and bobs along like the head of a stomping troll. With a lurching turn to the left, Box Top 22 – the twenty-second flight of Operation Box Top – took its position on the button of the runway.

"Temperatures are good, let's go."

"Okay, reverse two and three."

"Reverse check."

"Taxi check completed."

The pilots each placed a hand against the throttles to test the power settings. Bales' hand went to the throttle levers first, checking the action of the captain; Couch placed his hand over the knobs at the top. Both men gazed down the runway.

The Thule runway is 10,000 feet of where the hell are we. Because it is built on permafrost, the paved runway is painted white. In the summer months, this reflects the weak rays of the sun. If the runway were black, the rays would gather on the surface and melt the permafrost underneath. The runway would sag, and heave, and crack. The white paint is a stroke of genius in the summer months, and a blinding obstacle in the winter ones. The runway is bordered with white lights to provide both perspective and a boundary – but it is white against white. The imaginary centre line is difficult to estimate. Also, the white background provides camouflage for snow drifts on the apron. The propellers of the Hercules – even with a clearance of five feet, nine inches above the ground – have been known to strike these drifts during taxi. Frost also accumulates on the white surface, rendering the nose-wheel steering next to useless. Thule is a slippery strip.

"Box Top Two Two ready for takeoff," said Bales.

The throttles were pushed forward, and the Hercules

responded with surprising and loud enthusiasm. Couch, with his left hand, gently guided the nose wheel back and forth. The flight deck adopted the rocking and yawing motion of a twenty-five-cent ride-'em pony. The nose wheel began to lose contact with the runway.

"My wheel," said Couch. He took over hands-and-feet controls from Bales. "Vee one. Watch the torque on two."

The Hercules passed rotation speed, and the nose lifted from the runway. A few seconds later, the rest of the wheels followed. The sensation was quite unlike the cautious climb of a commercial airliner; in comparison, the Herc's takeoff is nearly vertical. It was no longer a clumsy creature of the ground, heavy with the burden of carrying sixty-seven tons. It had become weightless, shouldering itself upwards on fat, nimble wings.

Couch began a climb to 8,000 feet and banked to the right. Outside the window, the stars of Ursa Major were bright and close on the horizon of the perpetual night sky. It almost seemed that he was flying the aircraft into the ladle of the Dipper itself; then the constellation swung away to his left. Couch completed a turn of 100 degrees – more than a quarter of the compass – as he flew to intersect a flight path known as Foxtrot One.

Once the Herc was on this path, Couch would fly the aircraft without need of reference to the real world. He merely needed to consult a prominent instrument called the horizontal situation indicator, or HSI. There is a small white depiction of an airplane in the centre of the instrument, in a stationary position with its nose pointed straight up. But the window also contains a floating white line, called the track bar. This white bar corresponds with the wagon rut furrowed across the sky; and the little white airplane and the track bar together tell the pilot his position relative to the desired course.

To get on course, the pilot need only fly the little white airplane until it intersects the little white line, and follow it. To his senses, he is keeping a track bar centred vertically through the airplane on the HSI. In reality, he is piloting a boxcar of metal at speeds of 240 knots at a height of nearly two miles above the surface of the earth. (Aviators measure their airspeed in knots, or nautical miles per hour. One nautical mile is 1.15 miles or 1.852 kilometres. In other words, Couch's airspeed was 275 miles per hour.)

The white needle would take him to an imaginary target known as Way Point Frini, two degrees longitude to the north. From there he would steer a course to Way Point Henry, on the 80th parallel, about halfway to Alert. Then he'd enter uncontrolled airspace, and the flight deck of the Hercules would be navigating on its own resources.

———————

For weeks, it seemed, Carol Couch had been out of sorts. She had grown increasingly resentful of John's work, and the time it took him away from home; especially since the girls, aged three and one, had come along. When Couch had been called up for the Gulf War, she'd been beside herself. Why couldn't they send someone else? Couch had said it was his duty; but duty, she knew, would not raise the children if he were killed.

Some wives adapted to military routine, or lack of routine, and established their own lives independent of their husbands. Base wives formed a community with other base wives for support and companionship. Carol had no such support system. She and John had chosen to live off the base, in an Edmonton suburb not popular among the military. Their family friends were civilians. It was almost as though she pretended he weren't in the military at all.

"How long are you gone this time?" she had asked at their last dinner before the Box Top mission.

Couch had hesitated. "Ten days."

"You know," she said dispiritedly, "sometimes I think I only grew my hair long so that I could pull it out."

Perhaps to head off the well-beaten topic of his frequent absences, Couch added: "I really don't want to go."

This was odd; he never complained about his work. She waited.

"I don't. It's the crew. I don't want to fly with them."

This was equally odd. Couch seldom brought his work home.

"They're green. The first officer's a pipeliner. They're getting greener all the time."

When Couch got back from Alert, she promised herself, they would have another talk about finding work with the airlines.

"Well," she had said, "you're not getting any younger."

Box Top 22 passed Way Point Henry, continuing its flight to an imaginary line at which control of the flight was handed over from Sondrestrom, Greenland, to controllers in Edmonton. The aircraft was now flying on autopilot, 19,000 feet above the frozen Kennedy Channel. It was a clear night, without blemish. A half-moon buffed the wings of the old Hercules.

"Should I call up the weather?" Bales asked.

"Go ahead," said Couch.

"Alert radio, Alert radio. Box Top Two Two. Flight level one niner zero, en route to Alert. Estimating Alert at sixteen thirty. Requesting latest Alert weather, please."

"Box Top Two Two, latest Alert weather is ceiling and vis unlimited, temp minus two two, surface wind calm, altimeter two niner six four."

Perfect flying weather.

At about 100 nautical miles out, the Hercules was acquired by tacan at Alert. Tacan – tactical air navigation – is a primary navigational aid that will provide the aircraft with all the information it needs to reach the field safely. The tacan needle circled around the dial a few times, homing in on the signal. It then held a position as it locked on.

Box Top 22 was heading into port. It was time for Couch to begin the approach check with the flight crew. He briefed them for a precision instrument approach, using the mnemonic AMORTTS – approach, minimum altitudes, overshoot procedure, radios, transition, timings, and speeds. Reaching down, he set the bug on the radar altimeter to 380 feet. This was his decision height on the approach to Alert. At 380 feet, the warning light would glow yellow, reminding the pilot that it was time to decide whether to complete or abort the landing.

"Want to give Glow Worm a call?" Couch asked Bales.

"Yes, sir. Will request descent seventy-five miles."

Glow Worm is the code name for a precision approach radar. It tells the pilot whether the aircraft is to the left or right of the runway, and whether it is on the correct glide path. It is not normally part of the navigational aids at Alert, but it had been installed for Operation Box Top as a safety measure. The equipment is second to none, for if Air Transport Group lacked modern navigational aids in its aircraft, it was a whiz at setting them up on the ground. Given a flat, relatively hard piece of terrain, Air Transport Group can set up two self-contained airfields anywhere in the world, from the precision radar right down to 8,000 feet of runway lights and the generator to run them.

The Glow Worm in Alert was capable of seeing an aircraft in a plan display, or from above, out to a distance of 200 nautical miles. Within forty nautical miles, it can also generate an elevation, seeing the aircraft in altitude. The aircraft is not, however, switched over to this mode until final approach. The system was working, but the operator could not see how close the aircraft was to the ground.

"Glow Worm, this is Box Top Two Two," said Bales, "requesting descent in approximately fifteen minutes."

"Box Top Two Two is identified," said Glow Worm. "Ninety-two miles west grid. Pilot's discretion. You may descend to ten thousand initially."

The real problem with pipeliners, Couch mused, is you had to be riding them all the time. It was built into the system. The Hercules uses a pilot-monitored approach. The co-pilot actually does the hands-and-feet flying until the aircraft is close to the airport. Then the aircraft commander takes over. This doubled the pilot's responsibility. You had to fly the plane, and when you weren't flying you had to watch over the other guy flying the plane.

Pilots had to be tough on the first officers, but Couch did not like conflict or aggressiveness, least of all on his flight deck. There was enough stress in the military, there was enough on the street, there was plenty in domestic life; Couch was disinclined to wind the spring any tighter than it had to be wound. He decided to take over. "I have control," he said.

"You have control," said Bales, confirming the switch-over, as he'd been taught.

It had been hard for Couch in flight training. Instructors had berated him for his pliant attitude, tried to roughen his edges. In tactical airlift, which requires assertiveness at the controls, his instructor had told him: "John, you're a nice guy. Too nice, you know? You're too nice a guy for your own good." They had ragged his butt again when he took the aircraft commander's course. "You've got to be seen to be more of a leader," his instructor had told him. "You're not in the right seat any more. You can't just sit back and let things happen."

Eventually, it had become well known around the squadron.

Fellow pilots ribbed him: "Hey, John, did you take your aggressive pills today? Need any ugly pills?" It got to be a standing joke.

Couch was intelligent and well liked. He was regarded as a competent and cool-headed pilot. But it bothered him that people thought it a fault that he was easygoing. When something had to get done, he made sure it got done. He just didn't wring his hands over it.

The aircraft passed over the rocky coastline of Ellesmere Island and began plying an overland course to Alert. Couch decided once again to be a nice guy.

Box Top 22 had left Thule on schedule, but Box Top 21 – the twenty-first ferry flight of the mission – was actually behind him. It had been delayed by a small mechanical malfunction and was now twenty minutes' flight time to his rear. This did not cause Couch a problem, but he was thinking ahead, trying to be helpful. There is limited space on the apron in Alert, and the delay of Box Top 21 would mean that all three Box Top flights would be on the ground at once – his, the one behind him, and the flight running twenty-five minutes ahead.

Couch foresaw congestion at the bulk fuel storage tanks, where he was supposed to offload his cargo of heating fuel. The tanks were located on the apron by the approach end of the runway. Offloading took about fifteen minutes. If Couch could speed up his arrival at Alert, he could be nearly emptied and ready for takeoff by the time Box Top 21 arrived.

The easiest way of expediting his arrival was to make a visual approach. It would cut the time needed to fly the precision circuit for an instrument landing and save perhaps five minutes. It was a clear night with superb visibility. The runway lights could already be seen, fifty nautical miles away. They looked like a flat bar, running at right angles to the aircraft and directly ahead of its nose. The lights and the stars were all that Couch could see, but he could see them with brilliant clarity. The lights at Alert were a haven, and they suckered him.

Even in mid-afternoon, the frozen land of rock beneath Box Top 22 was in utter darkness. Couch had no night vision. The instrument and cockpit lights had been lit since Thule, and the Hercules flight deck is illuminated by white light. Even at low levels, white light bleaches out a pigment called rhodopsin – visual purple – from the rod cells of the eye, and without rhodopsin, a person has no night vision. It takes at least half an hour after exposure to white light for rhodopsin to form again. With the exception of the runway, the landscape was carpeted in black velvet. Couch could see neither terrain nor horizon. He was flying what pilots call a "black hole" approach. He could no more distinguish the degrees of darkness beneath him than if he were blind.

The graveyard of aviation is littered with pilots who attempted a black hole approach. Black holes throw visual tricks at the pilot. The first of these was uncovered by a Boeing scientist, Dr. Conrad Kraft, after accidents downed four Boeing 727 commercial jets in rapid succession in the 1970s at Chicago, Cincinnati, Salt Lake City, and Tokyo. In each case, the pilot crashed short of the runway during a clear night approach.

Kraft took twelve of Boeing's most experienced captains and had them fly a simulator. They had an average age of forty-four years and nearly 11,000 hours of flight time, just about the ideal profile of an aircraft commander. Kraft asked them to make an approach towards a well-lit city during clear night conditions. The only instrument they were denied was their altimeter. All felt the task would be easy. Eleven of the twelve crashed short of the runway. The only one who made it was an ex-Navy carrier pilot.

Even though the pilots' line of sight was in line with the runway, they flew the aircraft along a banana-shaped arc, consistently overestimating their height above ground. Kraft concluded that a black hole approach exceeded human ability, and the crashes were no more pilot error than if the pilots had been asked to fly an aircraft requiring stick forces far exceeding human strength. He determined that ideal conditions for a black hole include "an approach over dark land or water where lights to the side and below the aircraft do not exist." The problem is compounded on airfields that, like Alert, are lower than the surrounding terrain.

A report prepared for the United States Air Force School of Aerospace Medicine confirmed the black hole effect, adding that "the worst case is when only the runway lights are visible." The Air Force physicians had precisely described the flight conditions facing John Couch. The fact that he could see the runway lights was not a reason to switch to visual flight; on the contrary, it was a reason to pay strict attention to the dials.

So Couch was almost certain to misjudge his altitude; he was also certain to misjudge his distance. Depth and distance perception are even trickier on a clear night than on a cloudy one. Objects appear to be remarkably closer than they are. In clear winter conditions, distances are compressed by as much as a factor of ten. Couch was lulled into a sense of security by the very thing that endangered him: the clarity of the air and the brilliance of the runway lights.

"Joe," said Couch. "Clear us for visual, will you?"

Bales pressed the microphone switch and spoke to Alert. "Glow Worm, maintaining ten thousand. I have the airport in sight. Am going visual."

"Roger, Box Top. Cleared for visual approach."

Inside the flight deck, Couch turned the rotary switch on his horizontal situation indicator from "tacan" to "heading." The white needle on the HSI no longer pointed the way to the airfield, and the instrument no longer gave his bearing. If he wanted that information, he now had to look at a small instrument placed to the bottom right of the central display, the BDHI (bearing, distance, heading indicator). That instrument is not part of the T-shaped instrument scan.

The instrument scan is the very least attention a pilot is instructed to pay the dials, even in visual flight. The scan will tell the pilot with absolute certainty the position of the aircraft in relation to time and space. It will not, however, tell him the relationship of the aircraft to the ground.

For that measurement, the entire flight deck relies on the radar altimeter. It is tucked away in the lower left of the instrument panel, and, like the tacan, is not part of the T-scan. So, almost as though correcting an oversight, designers enhanced the role of the radar altimeter by connecting it to a small warning light on the top centre of the control panel. About an inch by an inch and a half, the light glows yellow when the aircraft falls below a determined height above the ground. The light reads, "Altitude low."

It is an old kit, and not considered terribly reliable. For one thing, the radar altimeter hunts for a while after being switched on, taking several soundings before deciding its altitude. While hunting, the needle swings back and forth, briefly illuminating the warning light. It can similarly become unsure of itself over rolling terrain, taking several soundings before it gets a sure fix.

For such a large transport, the warning system was ancient. But then, so was the aircraft itself. Couch's Hercules was an E series, tail number 322, built twenty-five years earlier. Its ground warning system was as old as some of the first officers that flew it. The modern alarm is called a ground proximity warning system, which pilots call "Bitching Betty" or "Bitching Bob," depending on whether the voice is male or female. In either, a radar warning causes a loud voice to pierce the cockpit, repeating, "Too low, too low, pull up, pull up," until corrective action is taken. Couch's Herc did not have Bitching Betty, but this shortcoming was not considered a hazard, certainly not for an experienced crew.

Scanning the dials, Couch read whether he was straight and level, his airspeed, and his altitude above sea level. But he knew neither his position relative to the airfield nor his height above the ground. He knew nothing, in other words, about his location in space. He was flying blind, no differently than if he were attempting to walk across a darkened room towards a point of light without bumping into the furniture.

The single point of light at Alert grew in the windscreen until it became twin rows. The airfield resembled a constellation in the shape of a pier, set against a coal-black sky. Couch was flying on a north-northwesterly course, with the airfield dead ahead. A few miles farther on, and slightly to his left, was a mountain peak rising 1,800 feet above sea level.

To his right, however, the hills were lower, climbing no higher than 1,200 feet. These hills were gentle in their roll and crest, being composed mainly of fragmented shale and covered with snow. Beyond them was the Arctic Ocean, a fearsome landscape in comparison. There, sharp blocks of ice ground one another into crested ridges and tore apart along sharp fault lines; ice floes the size of small farms collided and thrust pressure ridges hundreds of feet into the air. Couch swung his aircraft to the right, towards the coast. He began a descent to 3,900 feet.

"Commencing downwind leg, level and thirty-nine," Couch said. "Better tell Glow Worm."

Normally, pilots set up for the downwind leg roughly a mile from the runway. They fly parallel to the runway until past it, then double back and land against the wind. But Couch had turned off course a good twelve nautical miles from Alert. The airfield appeared much closer. Couch was impatient to get down to circuit altitude. Less than two minutes passed, and he hailed Moore on the intercom.

"Nav, I'm going fifteen hundred feet," Couch said. "Is that fine?"

Moore looked at his radar scope. Flat, smooth water shows up black on the scope, since there are no sharp edges to reflect the radar signal. Terrain, on the other hand, shows up orange, as the radar bounces off trees, buildings, cliffs, and so on. The aircraft was over the black; it was evidently over the water.

"Yes, that's fine."

Had Moore studied his tacan indicator, he would have realized there was something quite wrong with his radar reading. In the imagined world of night flying, tacan projects a giant bicycle wheel across the sky. Each spoke on the wheel is a numbered radial – there are 360 of them, corresponding to the degrees of a compass. Tacan also measures the length along the spoke between the aircraft and the runway. Tacan, in other words, projects bearing and distance – all that is needed to orient the aircraft in the horizontal dimensions.

On the Hercules, the tacan information is displayed twice: once on the tacan instrument itself, and again, if tacan is selected, on the horizontal situation indicator. But Couch had switched the larger instrument to show his heading rather than his relation to tacan. Nonetheless, the smaller tacan instrument still showed the radial. But no one, neither Couch nor Bales nor Moore, looked at it. If they had, they would have seen that the aircraft had not yet passed the 210 radial. As published on their approach diagram – all three had one – the aircraft would not be over water until it was east of the 170 radial. A glance at the tacan dial would have told them that a descent to 1,500 feet was unwise. It would barely give them clearance over the range of hills to the east.

What Moore had seen on his scope was a rare phenomenon called radar reversal. In the Arctic, there are no trees or buildings.

Snow is soft, ice is hard. The radar was indicating land where there was water, and vice versa. Somewhere in navigators' school they talk about radar reversal, but Moore failed to recognize it. He'd been suckered.

Couch brought the throttles back and the Hercules slowed to a speed of 160 knots. He selected 50-per-cent flap, to provide lift at lower speed. Although he had called 1,500 feet, no one alerted him as the aircraft slipped beneath that altitude. At slower speed, the Hercules dropped, even though it was still level. It passed 1,400, and 1,300, and 1,200, and below. Couch had fallen prey to the documented illusion of overestimating height in a black hole. There should have been a clue: for the Herc's distance from Alert, the airfield was much too high on the windscreen. But that made sense, since the airfield appeared much closer than it actually was. No one twigged. Couch began calling out the lengthy list of landing checks; the familiar, comforting routine. The Hercules veered slightly to the right, just enough for the airfield lights of Alert to disappear behind his left outboard engine. Couch realized, perhaps for the first time, and perhaps with a jolt of alarm, that he really was flying blind. He dropped his left wing 20 degrees, expecting that this would bring the lights back into view.

CHAPTER THREE

Death Roll

LIKE MANY of the thirteen passengers, Sue Hillier thought the pilot had merely made a hard landing. She was seated in the centre row of bench seats, facing the left of the aircraft, and she'd seen the airfield lights at Alert through the window. Feeling the Hercules bank to the left, she composed herself for touchdown. When the left wing of the plane slammed against rock, she remembered her own flight training as an Air Cadet. Kind of rough, she thought. Even I could do better than that.

Then all thoughts were chased from her mind; she stared, dumbfounded, at the floor of the cabin. A rock had punctured the floor and was carving it along the length of the bench seats.

A shark! The sight of this shark's fin slicing the metal floor of the Hercules caused such disorientation that her mind refused to make sense of any further information from the outside world. The lights of the aircraft flickered and then went black and she sensed herself leaving the cabin, still attached to her seat. All right then, she told herself, I'm still in my seat. But she could not accept what her seat was doing. It was not attached to the aircraft; it was moving outside.

Sue had braced herself by placing a hand down on the seat beside her, and she felt the science-fiction novel she'd been reading. If I lose this book, she thought, Adrian's going to kill me.

So she struggled to stuff the book into her pocket as the bench was catapulted through the torn fuselage and came to rest in the snow.

It's awfully quiet, Sue thought. Someone must have turned off the sound.

The Hercules made a tremendous explosion of noise as it began its death roll. Heading east, it had caught the crest of a small mountain peak. The left wing had hit initially, then the underside had struck the ground. The Hercules was plowing in an easterly direction along a plateau. The crash site sloped gently downwards to a broad and empty valley. To the north or to the south, the aircraft would have hit an area of rugged boulders. To the west was the steep gorge of the Sheridan River escarpment, at that point a nearly vertical cliff face of 600 feet. The Hercules had struck the one point where the passengers had the best chance of surviving collision with the ground. People would later say they were lucky, but they spoke without thought for the dreadful irony of their words.

The surface was frozen rock, covered with a light layer of snow. The aircraft had been travelling at 160 knots. It ground along for 1,600 feet, careering in a big slow circle to its left, before it came to a halt. The crash sequence took a full minute, perhaps longer. As it pounded the frozen ground, the aircraft split into three sections. The tail cracked off first, just ahead of the loading ramp. The loadmaster, Master Corporal Roland Pitre, was thrown out. He was the first to litter the crash trail.

The Hercules split again at the bulkhead, and all but two of the passengers were thrown clear of the fuselage. Behind them, the bulk fuel container ripped from its moorings. It was also thrown clear, and it burst open on impact with the ground. Nearly 24,000 pounds of diesel fuel sprayed over the site in an eruption of volcanic proportion, as though a railway car filled with liquid had been dropped on asphalt from a great height. The diesel splashed outwards and sprayed into the air, soaking the snow clear through to the underlying rock, soaking the wreckage, and soaking every one of the survivors.

Sue, strapped in her seat in the snow, drenched with diesel fuel, remembered that this had been a wet flight. Great, she thought. I'll never get the smell out of these clothes. And where's my hat?

———————

On the flight deck, Couch had responded with a pilot's instincts. He gripped the yoke and massaged the rudder pedals, as though the controls were still of use, as the severed cockpit roared along on its own, disintegrating on the jagged shards of rock.

In the co-pilot's seat, Joe Bales could still not grasp what had happened. He looked under his feet, and instead of the grey metal floor he saw white snow rushing past. He looked at Couch, but the commander was oblivious to everything but the controls. Couch's face was as taut as a clenched fist, and his fists were iron on the control yoke. Bales looked out the window and saw only a blinding cloud of snow.

It took all this combined evidence for Bales to realize that the aircraft had struck the ground. He was paralyzed by the realization. Near his right ear, he heard a single pop, and then a flushing sound not unlike the sound of an acetylene torch being lit. It was the aircraft's oxygen system. The lines had ruptured and caught fire.

Directly beneath Bales' feet was a cylinder, similar to the one on a propane barbecue, loaded with twenty-five pounds of liquid oxygen. Such a cylinder contains tremendous energy to feed a fire; oxygen by itself does not burn but will intensify any flame. Bales understood that he would be incinerated. He reached forward to a small window set into the curve of the windscreen and pulled a latch. It refused to give. The flame had flourished in the oxygen-rich atmosphere; it was now a solid, writhing wall behind him. Bales steadied himself, unlocked the latch, and pulled again. The window was small, about the size of a briefcase. But Bales is a slim man, and he was dressed in nothing more bulky than his one-piece flight suit. He dove through head first, fell more than four body lengths to the ground, and scrambled away.

Cut and bloodied, Bales was otherwise unhurt. He turned to look for Couch. He imagined that the captain had followed him out the window, but there was no one else on this side of the aircraft. The cockpit had become a cauldron, shrieking and hissing; balls of flame rose from it and coiled away into the black Arctic sky. The cockpit fell forward onto its nose as it was cremated. Aluminum and vinyl, glass and rubber, everything was turned to acrid gas or melted beyond recognition.

They're dead, Bales thought. He looked at his watch. It had been smashed and was no longer working. Bales accepted at once that the plane had crashed, that people were dead and wounded, and that he was in mortal peril near the North Pole. But he could not accept that his watch had stopped working. He shook his wrist and checked the watch again and again.

Then a question occurred to him. That was just the cockpit that was burning. Where was the rest of the airplane? All he could see was the skeletal outline of what must have been the fuselage, strung with a cage of wiring. Hearing moans from that direction, he hurried over. As he rounded the cockpit fire, he saw the other flight crew standing in a group. Three of them, all in flight suits. So they're not dead, he thought.

"Joe," said Couch. "You okay?"

Bales nodded. "What – "

"We'll worry about that later," said Couch. Like the others, he had scrambled down the crew stairs and fled the cockpit before its immolation. He was the senior officer on the ground. Here there was no routine, no script to follow, and he acted decisively. "First we have to find everyone. I want to know casualties, and I want everyone in one place."

It seemed an impossible task. In the orange light of the fires, they could see the dark shapes of bodies in the snow, and other dazed survivors walking about aimlessly.

"We'll work our way back up the crash trail," Couch said. "Spread into two teams. Joe and me. Paul, you stick with Mike."

Not far from the cockpit, one of the flight crew found someone burning in the snow. He rushed over and doused the flames, then tried to find a pulse. Captain Judy Trépanier, the dietitian, had been seated in the right forward seat, directly behind and below Bales, separated from him by the bulkhead. Although she would not have seen it, the oxygen tank had been a few feet from her head. She had been thrown into the path of the oxygen fire. The super-heated gases had scalded her lungs; she had died quickly.

Captain Wilma de Groot – the third woman on board, and the only medical doctor – had been seated on the same row of bench seats as Sue Hillier. As the aircraft had turned for its landing, Wilma had asked a fellow passenger for a laminated card of emergency procedures. Every aircraft, civilian and military, has one; they all strike the same reassuring tone.

"You are flying aboard a Hercules aircraft with an Aircraft Commander and Crew who are thoroughly trained and experienced," Wilma had read. "There is little likelihood that a situation will be encountered requiring use of the aircraft's built-in safety features; however, it is a good idea to be acquainted with them."

The card assured de Groot that an emergency landing would be preceded by an announcement and six short rings on the alarm bell. She should remove her eyeglasses, dentures, and sharp objects from her pocket, loosen her tie, and bend over with her hands over her head and her head tucked between her knees. There would be a final, long ring of the alarm bell, and the aircraft would land. She should remain in her seat until directed to the nearest –

Wilma couldn't finish reading. The lights had gone out. The side of the aircraft had been ripped apart and Wilma felt a freezing wind on her face that made her close her eyes. Something slammed her left temple, and her head filled with bright lights and swam with colours. She is a small woman, and she knew that her body, still strapped to the twisted frame of the bench, had been wrenched out of shape.

Wilma asked herself a question. How much pain can a person feel? How much can a person hurt before the pain kills them?

As a medical practitioner, of course, she knew the answer. Any amount of pain. Pain is limitless; it is a function not of death but of living. As a practising Christian, she knew that pain was the defining feature of this fallen world. The question really didn't lead anywhere promising. She decided to open her eyes.

She did not see, as she had hoped, the inside of a passenger cabin. She saw instead a clear night sky. She was still strapped to the bench seat, and she counted the people along the bench: three beside her, and two more at her back, still buckled up. That made six. Six people. That's something, she thought. That's a fact I can use.

She looked at her feet and saw snow. We've crashed the airplane, she thought. Then she chided herself for being foolish. Wilma, you're being melodramatic. This isn't bad enough to be an airplane crash.

She looked slowly around. Okay, then. If this isn't an airplane crash, where's the airplane?

She had herself stumped. There were pieces of metal strewn

about, and pots of fire here and there. But there wasn't an airplane, really. The fires gave enough light that, if there had been an airplane, she should have been able to see it. This was a situation that required more thought.

As Wilma was trying to make sense of things, Private Bill Vance staggered into her line of vision. He was on fire. The flames were lapping up from his collar and consuming his face. Wilma unbuckled her safety belt and managed to walk a few steps towards him. Bill fell into the snow, and Wilma fell on top of him, rolling her body over his, patting at the flames with her gloved hands until the fire was out. His face was charred, and black, and bloody.

Wilma was tempted, as a medical doctor, to study Bill's face more closely. It appeared as though his eyes had been burned out. That's when she decided she did not want to know more after all. Coward, she told herself, and got back to her feet.

Seven, she thought. Now there are seven. That's good. It's a number you can say, it means something.

A voice called to her from the bench seats. A woman's voice. "Hey, help. Help me get this thing off."

Sue Hillier had come to her senses and found herself trapped beneath the metal bars that had held the bench to the airframe. She saw someone's head near her foot, and another foot near the head. She couldn't move. A metal bar had been driven into her mouth, slicing off part of her tongue and smashing a tooth. She had pulled her mouth free of the bar and felt her face. She couldn't tell whether the blood on her hands came from her mouth or from her face.

Wilma made her way back to the bench seats. "I'll lift the metal," she told Sue, "but you'll have to pull yourself out."

Sue nodded. Her eyes, so striking and vibrant, were set and determined. Sue Hillier could stop a charging bull with her determined look.

"On the count of three," Wilma said. "One ..."

On "three," Wilma pulled at the metal bar and Sue shoved herself backwards with her hands. She managed to pull herself onto her knees but pain was shooting up from her hips in a nauseating wave, flooding her back and her skull. Her eyes opened in astonished distress, and she fainted.

It was then that Wilma saw the flesh of Sue's thigh and buttocks. Sue's boots had been blown off in the crash, her slacks shredded. The flesh was lacerated in several places and laid open nearly to the bone; but the wounds were not bleeding. No severed arteries, Wilma thought. The lacerations must be cauterized by the cold. The Arctic is an aseptic environment. That's good. That's fortunate. Lord, but I am in pain.

Wilma had been walking on a broken right ankle; suddenly it would no longer support her weight. Her twisted back was excruciating, and the pain got worse every time she expanded her chest to breathe. With each breath, she discovered a new threshold of agony. Strange that she hadn't felt it before. It occurred to her that she had a broken back. She fell face down in the snow.

Stay conscious, she told herself. You must stay conscious. There are seven. The airplane has crashed. You have a broken back.

After a time, Wilma could no longer breathe lying on her face; she decided to roll over. As she did, she saw Mike Moore and Paul West come into her line of vision.

"I'm okay," she said.

She told them there were six others, some with burns and severe lacerations. The men set off to help them. Wilma thought maybe she could breathe if she pulled herself up into a seated position. West returned with a box.

"Here," he said. "Sit on this."

Wilma asked him the time. If only she knew the time, that

would be another sure fact to cling to. West appeared to understand. Of the entire crew, he would be the one who would understand. He looked at his watch.

"Four-fifteen," he said. "Precisely."

She loved him for that, loved him for saying "precisely."

West told her the count. Four crew members alive and unhurt. The fifth, the loadmaster, Roland, was severely injured with massive traumas. Of the thirteen passengers, eleven had been found alive with various degrees of injury.

This blessed man, she thought. This man who knows the importance of precision.

West went off to join the other crew members who were back along the crash trail, ministering to Roland. It was not a case of preference; Roland was plainly the most severely injured of the casualties. Wilma was left alone on her box.

She looked up at the stars in the sky. They appeared so much closer than they did in the South. Polaris was directly overhead; she had never before seen it dead centre in the bowl of night. The air was clear, with just a few suspended ice crystals glittering in the light of the fires and the half-moon. The stars were close enough to pluck. The fires threw a flickering orange light over the snow; it was like a camp bonfire. It was remarkably calm, and Wilma did not feel the cold. Neither did she notice the stench of diesel, or of burnt flesh and wreckage, or the noise of incineration and human distress. Nor did she feel desolate. She felt instead an indescribable beauty and peace.

Sue Hillier thought for a moment that she would like to take an Arctic cruise with Adrian. A client at the salon had told her about it; the ship leaves from Victoria and sails all the way up the Pacific coast to Alaska. A cruise would be romantic, and it truly is beautiful up here. Adrian really should see it.

Then she felt foolish. She was trapped in a tangled hunk of metal with her legs ripped open and what felt like a broken neck. There were other people strapped around her, dead for all she knew. She was on the most northern tip of land on the planet, not far from the North Pole, and there was nothing but ice and rock. She had been in an airplane crash. The Lauraldo Hair Connection and Adrian and her family were more than 2,500 miles away. And it really hurt, goddamn it. The pain was becoming almost unreal.

"This is a nightmare," she said aloud. She waited a moment. "This is not real," she said more loudly. She felt her voice becoming hysterical. "This is a fucking nightmare!" she screamed.

Wilma felt the pain in Sue's voice and spoke matter-of-factly. "If this is a nightmare, then I'm in your dream. I'm here with you, and I'm real."

While Wilma was trying to comfort Sue, they both heard, in the distance, an odd moaning noise. It rose above the screams and groans and crackling flames that had been the constant background noise since the crash but that no one had noticed, just as no one had yet registered the cold. The moaning noise could have been the wind, Wilma thought, except that the air was still. She struggled to place the noise and finally recognized it. It was the sound of men in lamentation.

It was John Couch and his crew. They had been watching over their loadmaster, and Roland had just died. West had pulled a covering over Roland's face, saying, "Sorry, buddy, sorry, sorry," and the moaning was the chorus of voices of the remaining crew members, wailing like children into the beautiful night.

CHAPTER FOUR

Hercules Down

I N T H E freezing darkness of late afternoon, Major Don Hanson stood on the airfield at Alert, waiting for Box Top 22. A dark-haired fellow with the bearing of a thirty-year military man, Hanson was, in military jargon, the on-scene commander of the airlift control element – the officer in charge of Operation Box Top. He had come up from Edmonton the previous day to oversee the work of the thirty men and women stationed at Alert for the ten-day supply operation. There were no serious problems, other than some leakage from the new bulk fuel delivery system, and he was heading back to Edmonton. Box Top 22 would take him home.

Hanson stamped his feet. The air was cold and clear. He checked his watch – 4:25 P.M. The Hercules should have been coming into view. He scanned the horizon for the aircraft's navigation lights, but all the points of light in the sky were steady. Squinting, looking carefully for movement, he saw nothing but stars. He felt a stirring of unease. Where was the Herc?

In its first twenty years of Canadian Forces service, Hercules aircraft had had two accidents, both in April 1967. The first had been straight mechanical failure – the forward cargo door blew off, causing a sudden decompression. As proof of the Herc's claimed ability to land on short and austere airstrips, the pilot had landed in a field with no injuries. The second Hercules had crashed during a training mission. All six crew members on board were killed.

Pilots have a particular way of referring to pilot error. It applies to the most incongruous of circumstances. A pilot could be tasked to fly a Labrador helicopter up a mountain ravine in a howling storm with visibility shot to hell, and when he miscalculates and slams into the wall, his colleagues say not that the weather was too bad, or that the machine was not up to the job, but that he got suckered. This says much about the way pilots, at least in the Canadian Forces Air Transport Group, approach the question of judgment. The sky is a wily trickster, ready to lure you into a trap at every turn; the good pilot anticipates these traps and uses care and discrimination to avoid them. A pilot who falls into a trap has not been malicious, or wilful, or particularly negligent; he has been duped.

After the "pipeliner" system was introduced in the late 1970s, the following decade saw four Hercules accidents – a 200-percent increase over the previous twenty-year total. The numbers have no statistical significance, but the small, close-knit community of Hercules aircraft commanders began to draw their own conclusions. They began to worry among themselves whether more pilots were getting suckered.

The worry began after the first of these accidents, on October 15, 1980. A Hercules from 436 Squadron in Trenton had been called out to help in the search for an overdue Jet Ranger under the command of a pilot named Ryan. All search and rescue missions are named after the lost person, so this mission became SAR Ryan.

The search for Ryan had taken Hercules 312 to a position near Chapais, Quebec, northeast of Montreal. The aircraft was flying low over the woods in clear weather, searching for wreckage. The official version of what happened next has been released to the public by the Director General, Public Affairs, Department of

National Defence. Hercules commanders concede the official story is accurate, as far as it goes: "The aircraft commander did not exercise due care and attention to ensure that the aircraft remained within its operational envelope prescribed in flying orders. The pilot descended too low, the aircraft stalled and the pilot failed to recover."

A stall is a loss of lift from the wings, caused either by a loss of airspeed or by an increase in the wings' angle of attack through the air. The commander of the Hercules was on his first operational tour of duty, flying search and rescue with maybe a year and a half on the Hercules. A pilot of that experience can fly the Hercules, know a fair bit about its systems, and travel around the world on radar vectors. He can land the Hercules on instruments at just about any airfield with an instrument landing system. But he knows little about tight manoeuvres at low altitude in lousy weather, the daily grind of search and rescue work. Asking a pipeliner to assume command of a search and rescue aircraft is like putting a suburban commuter on a Formula One racetrack.

Hercules 312 did not have a stick shaker, a device that warns the pilot of an incipient stall by literally shaking the control column. The Hercules operating instructions explain the stick shaker; the circuits have been wired for one; older pilots remember a time when they were installed. But somewhere along the line the warning device was removed. Pilots are not supposed to induce a stall within the operational envelope of the Hercules prescribed in flying orders.

The search for Ryan had been going on for sixteen days; the Quebec wilderness was stubbornly refusing to yield her dead. The young Hercules pilot was crawling over the dense woods at an altitude of between 700 and 800 feet, trying to spot the shorn crown, the straight-edge slash, and the torn branches that indicate a crash site. He banked the aircraft to look at something. Banked, an airplane loses both airspeed and lift from the wings.

A heavy airplane loses speed fast. The pilot recognized too late that he needed to make a recovery. He went in with full power selected, 20 degrees nose up. He floated into the ground.

There were 34,000 pounds of aviation fuel on board, and ready ignition in the magnesium flares loaded in the search and rescue pallet. There was no hope of survival for the search and rescue technicians in the rear. The aircraft flopped in; the wings broke off and rolled underneath the airframe, soaking the fuselage compartment with fuel from the auxiliary tanks. The stricken Hercules laid down a fire trail as it ran aground, and the fuselage burned away like so much skin. The co-pilot and the engineer clambered out through an emergency window before the flames got to them. Everyone else – the remaining crew and an entire complement of search and rescue specialists – burned to death.

So the explanation given, that "the aircraft commander did not exercise due care and attention," was genuine. He got suckered. But error never fully explains how the parchment ripped, or why the surface tension suddenly burst beneath the machine. Was it an error of judgment or of calculation? Were the judgments and calculations demanded of the pilot beyond his personal "operational envelope"? If the aircraft was taken beyond the operational envelope, then why was the pilot not informed? Why didn't the machine scream out? Why was there a pipeliner in command? If rookies are going to be placed in command, shouldn't you at least give them a stick shaker?

Hercules aircraft appeared determined to take their share of rookies. On November 16, 1982, a Hercules from 435 Squadron in Edmonton crashed while conducting proficiency training. This one was mechanical error. If there are times when a pilot makes an error that no aircraft can be asked to forgive, the same must be said about aircraft; and Hercules 329 appeared to behave with wilful intent.

The Hercules is equipped with a low-altitude parachute

extraction system, which allows it to drop loads by parachute at low speeds from only a few feet off the ground. This is something the Hercules is really good at; the aircraft's party trick, as it were. The loads are stowed on pallets, which slide along metal runners the length of the cargo bay to the tail. The tail section of the Hercules, which resembles that of a lobster, is in fact an articulated loading ramp. In flight, the aft portion of the tail lifts upwards, and the forward section lowers to a level flush with the cargo bay. A drogue chute is propelled out this opening, which catches the slipstream and in turn drags out the main extraction parachutes. These three parachutes each have a diameter of twenty-eight feet; when they catch the air, they instantly produce a backward drag of 16,000 pounds. The pallets are yanked down the rails and out the ramp.

Hercules 329 descended from a circuit height of 200 feet down to about five feet and activated the drogue chute. A transfer mechanism jammed, preventing the drogue from pulling the main chutes out the door. The crew knew instantly something was wrong. They tried to jettison the drogue chute, but it was jammed; it also managed to release the extraction link, a small metal wedge that holds the load in place. The pallets began to slide back the length of the aircraft. They fouled on the extraction chutes, and a 29,000-pound load was suddenly lodged on the loading ramp at an altitude of five feet. This is beyond the operational envelope of the aircraft. All seven crew were lost on impact.

The crash of Hercules 330 and 331 was a messy deal. It reinforced the feeling that experience on the Hercules was vital. The two aircraft from 435 Squadron in Edmonton collided in mid-air on March 29, 1985. They were conducting a fly-past to entertain a mess dinner in commemoration of the sixty-first anniversary of the founding of the Royal Canadian Air Force. This may also have been a contributing factor, since the pilots decided to conduct a tactical fighting manoeuvre known as the "battle break," of little or no use in the operation of the Hercules. In this exercise, two aircraft flying in formation break off and peel away sequentially while gaining altitude. The procedure is no longer approved for the Hercules.

The lead aircraft was under the command of an American pilot on an exchange program, with much experience in the Hercules; the second aircraft had a former Snowbird display pilot at the controls and a pipeliner in the right seat. Prior to this first tour on the Hercules, the pilot had flown the faster, more responsive Tutor jet. The last propeller aircraft for both captain and co-pilot was the rubber-and-balsa Musketeer.

Entering the break, the lead aircraft did a gentle, Hercules-style climb and bank. The pilot was, in fact, faulted for delaying his own turn by four or five seconds. This is still a matter of some debate at the mess; some pilots maintain he was merely proceeding at the pace a Hercules pilot would naturally follow.

After the lead aircraft had broken formation, it was temporarily lost to the sight of the second Hercules. It floated above and behind the windscreen. Although the second pilot had lost visual contact with the lead aircraft, he had not lost his aggressive style from the Snowbirds. He gave his Hercules a hard, Tutor-style yank on the control levers.

It is never a good idea to yank an aircraft in the absence of visual reference to obstacles, especially ones above you. The pilot had been suckered. The second Hercules slammed into the belly of the first, and everyone died: six in Hercules 331 and four in Hercules 330.

The veterans of the Herc community watched as their co-pilots grew ever younger, and calculated whether there was a pattern. Then, on January 29, 1989, the last of this run of bad luck took place during Operation Brimfrost at the Wainwright army airfield in Alaska.

Hercules 318 was the second aircraft to fly from Edmonton to

Wainwright in the exercise. Both the pilot and the co-pilot were on their second tour, and experienced; but they were both new on the Hercules. The crew checked local weather conditions before landing and received a pilot report from the first Hercules, which had landed about an hour earlier. The report indicated that visibility was suitable for night landing but warned that it deteriorated sharply on landing rollout. In other words, the runway was visible from altitude, but ice fog obscured the runway as the pilot drew closer to the ground. Motorists have seen the same effect in fog; truckers peer down through the mist with good visibility, while vehicles closer to the ground are blinded.

The Hercules followed a precision-guided radar approach down the glide slope, but all precision radars leave the pilot 200 feet above touchdown. The pilot got suckered. His Hercules touched down early, striking the approach lights about 350 feet short of the runway threshold. The impact sheared the bottom of the aircraft and broke it into three sections. The tail section came to rest, intact, on the threshold. The right wing and fuselage slid another 500 feet, spinning in a half-circle and throwing passengers to their deaths. The wheels came to rest facing the plane's tail. Of the eighteen people on board, nine were killed.

The Director of Flight Safety issued another circular, this one warning pilots to refresh themselves on the numerous visual illusions the sky can produce, especially in the night Arctic sky. Once again, the authorities were dead right. And once again, the older hands wondered what the Director of Flight Safety had to say to aircrew whose knowledge of those illusions was dimly remembered from a lecture hall, but not from the indelible schooling of the flight deck.

Major Hanson spent ten minutes on the airfield at Alert, studying the sky intently, before the sick unease in his gut gave way to
dead certainty. Box Top 22 was overdue without explanation. He
headed for his air traffic control unit and raised the alarm. Hercules down.

Hanson checked first with the Glow Worm operator, who
reported that Box Top 22 had been lost from the radar scope five
nautical miles after cancelling instrument flight. The flight had
been missing for about ten minutes. Hanson, at fifty-one, was an
experienced search and rescue commander. He knew not to leap
to conclusions, to take things one step at a time. But it looked as if
Couch had been suckered.

"I want all radios to conduct a communications check on all
frequencies. See if you can raise them. Get hold of Box Top Two
One. Have them check all frequencies, too. Maybe they'll raise
something. Instruct Two One to begin a visual search over the
last reported position."

Hanson established a command post. He ordered samples
taken both from the aircraft fuel supply and from the blood-
stream of the Glow Worm operator, in case either was contami-
nated. Neither was. The radar and radio communications tapes
were seized and quarantined; so were the flight manifest and
records. The Hercules already on the ground at Alert was ordered
drained of fuel and replenished from a different source.

Next, Hanson called for a count of available ground vehicles
and medically trained personnel, in preparation for a search
party. And he needed a helicopter badly; the radio operators at
the Alert command post began a search for anything, military or
civilian, that could make it from Greenland. Then there was
nothing to do but contact the rescue centre at Trenton and wait.

———————

At the Canadian Forces base in Edmonton, 2,160 miles to the south, Major Don Blair was pouring himself the last coffee of his shift. Blair was in charge of Edmonton's rescue coordination centre; as long as he was on duty, he would take responsibility for every lost soul between the prairies and the North Pole.

The rescue centre was a modest office located just off the base operations room. It had a portable computer, and while just about everybody had elaborate software at home, they ignored the cheapjack software of the command post's computer in favour of the familiar radio sets, telephones, and teletype. Edmonton had a caseload of 300 call-outs a year. On the coastal stations, or at headquarters in Trenton, activity climbed to nearly ten times that amount. Edmonton was a nice, quiet station. Someone once remarked that the Edmonton command was like desert air for Blair's nerves.

Blair, a colleague and contemporary of Hanson's, was a wiry, ginger-haired man and a heavy smoker; hence his nickname, Smokey. He was deciding whether to take the walk of shame, down the stairs from the second floor of Five Hangar to the secure smoking area, when a duty officer called him over to the teletype.

"Hey, Smokey. Come take a look at this."

Blair sauntered over. The machine was hooked up to SARSAT, the search and rescue satellite-aided tracking system. The system was founded by Canada, France, the Soviet Union, and the United States to locate signals from emergency beacons using satellites in outer space. Over a dozen countries now use it. When a ship or aircraft triggers its emergency locator beacon, SARSAT detects the signal and sends a notice to the nearest rescue centre. Most of the time, SARSAT will raise a crash alarm within two hours and direct rescuers to within an accuracy of eight miles. Since coming into use in 1982, SARSAT has been credited with saving 1,500 lives, and it has drastically reduced the time needed to locate a downed aircraft or ship in distress. It is also a whining pain in the ass.

The SARSAT signal does not discriminate between a real and an imagined emergency. A pilot will leave the emergency beacon armed when landing, jostling it to life. A farmer will hit a parked aircraft with a tractor, sending an electronic "Help me!" into the ozone. Neither will realize anything is wrong until the yellow rescue aircraft comes flying overhead. As at your local fire station, false alarms are more plentiful than the real thing.

In the case of Box Top 22, of course, the beacon had worked as designed. It had been thrown a few hundred yards from the crash site and begun sending a signal on 243 megahertz – the distress channel – that was picked up by the computers at the search and rescue centre in Trenton. The computers routed the alarm to Edmonton, where it was printed over the teletype.

The duty officer showed Blair the printout: "We just got a SARSAT hit out of Alert."

Both men laughed. The previous spring, during an earlier Box Top airlift, an emergency beacon had fallen off a Hercules aircraft in mid-flight. The radio beacon is attached to an airfoil, or small wing, designed to fly clear of the crash site. The beacon had survived the fall to pack ice midway between Thule and Alert and had begun issuing a mayday. Designed to endure forty-eight hours in those temperatures, the alarm had in fact sounded continuously for two weeks. The rescue centre had to program its computers to ignore the signal.

"Christ," said Blair. "Another airplane's lost its crash position indicator. Now we'll have to listen to that for the next two weeks."

Blair went out for his smoke. An hour later, after tidying up some paperwork, he went home.

Don Blair had just walked out the door when the telephone rang. It was traffic control, advising the rescue centre that Box Top 22 was an hour overdue at Alert. The call was routine paperwork; pilots often forget to close off their flight plan after landing. The duty officer picked up another telephone and called Alert. Couch would get his wrists slapped for this.

When the duty officer in Edmonton raised Alert, however, he found out the matter was anything but routine. Don Hanson told him there was now confirmation: Box Top 21 had flown over the crash site and seen fire on the ground.

Bad news travels fast. Captain Wayne Todd, Blair's replacement on the evening shift, was hanging up his coat when the cleaning lady passed him, pushing a broom. "You're going to have a busy night," she told him.

Todd went over to the duty officer. "What the hell did she mean by that?"

"We've got a Box Top down at Alert."

"Jesus," said Todd. "Get Smokey at home and bring him in here. As a matter of fact, get everybody in here."

The crash of Box Top 22 was the first major air disaster ever to confront Canadian Forces search and rescue. A major air disaster is classified as an airliner down with more than ten people on board; in military abbreviation, the situation is called a MAJAID (pronounced "mayjade"). A MAJAID plan had been in the works for years, and drafts of the response plan were securely stored in several offices around the country. In the wake of the crash, the plan was activated, although never officially declared. No one broke open the book and followed procedure, because no one needed to. The book was also stored in the minds of Hanson, Blair, and Todd. They had helped write it.

The MAJAID plan called for loading a Hercules aircraft with airborne troops, along with a medical and survival kit capable of tending eighty survivors. There are two such kits, one in Edmonton and the other in Trenton. But these kits and troops were to be flown to the crash site in support of a team that would, according to the plan, already be in place. That on-site team would be drawn from a small unit of highly trained and motivated rescue specialists called SARtechs, search and rescue technicians.

Warrant Officer Fred Ritchie, the SARtech team leader in Edmonton, was in many ways an unlikely commander. He was forty-three years old, absolutely ancient by SARtech standards, and his favourite activity was inactivity, unlike many of the SARtechs, who count among their hobbies such hairy-forearm stuff as mountain climbing and skydiving.

Ritchie liked those, too, but he liked nothing more than to curl up on his sofa with his head in the lap of his once-and-ever child bride, Pam, and allow her to stroke what remained of his hair. He had enjoyed this particular variation on the theme of doing nothing since he had married her twenty-two years earlier, immediately started a family of three sons, and weathered poor pay and long absences until his marriage was as solid and expansive as his home in a civilian suburb just off the Edmonton base.

Nothing, in such sweet moments, could drag him from the hearth; neither his love of bonhomie and revelry, nor the call of the outdoors. Fred Ritchie was only half tamed and needed frequently to be allowed out to run. But when he came home, all of him was home. He had been a difficult man to unlock, but Pam had come to understand him.

Which is why it was that whenever the telephone rang – as it seemed to have a knack of doing whenever Ritchie was profoundly at rest – she was the first, figuratively, to hand him his bags.

"Fred, it's Kobe."

Master Corporal Mike Kobayashi, one of Ritchie's more

trusted SARtechs, went by the name of Kobe, as in beef. He was on stand-by duty at the hangar.

"We have a MAJAID," said Kobe. "Herc down at Alert with eighteen souls on board."

"I'll be right in."

Ritchie is smaller than average height and wiry as a hawser line. He has an erect and proud bearing, handed down to him by his father, the regimental sergeant major. But his every gesture has the quick smoothness of the cat. Wriggling into his flight suit, he looked as restless as the seven deadly sins.

"Going north, honey."

Pam handed him the bag with a change of underwear, socks, and sweatsuit, and kissed him goodbye.

A dozen SARtechs in the Edmonton area received such a call, and from the time they picked up the telephone, drove up to thirty miles to the base, loaded a Hercules with rescue gear, gathered the aircrew, fuelled the airplane, received a briefing, and took off into the air, one hour and twenty-eight minutes had elapsed. The MAJAID plan calls for a best-effort response time of two hours.

Fred Ritchie drove without regard for the Highway Traffic Act to the base, pulling up in front of Four Hangar, where the SARtech equipment is stored. He jogged towards the rescue coordination centre at Five Hangar, a hundred yards away, and met Major Jim Burger coming out. Good old Hamburger – thank Christ, thought Ritchie, we got somebody who knows what the hell he's doing.

Burger, thirty-nine, was one of the more experienced rescue pilots in the Canadian Forces. In an air force where many pilots serve one three-year tour with the SARtechs and then beg off, Burger had been flying Hercules rescue aircraft since 1978, with one two-year exception. In his thirties, he had joined an airborne regiment and became a paratrooper, training alongside soldiers ten years younger. Burger found the training arduous. He did it only because no other pilot wanted the posting, and he received a promise he could go back to flying rescue work for as long as he liked. He was, as he said, "converted, committed, and commissioned" to the role of flying search and rescue aircraft – or, as the pilots called them, SARbirds.

Burger told Ritchie all that was known. The Hercules was down ten miles from Alert. A fire had been seen on the ground. There had been no contact with survivors.

"Who's the pilot?" said Ritchie.

"Couch."

Ritchie had flown his last rescue assignment with John Couch, fifteen days earlier. He and Burger both believed there was no chance of finding anyone alive. Neither of them expressed the sentiment.

Burger's stand-by Hercules was already loaded with a twenty-person survival kit, but Ritchie wanted all available gear on board. There had never been an all-hands exercise before. SARtechs usually work in pairs, but now there were a dozen men hustling around the shop. They worked together with quiet precision. Ritchie assigned the duties. You, take all the extra parachutes you can find in the folding shed. You, bundle the personal survival kits in cargo nets. You, we need a dozen sets of Arctic kit.

Ground crew hustled the gear into the tail of the Hercules. It formed an enormous pile: strobe lights, flashlights, headlamps, marker lights, radio beacons, radio handsets, jump suits, poopy suits, parachutes, parkas, signal flares, magnesium flares, streamers, penetration kits, shell dressings, oxygen cylinders, tourniquets, shock trousers, saline solution, ringer's lactate, back boards, body bags.

59

Ritchie noticed Master Corporal Jim Brown strapping snow-shoes to his B-25 kit, a personal survival bundle. Nothing much that Brown did could surprise him. Brown came from a farm near Innisfail, ninety miles south, and he'd been known to drop in on the folks by parachute while returning from a mission. That was one of the more sensible things he did.

"Jim, what are those?"

"Snowshoes, Fred."

"Have you ever seen an Eskimo wearing snowshoes?"

"No, Fred."

"Get rid of the snowshoes, Jim."

Brown unstrapped the snowshoes but kept his helmet. Brown's helmet is easy to spot. Someone had attached a warning label to the forehead: "Explosive." It probably dated to the time Brown dropped down to a rubber liferaft in the stormy North Atlantic to hoist up two survivors from a sunken vessel.

The first hoist to the rescue helicopter went poorly. Brown placed the ring around the crewman's chest and held him to his own. Then he told him, as is standard procedure, "Grab your crotch." This is the best way to remind survivors to keep their arms down, so they won't slip out of the hoist. The advice was wasted, as the crewman didn't speak English. The two were swamped by a wave as they left the raft, and were pulled along for about thirty feet under water before they broke clear. By now the crewman was limp. Brown held him as the cable swung in a wild, 60-degree arc, all the while hoisting them up to the Labrador helicopter at 300 feet per minute.

When Brown returned to the rubber raft, the second crewman refused to be rescued. He just sat there, clutching the raft and shaking his head. Brown wasn't in the mood for arguing with some ungrateful son-of-a-gun over gale force winds and towering waves. He unsheathed his marlinspike and punctured the liferaft. As the raft deflated, Brown raised his eyebrows at the crewman. The crewman, wide-eyed, nodded in return.

Fred Ritchie admired that kind of spirit. He made a mental note to assign Brown as the team leader on the mission.

Two sets of aircrews had boarded the Hercules, so they could relieve each other at the controls. Burger and his co-pilot, Captain Derek Stobbs, would fly the first leg. The aircraft was loaded and ready for takeoff when two things delayed departure.

The first was a problem with the fuel gauges. Although the tanks should all have been filled, the gauges were showing that one auxiliary tank under the wing was 2,000 pounds short. While Burger was sorting out the calculations, it began to snow a freezing slush. Another delay was called while the wings were de-iced.

The SARtechs were waiting impatiently in the back when Master Corporal Ron Condly noticed the cause of the second delay: the morphine kits were missing. The pre-measured syringes were locked in the base hospital, about a quarter-mile away. He leaped out the aircraft door to get them. Ritchie yelled after him that they would not wait for him to get back.

Condly commandeered a passing Jeep and had the driver take him to the medical unit. He told the driver to wait, and ran inside. There, he was confronted with medical orderlies of a bureaucratic frame of mind and no understanding of the SARtechs' authorization to draw from the morphine supply. There was a quick and heated discussion. Condly impressed upon the staff his willingness to tear the narcotics stores from the wall with his bare hands if necessary, but that he would prefer to smash the cabinet open with their thick skulls; and in the end, reason prevailed.

A SARtech must be fit. The fitness standards are higher than those of the regular military; SARtechs must, for example, be able to run one and a half miles, do thirty-one push-ups, thirty-three sit-ups, and eight chin-ups, do another 500-meter run, and climb two twenty-foot ropes, all without rest and within seventeen minutes. Condly was grateful for this training as he ran out into the freezing snow with the morphine kit under his arm, for the Jeep and driver were gone. He sprinted back to the Hercules. When his partners pulled Condly into the door, the Hercules had already begun to taxi.

Three hours had passed since the crash. With any luck, Burger calculated, he'd have Ritchie's SARtechs over the scene in seven hours. Ten hours total since the crash.

He called up the Alert weather forecast and got disheartening news. Visibility and ceiling were falling, winds were on the rise. A fierce Arctic storm was brewing at the Pole, and it was headed towards Ellesmere Island.

Burger selected maximum continuous power. The turbine inlet temperature of the Hercules roared to more than 1,000 degrees Fahrenheit – the equivalent of red-lining a sports car's tachometer. Burger pushed the SARbird into the night sky towards its top speed of over 310 knots. It was suddenly a race between the aircraft and the elements, and the storm had all the advantages.

CHAPTER FIVE

The Wasteland

BOB THOMSON's journey into misery had begun with sudden cold and darkness. One moment he had been airborne, preoccupied with thoughts of his wife and the CANEX post at Alert, and the next moment his body had been pummelled by the equipment that had been on the walls of the Hercules. He had held his hands up to his face, warding off the blows, then had felt himself being launched.

The least I could do is get unconscious, he'd thought. Don't tell me I'm going to have to stay awake until I die.

Bob had landed in the snow, on the same metal bench frame as Sue Hillier and Wilma de Groot. His body was cruelly bent. His first lumbar vertebra was smashed, and his left leg was curled backwards, pressed up against his buttock in such a way that his heel was behind his ear. His right leg was splayed out at an odd 45-degree angle, twisted away from the thigh. He had no idea it was possible to feel such pain. Death in a plane crash was supposed to be quick.

Don't tell me I've got to live through this. Please. Not this.

Bob began to feel anger at being spared from death. He looked around, not so much for help as from resentment. He saw people walking, lit by the orange light of the fires. It infuriated him that other people could walk. They'd all gone through the same crash.

There they were, walking away scot-free, and here he was, contorted in metal and ice. It wasn't a question of fairness. Fairness hadn't entered his mind. Neither did he think it was wrong, or a waste. He only knew that he was deeply hurt and his response was anger. He was blind with anger that his luck had run out.

As a younger man, Bob had been a one-day celebrity in the Toronto newspapers for having survived an unusual accident. He had been engaged in horseplay around a railway trestle, and a boulder had rolled free and crushed his back. He'd been rescued after some hours, and he'd walked away with no lasting injuries. His entire life had gone like that. He had married the woman he set out to marry, and the marriage had worked beautifully. He'd got every job he wanted, at times through lucky circumstance. His jobs had allowed him to ski across Europe, sail off Bermuda, and build his ideal home. Bob Thomson envied no one; he had lived his dreams.

Now the charm was off his life, and it didn't make him despondent or baffled or humble. It made him mad.

Bob was able to hold his torso more or less erect by planting his hands in the snow; he found the most comfortable position was to lean slightly forward, over the displaced left hip. He decided to study just how much of the bloom had gone. When he'd been trapped under the boulder, he'd been unable to feel his legs. He had thought then that his back was broken, but it wasn't. The sensation was similar this time, except for the intensity of the pain. He allowed himself to hope.

"You've been through worse than this, Thomson," he said aloud.

But he knew it was a lie.

He tried to move the right leg. He consciously willed himself to bring the leg in, pull it under his buttocks, and raise himself to a squatting position. The behaviour of the leg astonished him. It began to flop about like a landed fish. It felt as though an electrical current was passing through it. It flopped frantically until he stopped trying to move it, and then it lay still, senseless and apart from him.

Thomson, he thought, this is really bad.

How bad? He decided to take stock. One hand was resting on a jagged spar of square metal, which seemed also to have impaled his legs and back. He had no gloves, but he was wearing a parka, wind pants, and lined galoshes. He could hear moaning. The air was calm.

He noticed that he was sweating profusely. Then he realized that his heart had begun pounding in his chest. Not the regular, hard beating he could get from a workout on the bicycle, but an insanely rapid-fire hammering. His chest was exploding; he could actually feel the walls of his chest throbbing outwards as if someone were in there, beating the ribs with fists. The pressure filled his throat, distended his skull, and caused his eyes to swim. He waited for his heart to burst, but it would not. He could hear each heartbeat clearly, more a whack now than a thump, and he expected at any moment to hear silence.

Bob did not realize that this was his body's moment of decision. His autonomic nervous system was going to either shut down all engines or else transfer remaining power to those that still worked.

Bob waited for his body's decision. He sat that way for perhaps half an hour, oblivious to everything but his body's bizarre torment. Then the beating subsided, winding down so much that he thought it was winding down altogether, that this, finally, was his exit. Then it levelled out at a normal rhythm, and the pressure from within disappeared. He stopped the profuse sweating, but by then he was soaked through with both sweat and diesel fuel.

He looked up, returning to the world. Sergeant Paul West was standing above him.

"Anything I can do?" said West.

Bob thought for a moment. "I'm getting cold. I could use a hat."

The pain from his chest had allied itself with the stabbing in his lower back, a continuous circuit of pain; below that, he could feel nothing. Half his body had been taken from him; the other half tortured him.

In the few minutes immediately following the crash, Bob Thomson believed he had hit bottom. To remain conscious through your own destruction seemed a fate that could not be surpassed. He believed his misery had been the worst that life could deliver.

Now, as the sounds of human grief registered in his brain and the breathtaking cold began its slow, insidious invasion, he understood that the misery had barely begun.

———————

It is hard to imagine the place where the survivors found themselves. It was as alien to them as the surface of the moon. Those from the cities had to begin by taking away. There was no built environment of any kind. The works of people had not reached this place; the foot of man had perhaps never trod it. The Inuit had never dared to live this far north; in their tongue, the name for this place was "The land of the land beyond people." Explorers had seldom wintered its coast.

There were no straight lines here, and the survivors' eyes had learned over a lifetime to order the world along straight lines. So their perceptions drew inwards, away from this alien place. Many maintained little awareness of anything beyond the span of their own arms and legs.

They were, oddly, in a desert environment, a region that receives scant precipitation, most of it in the form of snow that blows and drifts to varying depths. In the summer, the survivors might have found blue grass, chickweed, arctic poppy, saxifrage, arctic willow, and mountain aven. These are pretty plants but would have provided little sustenance. Perhaps they could have found reindeer moss, and boiled that. In summer, they might have seen glaucous and ivory gulls, long-tailed jaegers, sandpipers, snow buntings, oldsquaws, and, perhaps, snow geese. But it was not summer.

It was almost November, and the stillness of the land was disturbed only by arctic hares and the swift movement of the arctic fox. Both were white, and nearly indistinguishable from the landscape. They were as difficult to see as the little people who, according to the beliefs of the Inuit to the south, also lived among the snow and rocks. Even more rarely seen were arctic wolves.

Insect life, which causes intolerable suffering in the tundra, had virtually disappeared this close to the Pole. Spiders, deer flies, and warble flies are seen on Ellesmere Island in summer; but by this last day of October they were gone. Not even microbe life was active, a blessing to those lying on the snow with dreadful wounds – a torn scalp, a smashed eye socket, a compound fracture, or a puncture – that at least would not develop infection.

The land was as God began, before the first day of Creation. It was formless and void, and darkness lay over the surface of the deep. There was no light. From the 10th of October there is no direct sunlight, but each day has a few hours of twilight. The last official day of twilight is October 30, the day of the crash. There were a few hours around midday when the darkness would slightly lift; but this was neither daylight nor twilight, merely a subtle lessening of the gloom.

The surface of the land consisted entirely of broken slates and shales. These were in flat shards, for the most part the size of a plate or a foot. Where the rock had not broken down, it formed square-edged boulders; where it had, it formed undulating hills that fell into steep ravines. On the shoreline, the rock turned to a fine dust. It was a primitive land. The ancient snow among the rocks turned to ice; ice and rock were the foundation. Above that, the snow was blown about until it lost its fringes and became a hard, granular sand of depth hoar. The newer snow was layered above this frozen grit. The surface was driven by the wind into a hard, icy crust. The snow was poor for insulation and poorer still for walking. It was the worst of snows.

And it was cold. The temperature was 22 degrees below zero on the Celsius scale. At the moment of impact, the temperature of the air enveloping the survivors had plummeted 40 degrees Celsius, or more than 70 degrees Fahrenheit. In still conditions, a temperature of -22 Celsius gives a wind chill categorized by meteorologists as "cold." Even the slightest wind intensifies this cold dramatically. Wind speed of three miles an hour – the wind generated merely by walking – doubles the heat loss caused by wind chill. Simply by walking, in other words, a survivor subjected himself to a temperature that meteorologists categorize as "very cold."

———————

When Paul West returned to Bob Thomson with a wool tuque and gently pulled it on Thomson's head, Thomson thought it was on crooked. He wanted it straightened and pulled down, but West had gone away again.

There were others in more serious trouble. Bales and Couch had followed the sounds of moaning back along the crash trail to the remaining portion of the fuselage. It was a jumbled mess of wiring and twisted spars, charred to blackness. Bales had spotted a body straddled over the wiring, high in the wreckage and in a prone position. Fires were lapping around the man, and he would soon be burned alive. He was calling for help.

Bales climbed up to get him. He tugged the man free, pulling him out through the clutter and onto the snow. He went around the fuselage to the other side, where Couch was already at work pulling out a second man. With these last two survivors clear of the wreckage, Bales went back to where he had left the first man, Master Warrant Officer Tom Jardine.

Among his many wounds, Jardine had evidently punctured his lungs. He was having great difficulty breathing, and Bales wrapped his arms about him, trying to find a position that would allow Jardine to inhale. It was a lost cause; his ribs had punctured the lungs. With each breath, air was drawn into the chest cavity, squeezing the lung and reducing its capacity. He was suffocating by his own attempts to breathe.

"What's your name?" Bales asked.

"I'm Tom," the man whispered.

"Where you from?"

"Moose Jaw."

The words were banal and small, Bales knew, but they were important. No one should die without a name.

"My wife is in Moose Jaw right now," Bales said. "Her name is Dianne. I'm Joe."

"Help me, Joe. It hurts bad."

The words made a simple request. This is a gentle man, Bales thought. A good man. He searched himself for some knowledge that could be of help, but came up with nothing. He tried instead to comfort him.

Bales held Tom Jardine in his arms, the dying man's head against his cheek. He prayed that the man would be given just one good breath. Then the blood spilled from Jardine's lungs, and Bales felt helpless and ashamed. He was miserable at his own escape from injury. Abruptly Jardine stopped breathing.

"Tom. Tom?"

Bales had never before been this close to death. He got up,

disoriented, and walked over to Couch. "He died. He just ... died."

"This one's alive," said Couch. "Let's carry him to the Doc."

The crew had been gathering bits of scattered survival gear while they searched for the survivors, and had uncovered an intact sleeping bag. They now put the man Couch had helped, Warrant Officer Robert Grimsley, into it. The bag was a mummy style, without closure or zipper; it was difficult to get an unconscious body inside. But once Grimsley was securely wrapped, they could half drag, half carry him to where Wilma was seated.

Bales was heartened to be doing something of use. They set Grimsley down by the fire, and Bales bent over to speak to him. But the air around Grimsley's mouth was perfectly still; his breath did not fog the air.

"He's stopped breathing."

Bales placed a hand on the man's neck, searching for a pulse. "No heartbeat." Bales began to pull down the sleeping bag, calling for his crewmates to help him perform cardiopulmonary resuscitation. He looked to Wilma de Groot – she was a medical doctor, after all.

"Don't," she said.

"What?" Bales snapped. His frustration and anxiety were near the breaking point.

"It only works if you're close to a hospital. Are we close to a hospital?"

"We have to try something," Bales said urgently.

"Joe," Wilma said gently, "we don't know what killed him, but CPR won't bring him back. I know it sounds cut and dried. But if it was enough to kill him, we don't have the resources. He didn't die of a heart attack."

"This is something I can do! I can do this!"

"Joe, let it go."

He glared at her, but he knew she was right. Gingerly, he

removed Grimsley's tuque; it would be needed. But it was a good half-hour before he could bring himself to claim the sleeping bag.

Wilma de Groot stared at Grimsley's lifeless body and wondered whether God was a hypocrite. She was a practising adherent of a small Mennonite denomination. But, in a society that anaesthetizes pain, she had never before grappled with the problem of suffering.

She wondered if a loving God would allow the airplane to crash. God the Creator had made the beautiful night, but he had also made this desperate land. God had allowed her to live, and taken the life of this man. He made it to rain on the good and the bad alike, and the sun to shine also.

Except there was no sun in this place. Wilma thought of profound matters, but no profound insights came to her. Bad things happen. She had always, in a detached sort of way, known that. It was not a perfect world.

She remembered that once, in Rome, she had visited the Sistine Chapel, and she had taken the steps up the dome of St. Peter's. They were so steep and high, it seemed she was entering the vault of Heaven itself. She had been frightened then, and she had calmed herself with a hymn. She began to hum it now to herself: "It is well with my soul." It is a slow, melodic, soothing melody, and it carried over the surviving passengers, over the blood and snow, and over the dead.

God had allowed her to suffer, and she could not understand that. But she had to choose. She could turn to him, or turn her back to him. She was free to decide, and her suffering had brought about this freedom. Curious thought. She knew that love must be given freely, or it becomes a sort of death.

She resigned herself. All right, then, I choose to let you help me. But I'm not going to become more religious. I'm not cutting any deals with you. You can help if you want. But I'm not promising anything.

Wilma de Groot did a mental calculation, performing the subtraction. We were eighteen, she thought. Now we are fourteen.

CHAPTER SIX

Good Buddies

THE THOUGHTS of Warrant Officer Arnold Macauley were not, on the afternoon of October 30, dwelling on the mysteries of God and his works. They were verging on the blasphemous, and occupied with the works of a Honda marine pump.

Arnie had spent the day trying to kill the pump, but the pump was not a quitter. He had it rigged up to a water barrel and ran it through a few trials. At first, he just held a garden hose in his hand and made a few threatening passes at the pump. That was usually enough to stop the marine pumps supplied to Arnie and the other SARtechs in Greenwood, Nova Scotia. The regulation marine pump was afraid of water. Not this Honda, though. Arnie held a jet of water steadily over the motor. The Honda didn't even cough. He sprayed water directly into the air filter. Didn't matter.

A big, handsome, square-shouldered man with tattooed forearms and a prairie way of talking, Arnie Macauley was the team leader of the SARtech unit in Greenwood. Most of their call-outs were to rescue ships in distress. Much of the time, the ships were taking on water. So the SARtechs had devised a SKAD kit – Sea Kit, Air Droppable – to help out such boats. It was a watertight steel drum that could be dropped upwind of a struggling vessel, with a retrieval line passing over the decks. The sailors hauled it on board and helped themselves to the items inside, including the marine pump.

Except that the regulation pump was an abject failure. It wasn't a marine pump, really, just a small two-stroke Briggs and Stratton engine with a pump on the side. The air filter was made of the same paper that filters coffee; as soon as it got wet, the engine would choke to death. Arnie had started trying to get a replacement pump more than four years earlier. In the military, these things take time.

A lot of time. The average wait, between filing a Statement of Operational Requirement and getting the replacement, is five years. Unlike most standing forces, Canada's military is not trusted simply to go out and buy things. Proper channels must be followed. The SARtechs' request for equipment must fit into the global budget of the Air Command, must not be pushed off the ledger by, say, a new whatsit for the Twin Huey helicopter. If approved by the commander of the Air Command, the request is handled by the federal Department of Supply and Services in Ottawa, which invites tenders from suppliers. Canadian suppliers receive preferred treatment. The tenders are for the specifications, not the gear itself – if SARtechs admire an all-singing, all-dancing, waterproof, fireproof Japanese radio, then a Canadian manufacturer must be given the chance to produce a cheaper equivalent. As if.

War, von Clausewitz suggested, is the pursuit of politics by other means; the Canadian Cabinet has broadened that dictum to include the pursuit of patronage. The federal Cabinet is not interested in articulating the role and policy objectives of the Canadian Forces, but it is keenly interested in getting its hands on all that loot. The purchasing program of the Forces comes under Cabinet review and has become a convenient means of distributing federal largesse to preferred regions and companies. Whether the contract is to service a fleet of CF-18 fighters or to build a new fleet of frigates, the Cabinet tends to make the decision as inefficient and corrupt as legally possible. In the face of such political stakes, the needs of a few SARtechs are easily overlooked.

SARtechs jump, for example, with parachute canopies that are, with minor changes, identical to those used at Arnheim during World War II. The square parafoil canopy, which is safer, more responsive, and in worldwide use, is being tested by the Canadian Forces. It has been in the testing process for twelve years; in the meantime, there have been a lot of broken limbs. The SARtechs' request for a new radio battery is, at this writing, five years old. Their marker lights routinely fail or bust up. They have no night vision goggles, although they often jump at night. They don't have the global positioning system, which uses a common, hand-held navigational unit that can be purchased wholesale in the U.S. for about $4,000. In the Gulf War, U.S. forces used the units to deliver pizza.

Cabinet meddling in the procurement policy is a great way to bestow favours on Quebec when that province needs stroking, or to create jobs in the Maritimes when times there are tougher than usual. But it's a lousy way to equip an army.

When the Briggs and Stratton pump failed on a marine rescue in the North Atlantic, forcing one of Arnie's boys to hoist down and end up perilously adrift in heavy seas, Arnie, tired of waiting, took matters into his own hands. He telephoned the American supplier of the Briggs and Stratton. The supplier told him they had stopped making that model eight years earlier. Couldn't be a worse marine pump in the free world, the supplier reckoned. You ought to try our new model – you'd think it had gills. Arnie asked if anyone still bought the old model.

"Just one buyer," the supplier told him. "The Canadian military."

Arnie decided to find out what else was out there, which was

75

how he came to be standing in the sARtech shed with a garden hose and a Honda pump. The Honda had not come through official channels. Arnie's boys had ... well, kind of noticed it fall off a Coast Guard vessel. What with all the paperwork, it would take a couple of months to send it back.

Arnie put down the pump to answer the phone. It was his little brother.

"I don't know what the hell's going on," said Marv Macauley, "but there's a plane down. You better get all the boys out."

That was one of the good things about life in the military. In what one of their colleagues, with a wink, called an "extraordinary coincidence," Arnie had spent the past ten years on postings with his brother. In Greenwood, their two families lived a block apart.

Five years Arnie's junior, Marv was the more explosive of the two, and even bigger, with a thick moustache and a six-acre voice. Despite his bluster, though, he felt perpetually in Arnie's shadow. Arnie was golden. Arnie had so much ability that Marv never felt he was even playing on the same field. Marv was under a hockey suspension for his habit of losing his temper and dropping the gloves. Arnie was more the type to take the cheap shot without retaliation, then score while the other guy was in the penalty box. Marv held Arnie up as a standard. Which is probably why he had followed his older brother through Air Cadets and basic training into rescue work.

A pilot, Marv had risen to the rank of major – he outranked his older brother – and was flight leader for the Hercules aircraft out of Greenwood. Arnie led the sARtechs; Marv led the sAR-birds; they worked under the same commanding officer. They were a good team. Indeed, they had won national exercises, proving they were the best team in the country. They'd proved themselves to the world, but Marv had yet to prove himself to himself – to cease seeing himself as Arnie's little brother.

At that moment, Marv felt he'd been at the centre of a monumental screw-up yet again. The base operations officer in Greenwood had telephoned him with breathless news about a big plane crash and asked him to hold while he was patched through to the rescue centre in Halifax. The officer didn't stay on the connection, and the line went dead.

Marv had tried a WATS line, but it was busy. He nearly drove a thick finger through the telephone dial, raising the Greenwood air base telephone operator. The operator didn't have the number for the Halifax rescue centre. Marv had wondered aloud, employing several Saxon euphemisms, why this was so.

He slammed down the receiver, then called Arnie, then raised the duty officer again. Finally, he got through to Halifax and learned the scant details: Hercules down near Alert, eighteen souls on board. Marv told the duty officer he wanted a hundred extra flares on the stand-by Herc, pronto, and an uplift of 63,000 pounds of fuel. One hundred flares weigh 2,500 pounds. With the additional fuel, Marv's Hercules would be 4,000 pounds over maximum allowable weight at takeoff.

"You'll need Air Transport Group Headquarters to approve that," he was told.

"Screw Headquarters," Marv replied. "Those are peacetime rules."

––––––––––––

The idea of air rescue was conceived by Canada's legendary flying ace of World War I and pioneering bush pilot, W.R. "Wop" May. In 1944, May was manager of the Number Two Air Observer School in Edmonton. He was concerned by the number of aviators who became stranded in the northern wilderness. All too often, a machine or human failure in the bush meant the pilot was lost for all time.

"The only way to give downed survivors a chance in this terrain, so far from roads and railway, is to drop medical men by parachute to patch 'em up," May said. "Then teach them how to survive until they can walk out or we can get in by dog sled."

The call went out for volunteers who not only were in good physical condition and knowledgeable about bush lore, but also were "temperamentally stable." Stability remains the most important quality in the trade. Recruits cannot enlist directly in search and rescue; SARtechs are drawn from the other services. Few enter the trade before their late twenties; few practise after their mid-forties. Great mental and physical resilience is required, and in most people these years offer the best blend of maturity and youth.

For many years, theirs had not even been a "trade," or occupation, in the Canadian Armed Forces. It was merely a "specialty" that borrowed its rescuers from other ranks: usually parachutists, medics, or explosives experts. Often they were drawn from the ranks of parachute folders. The reasoning was that they could fold their own chutes, saving the military money.

Arnie Macauley lived on the Greenwood air base with his wife, Darlene, two children, and a beagle named Star. On his bookshelf, he carried reminders of his former life, including a small statuette of an airborne commando. Around it were the insignia and symbols of the fighting trades, all hairy forearms and winged daggers. Arnie had sickened of that work; indeed, like many SARtechs, he had tired of the military altogether. He had been conditioned to a mental and physical prime, had been trained at great expense to jump from the sky, climb mountains, swim under water – all to the purpose of killing someone. Even if there were honour in arms, he knew that his life would be wasted on exercises; that he would, in all likelihood, spend his days playing soldier.

Then he had heard of a little-known trade in the forces that took the same energy and training as an elite para-commando, which he was, but put it to work saving lives. It was an operational detail – he'd be called to do real work. He thought it would be better for his mental health. He signed up and became a SARtech, as did his little brother.

Over the years the Macauley brothers had learned about the country in a way few Canadians ever do, even those within the Armed Forces. Canada, to them, was a vast and splendid land. They knew little about its cities and less about its neuroses. It was not the mind of Canada that they admired but its magnificent body.

To Arnie, the country began with a blue coast of high timbers that would catch him in its limbs as he fell from the sky. There, you always jumped with the coiled rope on your thigh and let yourself down gently to the forest floor. Then the high mountains, where the air was thin and you landed hard. Arnie knew the alpine snows, could read the course of a season in them and predict their intentions. He was an avalanche and survival expert; his skills were demanded around the world. The Canadian Rockies had been his teacher.

Then there was the northern bush, measureless and deep, and marshland, and tundra, each with its own lore. Arnie had been with Fred Ritchie then, and their friendship grew in the north country. They had foraged in the wild, as they foraged in the supply depot. Ritchie told him of how the northern bush tore up parachutes, and of how, in the old days, he had been forced to scavenge time-expired canopies from the U.S. military. They had cut steering holes in them and operated the vents with nylon cord and toggles cut from branches. You can jump on a torn chute, Ritchie taught him, but the crown must be intact; that's the high-pressure area.

"You can do anything you like as a SARtech," Ritchie had said, "just so long as it doesn't cost the Canadian taxpayer any money."

Macauley had been to Ottawa once to be presented to the

Governor General. They played a fanfare on the trumpet and gave him the Medal of Bravery, which now hangs in his dining room. He has no use for the city otherwise. To him, it is a place where few airplanes crash. It is to the south of the northern Ontario bush. It is a place where the elected go to become incomprehensible. He watches the news from Ottawa at night and admits to feeling like the "Peanuts" character Lucy. The teacher is saying "Waa waah waaah wah," and Lucy has no idea what she means.

After Ottawa, though, you get into northern Quebec and Labrador; and they are rugged. To Arnie, the Great Canadian Shield is not dimly remembered from geography class; it is hard rock to fall upon, difficult terrain to hump across. And then there are the Maritimes, composed of tiny boats upon heavy seas, always in miserable weather. And high winds. Atlantic Canada is, for Arnie, an adversary made of wind.

The trade seldom lost its people, except to injury or, in one case, to suicide. Arnie had always been aggressive; the SARtech life also made him tranquil. His job allowed him the outdoor life, and he fished streams known only to anglers who arrived in orange jumpsuits from the skies. He had never known of a criminal or disciplinary problem among his detachment. There was a rare camaraderie. His men – all SARtechs are men; although the trade is open to women, none has yet passed the course – were like a clan to him. They weren't just his men. They were also his buddies.

Details of the crash were sketchy because the rescue coordination centre in Edmonton was, in the first hours, as overloaded and jangled by shock as Bob Thomson's spinal column. Some things went more smoothly than others. It took only one hour and twenty-five minutes to set up a network of notifying the next-of-kin and assigning officers to assist the families. At the same time, word had been received from Alert that a Greenland Air Bell 212 helicopter had been launched from Thule and was on its way to the crash site. But a Bell 212 would never make it. It didn't have the range, and it couldn't be refuelled in the air.

In the Edmonton control room, everyone was busy, everyone had a job to do. A wall chart was being completed, listing all resources in North America that could be called to the task. Someone was talking to Scott Air Force base in Illinois, trying to determine if there were U.S. helicopters in Thule, or anywhere else in the Arctic. Others were on the line, raising the Macauley SARtechs and ordering a Labrador helicopter launch from Gander, Newfoundland. A second Lab was requested from Trenton, a third from Greenwood.

The last word from the circling Box Top flight near Alert was of "slim" chances of survivors.

Amid all the energy and slackening confusion, Captain Wayne Todd noticed something else. People weren't quite looking at one another. Everybody was engaged in their own tasks; when they spoke to others, they tended to keep their heads down, avoid eye contact. Everyone in the room had personal knowledge of at least one person on board. Some had had good friends on Box Top 22.

Then the bad news started coming back. It was taken quietly. The Labrador helicopter launched from Greenwood hadn't even been able to make it over the Gulf of St. Lawrence, because of closing weather, and had been stood down. That aircraft was struck off the wall chart. A helicopter from Goose Bay had also been stood down – the distance was too great. The rescue effort seemed to be falling apart before it had even begun.

––––––––––

In Greenwood, meanwhile, Marv Macauley was getting annoyed. He'd hurried over to the operations centre to pick up the briefing fax from Halifax. The fax hadn't arrived; he had no brief. His information was limited to a rough latitude and longitude of the crash site. Then he found out that the extra flares hadn't been loaded, because no one could find the duty armourers. Why weren't things happening faster?

In fact, the SARtech departure from Greenwood was moving along smoothly. The rescue squadron had been on two-hour stand-by, meaning a state of readiness requiring two hours to launch. Within eighty minutes of getting the original call-out, Marv and Arnie would be airborne in the Greenwood Hercules, Marv on the flight deck with the rest of the crew, Arnie in back with the rest of the SARtechs and the flares.

Marv may have stepped on a few toes, but he wanted to get to Alert as quickly as possible, with every resource at hand. He didn't yet know where he fit into the organization of the rescue effort. He didn't even know which rescue centre had command and control of his aircraft. He didn't know the weather at Alert, and he had only a rough idea of what he'd do when he arrived.

But he knew he had to get up there, and fast. He knew John Couch, had taught him tactical airlift, instructing him in such difficult manoeuvres as flying a Herc five feet off the ground. As for Paul West, Marv had flown rescue missions with the guy. So had Arnie. You don't share those kinds of experiences without becoming good buddies.

CHAPTER SEVEN

Shelter for the Mind

MASTER CORPORAL David Meace sat on a green duffel bag, trying to make sense of the past few hours. It was hopeless. He could remember certain things and even comprehend them; but his comprehension did not stir him to action. He was recovering from adrenaline shock, his brain sugars were depleted, and he knew he should move about or the shock could kill him; but he did not move. Even more than sinking into unconsciousness, he was afraid he might wander away into the night.

Meace remembered there had been a bang and the lights had gone out. He remembered reaching across the bench seat to brace himself, and his arm crossing the chest of Captain de Groot. His hand had clutched at some webbing; he remembered it had burned into his palm.

When he'd regained consciousness, he'd found himself lying in the snow under some wreckage. He hadn't moved at first; instead he looked up at the sky. There were stars out, and the moon looked much larger than it would at home in Montreal, or at the base in Kingston. It was a half-moon, as pregnant as it got in the fall, and there was something else reminding him of autumn – an orange, flickering firelight. He turned his head and saw flames billowing from the airplane's remaining sections, swirling upwards and disappearing in the darkness.

He noticed he was absolutely calm. He stood up and began speaking to himself: "Well, you can stand up. Your back hurts a little, but not too bad. You'd better walk around."

He stumbled over to the overturned wing and stood there awhile. His lungs had been seared by fire, and he tired instantly.

He had seen Bill Vance in flames, and Wilma de Groot rolling him in the snow. Then de Groot went away, and another figure pulled himself from the wreckage and began to crawl over to Vance's side. It was Vance's friend Mario Ellefsen.

Ellefsen had come to his senses and, upon realizing he was still alive, had kissed his wedding band. He then heard Vance calling for help. Although his hips were broken, he dragged himself along on his forearms.

Couch ran past him towards the fuselage, where someone else was calling out for help. Couch stopped briefly at Ellefsen: "You all right?"

"What happened?" asked Ellefsen.

"I don't know," said Couch, then ran towards the fires to rescue the two passengers caught in the fuselage wiring.

Meace had seen all this activity, and it had vaguely dawned on him that he was merely standing around. Everybody's doing something, he told himself. You'd better do something. He went over to Ellefsen and Vance.

Vance was a mess. Blood was flowing from his head. The scalp had been lifted away like a toupee and had fallen back roughly in place. Blood was coursing down the blackened skin of his face. His eyelids had bloated to the size of charcoal briquettes, charred black and greased with blood. The lids were nearly swollen shut.

Vance could make out a pair of feet stumbling towards him through the snow; then Meace was kneeling beside him and whispering in his ear. "Stay with us, buddy, stay with us."

One of the aircrew came by with sleeping bags. Meace knew it was a member of the aircrew, because they stood apart in their light blue flight suits. He dropped four of the bags and briefly examined Vance. "You'd better get him into a bag," he told Meace.

Meace picked up a bag. It was a thick Arctic bag, down-filled, with no zipper. A person had to crawl inside, and Vance could not move. Instead, Meace draped the bag carefully over him, tucking the sides against the snow.

The crewman returned and looked appraisingly at Vance and Ellefsen. "We'd better get them both inside."

So Meace and the crewman had struggled to get the men into the sleeping bags. It felt good to be working; it gave Meace purpose. When the job was done, the crewman left. Meace felt himself slipping back into shock. He wanted to wander away. He didn't know where he would go. He just wanted to go somewhere.

Instead, he dragged a duffel bag between the two men. Then he announced: "Jesus, I can't stand any more." And sat down.

Ellefsen wondered what he meant by that; whether he couldn't stand any more in his body or in his mind. Meace meant both. His back felt painfully swollen; he wondered why he had not felt the pain before.

Ellefsen was talking to the blinded Vance, an endless recording of the same text: "I'm here, Bill. Are you still here? Buddy, are you still with me? I'm here, Bill. Are you still here?"

Meace didn't say anything. He felt he would be intruding on their conversation. He sat in silence until Paul West came over to their group.

"I'm goddamn freezing," Meace said. "Is it safe to go by that fire over there?"

He pointed at the wing. It had flipped over in the crash, and the underside – which was now on top – had been ripped away, exposing its reinforcing ribs. The leading edge curled upwards, providing a wall of sorts. A fire was burning between the ribs. Altogether, it looked like shelter.

From his years on rescue aircraft, West knew that a psychological shelter was nearly as good as the real thing. The wing would provide scant protection from the cold. But it would provide a sense of home for the mind, and that would enhance the passengers' will to survive.

"Sure," he said.

The slow procession to the wing began. Most of the survivors were scattered nearby. Some could walk. Others were carried in their sleeping bags or dragged with their arms around the shoulders of the flight crew.

David Meace, being in fairly good shape and wanting something to do, was put in charge of preparing fuel to keep the wing fire burning. The flight crew brought him anything that would burn – webbing, the aircraft log, the operating manual, technical orders, paperbacks. He tore the pages from the spine and crumpled them. Then Michael Moore, the navigator, added them to the fire.

Moore was in charge of the fire, and it was tiresome work. The ruptured fuel bladder was about fifty yards away and still contained a few dozen gallons of diesel. But there was no suitable container to transport the fuel to the fire. After a search, he found a piece of wreckage in the shape of a cup. He and West carried the diesel, a few ounces at a time, back to the wing.

It was a journey of one hundred paces for eight ounces of fuel. The icy crust sometimes broke underfoot and stabbed at their shins. They struggled to keep their balance and tried not to spill the precious fuel. From time to time, they would break through the crust, falling over onto their knees or face. The diesel would spill onto the snow, and they would go back and try again. Barely had they added fuel to the fire when it was time for the next trip. They wore thick, absorbent gloves of wool or felt; soaked with diesel, the gloves weighed several pounds. The diesel parched their frozen skin, and their hands were soon cracked and raw. But still they carried the fuel.

Wilma de Groot sat by the fire, with Vance's charred head in her lap. She asked West how long it would be until they were rescued.

"We're only about ten miles from the station," he said. "Help is on the way. I'd say we should be out of here within, maybe, an hour or two."

Why, then, Wilma wondered, had the crew not stopped to rest? Why, if they'd be rescued in an hour or two, were they still striking off to gather up duffel bags and other potentially usable things? And though Paul West had sounded optimistic, why, she wondered, had his perfect precision suddenly failed him?

———

With Bob Thomson, Couch knew, there was no decision to make. The man had a broken back, as well as other fractures and possible internal injuries. His legs were grotesquely arranged. He simply could not be moved.

Sue Hillier was more difficult to diagnose. Couch had asked her many times how she felt, and at first she had said, "I don't know, I can't feel anything." But she had also complained of pain all over. He had tried to move her; twice, in fact, he had placed his arms under her shoulders and attempted to lift her to her feet. Each time she had fainted, and the deep lacerations on her thigh and buttocks had started to bleed. So he had left her there.

Despite Sue's injuries – both her legs were broken and badly burned, her right shoulder and elbow were broken, several ribs

87

were broken, and she was haemorrhaging internally – her mind remained remarkably clear and active. Each time she woke from her faint, she fixed Couch with those penetrating eyes and asked questions. She wanted to know everything. What happened? Why had they crashed? Where were they? When would they be rescued?

Couch let her talk. There was time enough for knowing. When she finally lapsed into silence, he told her he'd be back and walked over to Wilma de Groot, who was sitting inside the wing with the blinded soldier's head on her lap.

"I need your opinion, Wilma." His face was pained and grave. "I don't think it's safe to move those two. Think we should leave them outside?"

At first, Wilma didn't understand. "You mean we can?"

Couch nodded.

"Then of course. If you can leave them where they are, it's much safer. Even if their spines aren't broken, you could cause spinal shock by moving them."

Couch did not appear convinced.

"They could die, John."

It seemed to be what he'd needed to hear. He returned to Sue's side, kneeling and speaking softly. "We're going to have to leave you here with Bob. I'm sorry. But if you have a broken neck, any movement could kill you."

Buried deep in each heart is a great idiosyncratic fear, an irrational dread of something most other people accept with equanimity. Sue's great fear was of abandonment, a fear she had transmuted into a love of company. At home, she was always surrounded by other people, hardly giving herself a solitary moment. She had become a hairdresser for the same reason, to ensure community, a constant human context. It was clear that this balding man cared for her, and she tried desperately to control her anxiety.

She did not know who the man was, only that his name was

John and that he appeared to be in charge and that the cold was starting to get to him. He was wearing nothing more than his polycotton flight suit and a cotton jacket – not even a hat – and his speech had become affected by the cold. His tone remained quietly authoritative but the words had lost their crispness, running together in a numbed bumble.

"Where are you going?"

"The others are over at the wing. We'll make a fire here for you. We're going to make you as comfortable as we can."

"No," she said. "Where are *you* going?"

"I'm not going anywhere. I give you my word. I'll stay with you as long as I can." He added, in a voice suddenly emotional, "I won't leave you, Sue."

Now the roles had changed; Sue realized that he was distraught. She had not meant to upset him. "It's okay. I believe you."

Couch and Joe Bales began the slow work of building a shelter from the depth hoar surrounding the maimed bodies of Sue Hillier and Bob Thomson. Six inches of packed fresh snow, of the sort found hundreds of miles to the south and used in the building of igloos, has an insulation value of R-70, about the same as most homes. A resting body throws off the same amount of heat as a burning candle and can warm a shelter built of such snow to a temperature of one or two degrees above freezing.

Here, though, this close to the North Pole, the snow was dry and granular, almost useless as insulation and impossible to carve into snow blocks. The depth hoar around Sue and Bob had a tiny fraction of good snow's insulating value, and the permafrost beneath them was as cold as the ambient temperature. The primary value of the cave that Couch and Bales made for them was as a shelter from the wind.

Seven sleeping bags had been recovered, and the flight crew used four of them in sheltering Sue and Bob. First, they dug as much snow as possible away from their bodies and shoved a sleeping bag underneath. Then they packed snow between Sue's legs, covered her body with another bag, and piled snow on top of that. From the chest down, she was immobilized. They coiled a rag over her face, leaving her mouth clear. The rag was noxiously soaked with diesel fuel, but she found it warmer than having her face exposed. Sue, the woman who loved company, felt as alone as a mummy.

Bob was more difficult to cover because of the awkward skew of his legs. His left foot was still up behind his head, his right cranked outwards and exposed. Someone found a curled piece of torn fuselage and drove it into the snow, creating a windbreak. Bob's face was canopied with a piece of canvas tarpaulin. It was completely dark inside this structure, and Bob was still nearly insensate from shock. He was slowly pulled to awareness by the irritation of down feathers being drawn into his mouth and nostrils. The bag had torn and he began worrying his tongue over his lips, wetting the down, trying to keep his breathing clear.

"Box Top Two One, this is Paul West. Do you read me? Over."

Static.

"Try another channel."

Bob Thomson gradually came back to his senses in a blur of sound and blackness. The drone of an aircraft overhead was mixed up with the sound of radio static.

"Box Top Two One, do you read me? Over."

"Try the flares."

When the sharp report of three flares fired at close range registered in Bob, his nervous system could not handle the shock. The crack of the flares made him feel as though he were at the centre of a huge concussion. His body began to shake, and the image went through his mind of a sparrow quivering on the ground, having struck a pane of glass.

Your nerves are shot, Thomson.

The fingers of his right hand were close to his cheek, and they trembled over his skin. He wrestled to bring the hand under control. He heard voices again.

"They've seen us! It's only ten miles. They'll be here soon!"

Hear that, Thomson? Ten miles. You can hold out for a couple of hours.

Bob focused on the uncontrollable quaking, trying to settle his body. As he concentrated, he noticed he was not trembling from the waist down. He was nothing from the waist down. He was paralyzed. It was something he could no longer deny, but he could put off thinking about it.

"How are you?" a voice asked.

"Okay," he said. "A lot of pain."

"We're building you a fire."

He began to orient himself. Another voice was off to his right, a woman's voice – Sue's. It seemed as though his head was near her feet. She was going through a period of hysteria, the words impeded by the lacerated tongue that had swollen in her mouth: "Oh God oh Jesus how did this happen? Oh my Jesus oh God."

He let her ramble for a while. He begrudged her none of the words; he felt much the same way.

"It's okay, Susan. Hang in there."

Bob found it difficult to speak loudly, but even these few, barely audible words had an immediate effect.

"Bob?"

"I'm here."

Sue was not alone after all. She began to pepper him with questions. What did he know? What kind of shape was he in? How was his snow cave compared with hers? Could he see anything? When Bob described his injuries – that he had no feeling below the waist, that one foot seemed to be up behind his head, and that his buttocks seemed impaled on a piece of metal – Sue felt faint.

Then, to her surprise, the swoon yielded to a surge of purposefulness. She began to worry about him. She tried to engage him in talk about his life, but he fell suddenly unresponsive. Sue cast about for a common topic of concern. She settled on the fire.

Paul West had brought over a fire in a pot-shaped piece of metal and placed it in the crook between them. Bales and Couch were combing the snow for pieces of material to soak in diesel fuel and bring to the fire. It was throwing more light than heat to Bob, who watched the flickering light on his diesel-soaked tarpaulin and suddenly realized that a spark would carry over and ignite the canvas over his face.

"It's nice, guys," Thomson said, spitting down feathers from his mouth, when he heard the crew return. "But a lot of work for not much return."

"I'm burning on one side," Sue said. "I'm freezing on one side and burning on the other."

The crew agreed to let the fire die down. The darkness grew even darker. Sue felt the falling temperature and deeper darkness and associated it with nightfall.

"Well, Bob," she said as cheerily as she could, fighting her ungainly tongue, "we're in for a cold night, but it'll warm up at dawn."

"Dawn," Bob said hopelessly. "There's no dawn."

"It'll warm up," said Sue.

"There's no dawn. There's no dawn until spring."

Mike Moore was stoking the fire at the overturned wing. Here, at least, there was some semblance of shelter and kinship. The survivors all felt they had seen the worst; their fortunes were on the rise. They could hear the aircraft overhead, knew they were mere miles from the station. Intent on these hopeful signs, they had not really noticed the slow creep of the wind, the stars being extinguished one by one, the gradual fall in temperature.

Few of the survivors knew one another, and fewer could have recognized one another even if they did. Their faces were smeared with blood, diesel, and charcoal. Most of the passengers had parkas, which were also filthy and wet. Their feet and hands were covered with an assortment of boots and gloves, mostly torn, all of them fuel-soaked. They had started to shiver with the cold, and their injured bodies had become stiff.

Vance, blinded with second-degree burns to his face, had been wrapped in a sleeping bag and was resting his head on de Groot's lap. Ellefsen, with a broken pelvis that ground audibly when he moved, had been placed along the wing in his sleeping bag. Beside him was Master Corporal David Montgomery, who had lacerations to his scalp and left arm and a skull fracture that had left him drifting in and out of consciousness, rambling and incoherent.

The other injuries, while painful and gory, were not immediately life-threatening. Captain Richard Dumoulin had smashed the orbital bone around his right eye. His friend Master Warrant Officer Marc Tremblay, who'd suffered lower back injuries, did not tell him how bad he looked, even though the sight of Dumoulin's face turned his stomach. Master Corporal Tony Cobden was equally grisly, with a massively swollen bruise around his right eye and a long laceration in his scalp. Virtually everybody, including the flight crew, had deeply bruised and swollen backs.

The flight crew all had damage to their backs. West, perhaps the most energetic of them all, had slipped off his shoulder harness just before the crash. In addition to a bruised back, he had bruised his knees and shoulders. This was bruising of such severe nature that it caused several passengers to think their backs were broken. The flight crew worked despite the pain. Although they had the least useful clothing, they stayed warm by movement. Their bruising did not stiffen, and they did not feel the cold, because they remained active. They burned calories – their bodies were throwing off twice the heat of those on the wing – and they worked up a sweat. This would exact a terrible price later; but for the moment, they were in good shape. Besides, they felt sure of imminent rescue.

Because of Canada's size and climate, the Canadian Forces have developed a body of knowledge about survival rivalled nowhere else in NATO. Although none of the flight crew had completed the rigorous Arctic winter survival course in the Northwest Territories, all had learned the basic principles of survival in flight crew training.

Canada differs from its European NATO partners in its approach to survival. In Europe, crews are taught to be aggressive; the Canadian approach is passive. Downed over Europe, a flight crew stands a better chance of reaching safety than it would in the Canadian wilderness. Canadian crews are taught to wait at the crash site. The European model also emphasizes bush lore and skills; the Canadian model recognizes that nature is an impossible adversary. It teaches some lore but recognizes that the most important survival skill is mental resilience.

Cold is a physical reaction to the elements, but also a psychological one. Fire and shelter create physical warmth but are of far greater importance to the mind. Of the four benefits of a fire, only one is physical: the provision of warmth and the control of mild shock. The other benefits are psychological. Fire acts as a signal, giving reassurance to survivors that the crash site can be found. Building a fire provides first a goal and then a feeling of accomplishment. Fire also provides a sense of well-being. In controlled experiments, the sight of a fire has raised the body temperature of subjects even when the fire provides no warmth. Although the Hercules survivors' small fire, burning between the metal ribs of the overturned wing, provided not a single calorie of warmth to the survivors, West and Moore knew it was well worth the effort of sustaining it.

Fire also helps to overcome psychological cold, a term for the physical reaction to a mental attitude. Flight crews are taught that virtually everyone in a survival situation feels guilt – either for the blunders that got them into the mess or for the efforts being made to rescue them. But shame, along with fear, anxiety, and pessimism, can kill. These emotions contribute to shock. They cause perspiration, which leaches heat and later freezes. They dilate the blood vessels, bringing more blood to the surface of the skin and increasing heat loss. The best way of overcoming psychological cold is to set goals that contribute to the chance of rescue. For their own sakes, then, as well as for the benefit of the passengers, the flight crew knew the importance of keeping the fire alive.

It was working; the survivors were settling into something approaching a routine. The flight crew were busy, and the able passengers all had some chore to occupy them on the wing. Wilma comforted the blinded Vance. Meace tore apart the flight logs as fuel for the fire. Dumoulin opened the green duffel bags brought to him by West.

The duffel bags containing the lifesaving equipment on board the aircraft had been stored high along the right side of the fuselage, an area completely destroyed in the crash. They were green Defence-issue bags, and although some had a strip of orange fluorescent tape on one side, so did many of the passengers' duffel bags. As West searched the crash for useful items, he had no way to tell whether a duffel bag contained a fuel stove, for example, or some of Bob Thomson's CANEX stereos. He simply hauled everything back to the wing, where Dumoulin, his eye grotesquely displaced, pried the frozen zipper free.

This process took on the expectation and surprise of a Christmas morning. The other passengers watched eagerly as Dumoulin reached inside each duffel bag. Once, he pulled out several tubes of mosquito repellent. He held them high, and they drew a laugh from the survivors, at the expense of the Canadian military. He also found useful items, such as a Swiss army knife. But he put it in a pocket of his parka for safekeeping. He had not noticed the pocket was torn, and the knife – along with his Arctic mitts – was lost in the grimy snow.

It was a small mistake, just as the flight crews' working hard enough to perspire was a small mistake. The Arctic seldom kills by big mistakes.

Dumoulin was delighted with one discovery – three packages of survival candies. The candies were flavoured gelatin cubes, cling-wrapped in clear plastic. They had frozen solid.

"Here, Doc," he said. "You better take these."

Wilma read the instructions on the candy wrapper. Each package provided enough calories for one person for two days. That was six person-days. We are fourteen. We have enough sustenance for twelve hours each. She would ration them accordingly.

The survivors had purpose, the expectation of a quick rescue, and a degree of comfort. The initial shock had worn off, they had reconciled themselves to their various injuries, and they had taken an interest in their surroundings. Although they were beginning to register the terrible cold physically, they had mental warmth and security.

They even ventured into ribald humour. Wilma, with Vance's head in her lap, reached down into his sleeping bag to warm her hands.

"Look out, Bill. Doc's taking advantage of you."

"Hey, Doc, is that first aid?"

"Sure, Doc, the old 'my hands are cold' routine."

"You guys are just jealous," she said. "Aren't they, Bill?"

Vance forced a chuckle – a good sign, she thought. If we can keep our spirits up, maybe we can ignore that the weather is getting worse. She shivered, tucking herself more closely around Vance.

Moore was bringing a new container of fuel to the fire. Wilma had never seen his face, which had been covered since the crash by a wool-and-polyester knit balaclava. She was surprised when she first heard his voice. Why, she thought, he's just a baby.

Moore leaned down, bending close to the fire, and began adding the new container of fuel. The scene was abruptly fixed in time, as if caught in a strobe light. There was a whoosh, a blinding flash, and then a fireball erupted from the blaze, lighting the darkness and racing the length of the wing. Wilma curled over, covering Vance's face with her chest and tucking her own head.

Dumoulin and Tremblay were blown over backwards; the fireball had struck Dumoulin in the face, singeing his hair and flesh. In the ensuing panic – screams, incoherent shouts, bodies scrambling away on hands and knees – Wilma looked up and saw Mike Moore lurching away, his head in flames, screaming. He collapsed to his knees, burying his face in the snow, then fell motionless.

"The bag!" Dumoulin shouted. "Get the bag off him!"

Bill Vance's sleeping bag was highly flammable, and flames were creeping up the cotton cover. She beat at the flames with her hands, while someone yanked at the foot of the bag, tugging it off and throwing it away. It landed on Tremblay, who rolled it in the snow.

Then shocked silence. What had caused the fireball? The Hercules uses NATO-standard JP-40 fuel, an explosive blend of kerosene and diesel. Perhaps Moore had unwittingly scooped up aviation fuel rather than the slower-burning diesel. Perhaps a pocket of fuel in the wing structure had heated up beneath the fire, rupturing at the moment that Moore leaned forward. That would explain the force of the fireball. Whatever the cause, Moore now had second-degree burns to his face, and the number of useful flight crew had been reduced to three.

Wilma suddenly felt her husband looking for her, probing her. He had found her, and she felt his anxious telepathic questioning. No, George! She fairly screamed the words in her mind. No! She had never cut him off before, but now she slammed steel doors around her thoughts. Go away! I don't want you. Go away now!

It seemed to have worked. She felt his confusion, then sensed him drawing away.

Wilma limped over to Paul West, to ask what should be done next. West was switching on an emergency locator beacon.

"You don't leave that turned on all the time?"

"Can't. We're out of flares. This is all we have left. The batteries only last twenty-four hours. Batteries are no damn good up here anyway."

Wilma digested this information. It was the first concrete indication she had that rescue might not be imminent. The fireball had left the survivors shocked and demoralized. They had lost their precarious and hard-won sense of shelter and safety. Now, as she struggled back to her place, feeling the cold invade her body and trying to keep the weight off her broken ankle and wondering again if her back was broken, a gust of wind drove ice spicules into her face. They were as painful as tiny needles at first, then seemed to numb her flesh. The wind was picking up and the temperature was falling.

All at once, everyone became acutely aware of the gradually worsening weather.

Settling herself, cradling Vance's head in her lap, Wilma realized that the fireball had cost them more than their shelter. Like West's abruptness, and like her own rejection of George's attempts at psychic connection, it had marked, at some deep level, the beginning of the death of hope.

CHAPTER EIGHT

Operation Arctic Storm

CORPORAL Steven Cann, a man of simple tastes, would soon be leaving his six-month tour of Alert behind him. He had found his time at the polar station interesting, but long. When he got home, the six-month-old baby girl he'd left behind in Edmonton would be celebrating her first birthday. He thought of writing her. Emily. Or was it Emilie? He could never remember.

Cann was a mechanic. In the armed services, he's called a "vehicle technician." He might be asked to work on anything from a motorcycle to a ten-ton crane. It didn't matter to him. He made things go. At Alert, he shared a barracks with other mechanics, and their barracks had a reputation. It was called the Monster House.

Cann had knocked off his shift and ambled into the cafeteria and was just sitting down to an early-evening meal when a buddy from Monster House came through the doors double-time, spotted him, and waved him over.

"Get back to the shack. We'll be in touch with you."

"What's up?"

"There's a Herc down. I'm rounding up service techs for a ground party."

Cann bustled back to his barracks and waited. He didn't bother to take off his parka. He hadn't even finished his meal, but he was no longer hungry. The other mechanics assembled, with instructions to prepare all vehicles for a ground search party. They stepped outside to the vehicle shed, stamping their feet to keep warm while they topped up fluids, checked track, and warmed crankcase oil.

The station had nine vehicles capable of mounting a search for the downed Hercules. Two of them were Red Devils, half-tracked vehicles with enclosed cabins. They resembled pick-up trucks with two wheels forward and tracks under the box. There were also seven Bombardier Go-Tracks, fully tracked vehicles with enclosed cabins. Four of the seven Go-Tracks belonged to the eight-cylinder 800 series, three to the rather underpowered six-cylinder 300 series. The fastest and strongest were the 800 series, but even these had a top speed of only about thirty miles per hour – and that, as Cann said, was "going downhill with a stiff wind to your back."

The command post at Alert had decided the best chance of saving any survivors rested with a quick dash overland, retrieval of the wounded, and return to the station. The estimate was that this could be accomplished within seven hours, before any of the Hercules rescue flights en route from Edmonton and Greenwood had even arrived.

Twenty-four personnel were selected to go out, of whom half had some first-aid or medical training. The senior medical staff at the station were a sergeant and a warrant officer trained as medical assistants; they were known as "Major Duff" and "Minor Duff," the term "duff" referring to a fake. The station was not equipped for an overland rescue, and none of the personnel were trained in rescue work.

Still, within two and a half hours, the vehicles were loaded with warm clothing, sleeping bags, and first-aid kits. The search party set off in convoy into the darkness: the yellow Go-Tracks blazed trail, followed by the Red Devils, followed in turn by a bulldozer. The dozer was hauling a stoneboat loaded with forty-five-gallon drums of diesel fuel. Amid belching diesel and steam and mechanical noise and eerily lit darkness, the departure was like the launch of an all-tracked rally race.

The leaders of the convoy had a rough idea of the crash location, transmitted from the Box Top flight that had spotted flames on the ground. The bearing was reliable, but the estimate of the distance was optimistic. They believed, mistakenly, that the crash was about five miles away, and on their side of the most formidable obstacle in their path – the Sheridan River gorge.

Steven Cann drove a Red Devil. This is all wrong, he thought, as the convoy made its way in the frigid darkness. The medical staff were up front, in the Go-Tracks. The mechanics brought up the rear, in the Red Devils. It was not that Cann wanted to cover himself in glory by being the first to arrive at the scene. But what if the Go-Tracks broke down? He had covered this terrain in the summer months and knew how treacherous it was. The broken shale could slash the Kevlar-reinforced track tread, and loose shale rendered even a gentle slope dangerously unstable.

The convoy headed due south along a route used in the summer months to reach the twin peaks of Dean Hill and Mount Pullen, two prominent hills visible from the station. The night was clear, the winds were low, and the convoy was able to follow the compacted foundation of a summer road. There was a bridge across the first creek they had to traverse, and they reached the hills within an hour. They expected to find the crash nearby.

Cann had never felt so pumped up in his life, but his spirits soon flagged. The lights of the convoy lit only the desolate landscape; there was no sign of the wreckage. The convoy pressed on, and within minutes they hit a ravine, probably a tributary of the Sheridan. It fell steeply about forty feet, then climbed more moderately on the far side. The searchlights revealed that, although the prevailing winds had compacted the snow on their side, it had left the shale exposed on the other embankment. It would be tricky going.

The Go-Tracks risked the crossing, sliding down the slope and climbing up the far side. The Red Devils were forced to stay behind.

What if they break down? Cann thought. What good are the vehicle techs back here?

It was a mere two miles to the Sheridan River gorge, two miles beyond that to the survivors. The Go-Tracks made it nearly to the river's edge before two of them broke down within a minute of each other. One was no longer charging its own batteries, which quickly lost power in the cold. The other had an overheated differential.

Not that it mattered any more. The Sheridan, the searchers realized, was impassable, a sheer ravine of 240 feet. They drove back and forth along the embankment to find a crossing, but without success. The searchers got out of their vehicles to ponder and commiserate. From where they stood, cold and thwarted, they could see the orange light from the burning wreckage of the Hercules glowing on the horizon.

Then came the problem of getting back to the station. The convoy was itself in trouble and had to call back on the radio for mechanical help. The bulldozer paved the way, slipping over the edge of the creek ravine, blazing a path. Cann gingerly drove his Red Devil across the ravine with trepidation, but without incident.

By then the stars were blinking out, and Cann noticed the wind was rising. He had imagined himself in heroic terms, bounding across the snows on foot, bringing help to the survivors. He realized soon enough that it had been a foolish notion. By the time he had repaired the ailing Go-Tracks, fighting the numbing cold and darkness, a full Arctic blizzard was brewing.

The convoy proceeded at full speed back towards the station, trying to beat the storm. Two of the Go-Tracks broke down again and had to be abandoned. The blizzard was now at their heels; by the time Cann finally spotted the station lights at Alert, the conditions were approaching white-out. A button-up had been declared, meaning all personnel had been locked inside and a rope perimeter bordered the station.

Relieved to be back in the warmth and comfort of the station, Steven Cann realized for the first time how torturously difficult it was going to be to reach the survivors. It struck him how easily the convoy could have become lost, how quickly a heroic outing could have turned into a second disaster. For the first time since the adrenaline rush of setting out, he felt scared.

―――――――

At the rescue coordination centre in Edmonton, Smokey Blair took the news of the failed ground party from Alert at about the same time that a new weather forecast arrived. Just what I need, he thought. Cannons to the left of me, cannons to the right. And now cannons in front of me.

An hour earlier, Box Top 21, circling the crash site, had seen the three green flares Paul West had fired from the ground. It was the first confirmation of survivors from the crash. It was news nobody had even dared hope to receive. When Blair had arrived at the rescue centre, he and Todd had cautioned each other not to expect survivors. When the bulletin had come in to the contrary, Blair expected staff in the rescue centre to react with whoops of joy. But the news hadn't had that effect on the others, or on himself. It had merely tightened the knot in his gut.

With survivors on the ground, the rescue centre increasingly despaired of reaching them in time. It would be infinitely worse to have them die in their hands, as it were, than in the crash itself. But that tragic outcome looked more inevitable with every hour.

The failure of the ground party was a major defeat. Especially when Blair read the sheet of teletype in his hand:

YLT AMD 310617-X C10 BKN 8 BKN 2 S-BS 3320G30 OCNL-X C10 OVC1/2 S-BS.

To Blair, the coding drew a clear picture of a rising storm and closing weather. The amended forecast called for a ceiling of 1,000 feet, with reduced visibility in blowing snow. The winds had picked up out of the northwest, gusting to thirty knots. It was bad news all around: bad for the parachute rescue team en route to Alert, worse still for the survivors on the ground.

Winds of thirty knots would push the real temperatures at the crash site to less than -50 degrees Celsius. That is some 70 degrees colder than room temperature. Christ, Blair thought, that was 130 degrees Fahrenheit colder than the control room. Poor bastards.

Such fierce cold was nearly inconceivable; without shelter, exposed skin would freeze in less than thirty seconds. Death by hypothermia would follow in a matter of hours. It was as though Blair were trying to coordinate a rescue from a foundered submarine, with only hours of oxygen remaining. And the storm was not content merely to sap the remaining heat from the survivors; it had to foul a rescue attempt as well. No one jumped out of an airplane into winds of thirty knots, period. Let alone at night. Let alone over unknown terrain. Not even SARtechs.

"They'll never get in, not with this weather," he said to Todd.

It wasn't like Blair to be this far down. Todd put on his bravest grin: "I think they'd jump without parachutes, Smokey, if we let 'em."

Right now they needed a helicopter at Alert, and badly. If the SARtechs did manage to get into the crash site, they'd need a helicopter to get them out. If the SARtechs couldn't jump from the Herc, they'd need the helicopter to get them in.

When Blair called over a junior officer for a situation report on helicopter resources, the news only added to his frustration.

There was no word on the Bell 212 helicopter, which Blair was beginning to believe was a mythical creation arising from some Nordic mist. "Launch at first light," the last message from the Americans had read. The North Pole, October 30. What light?

The Labrador helicopters were all dead in the water. The Greenwood Lab hadn't lasted even an hour. The Gander Lab had been stood down in Iqaluit as unserviceable. The Lab from 424 Squadron in Trenton was still flying, but it was a pipe dream to think a Labrador could hopscotch from southern Ontario to the North Pole. It was a mad caper even to launch. He expected word of a stand-down at any moment.

It seemed the best bet among Canadian resources was a plan to scrape the belly of a Hercules from Edmonton's 435 Squadron and stuff a stripped-down CH-135 Twin Huey helicopter into the cavity. The Hercules would carry the helicopter to Alert, where it could be re-assembled and then flown to the crash site. It was a time-consuming plan but appeared to be the only realistic one. Maintenance crews in Edmonton were already at work tearing down the single-rotor Twin Huey.

"What's the situation report on Rescue Three One One?" Blair asked a junior officer.

"Estimated time of departure with Huey on board at fifteen hundred Zulu, sir," the officer said.

Blair needed a smoke. He patted his pockets for some chewing gum. Fifteen hundred Zulu was damn near ten hours away.

"Except I just contacted the squadron and I think the launch time is optimistic, sir. The flight crew for the Huey were in B.C. on exercise. They're not even due back until seventeen hundred Zulu, sir."

"Jesus, Mary, and Joseph. What about Elmendorf?"

He was referring to the large U.S. air base at Anchorage, Alaska; the U.S. base at Thule had already reported that no helicopters were available in Greenland.

"We've contacted Scott AFB and established a liaison to Elmendorf, sir. They have two Pavehawks available, ready, and configured to SAR."

A glimmer of hope. Blair raised his eyebrows: "When can they be on site?"

"They have air-to-air refuelling capability but no refuellers. And they won't use them on a polar routing. They'll have to fly south and around. Scott estimates two days max effort, sir."

Two days? In a wind chill of -50 Celsius? Those poor bastards. Game over.

Wednesday night was "Wings Night" at Rumours in Trenton. Rumours was the sort of tavern that appeals to men in the Armed Forces, and Wings Night was an inside joke among those at the Trenton air base who had earned their own wings. The place served chicken wings on Wednesdays.

The Wednesday night of October 30 found the Labrador pilots and flight engineers of 424 Squadron deep in beer and conversation. The evening of camaraderie and routine bitching was well under way by eleven o'clock, when a server came to the table to ask, "Is there a Major Shyiak here?"

The squadron's flight commander was, indeed, present and accounted for.

"Telephone for you. You can take it at the bar."

Shyiak strolled over, pursued by the expected ribbing. What's her name, Major? The expression on his face when he returned stopped the wisecracks cold.

"Okay, boys," he said. "Don't drink up. Go home. There's a MAJAID, Hercules down at Alert. We're launching SAR."

Like the others at the table, Captain Mark Levesque was dumbfounded at the idea of launching a Labrador to the Pole. He bent forward to hear what Shyiak had to say next. A Labrador helicopter had been on another mission, at the end of a crew day, when the call-out came. Levesque's colleague, Captain Don Paul, had been attempting a dash up the eastern shore of James Bay and Hudson Bay. But the weather had soured, and the twin-rotor Labrador had been beaten back as far as Chibougamau, in northern Quebec. Paul was now trying to reach Wabush in Labrador. He had already been flying thirty-six hours, and his crew was reaching the point of dangerous exhaustion.

The mission Shyiak outlined called for two complete flight crews to deadhead, or fly as passengers, on board a Buffalo aircraft to Wabush. There they would be joined by two teams of SARtechs and proceed to Alert. Flight crews at Trenton were to return home and await orders. Any one of them could be tapped for the rescue mission, which had been dubbed Operation Arctic Storm.

Levesque drove home convinced it would never happen. The very name of the mission had a dark irony. It was every bit as audacious as the military campaign in the Persian Gulf, but there the similarity ended. The campaign against Iraq had been planned and executed with a high likelihood of success. The odds against the Labrador mission's success were formidable.

For one thing, a Labrador had never made such a flight. To his knowledge, a Lab had once flown as far north as Cornwallis Island, about two-thirds the distance of this mission. The flight had taken three weeks, in the daylight months, as part of an expedition. It had support and a mobile repair party. This mission called for an unsupported flight of 3,600 miles. There was – what? – maybe one serviced airport over the whole flight plan. It would take a Lab some forty hours to cover the distance, and aged Labs simply did not fly forty hours without breaking down.

For another, it would be night visual rules all the way. The Labrador's navigational aids, although sophisticated, were useless that far north. The magnetic compass would be spinning in its socket. The directional gyros had been unserviceable for northern flying for years; someone in Ottawa was working on the problem, but the gyros could not be trusted. The other navigational aids did not work over long distances, because the Labrador had a ceiling of about 10,000 feet and a correspondingly reduced radio range. They would be flying blind. It simply couldn't be done without a fixed-wing aircraft to provide guidance from a higher altitude, known as top cover; and there hadn't even been mention of top cover.

Levesque figured he'd end up losing a night's sleep over this. He'd probably fly halfway up there through crappy weather, then be turned back with news that the Lab wasn't needed. No, they'd realize how misguided an idea it was.

Still, he went to bed with his flight suit folded at his side. He could not sleep. He could not help telling himself that no one had flown to the North Pole in a helicopter, unaided, at night. He wondered if it could be done. He wondered if he'd be the one to try.

At three in the morning, his phone rang.

"You're on," said the operations officer. "Departure in thirty minutes."

Fifteen minutes past midnight in Edmonton, about ten hours after the crash, a bulletin flashed through the rescue centre. Smokey Blair had trouble believing it. According to the message, Fred Ritchie's group of SARtechs from Edmonton had landed. How? It was impossible to conceive that they had jumped from the Hercules and reached the crash site by parachute.

"Hate to say I told you so," Todd beamed.

"Just a damn minute," Blair said. "Get Alert on the radio-phone. I want this confirmed."

But confirmation was slow in coming. The rescue centre was unable to raise Alert on the high-frequency radio and had to wait for the station to call south on the land line.

If Ritchie's SARtechs were on site, they would need a helicopter to get them out. Just one goddamn helicopter.

"What's the latest from Scott?" he asked.

"Still two days."

Finally, the command post at Alert telephoned the Edmonton rescue centre. Ritchie and the Edmonton SARtechs had landed, all right, but not at the crash site. They had landed at Alert, and were at that moment in the command post. The weather over the crash site prohibited entry by parachute.

———————

It was ten to one in the morning when Blair, in Edmonton, received word that the Labrador helicopter from Trenton was limping to Wabush. Trenton's 424 Squadron was sending flight crews to Wabush to take over the aircraft and fly it up to Alert. They needed assistance drawing up a flight plan.

Blair was stunned. The last he had heard, the flight had been stood down due to weather. He knew they could not make the flight without frequent refuelling stops and directional guidance from an aircraft flying top cover. It seemed unlikely that the Labrador could get through; but it was still Blair's best chance of reaching the survivors alive.

Blair was fortunate in one regard. The commanding officer of his base, Colonel Mike Wansink, who was new to the Edmonton posting, had done what a good commander does: stand back from the operation but run interference with higher command. In a matter of hours, a fluent command structure had been established from the command post to Air Transport Group, flowing upwards to the headquarters of Air Command, and from there to

National Defence Headquarters itself. Which meant that Blair, a mere major, had the resources of the entire Canadian defence establishment at his disposal.

The Trenton squadron had intended for a Buffalo aircraft, a twin-engine light transport, to fly top cover for the Labrador helicopter on the run up to Alert. But the Buffalo lacked endurance and sophisticated avionics. Blair cast his eyes over the wall map.

"They'll need the Auroras out of Greenwood," he said. "An Aurora can pick the fleas off a fly's butt."

The Aurora – the most advanced surveillance aircraft in the Canadian fleet – has range and endurance. It is used in anti-submarine warfare off the east coast. Its primary job is to find and follow submarines; as a result, it carries a sophisticated array of navigational and detection instruments. It has dual inertial navigation systems, a working transponder, a mainframe computer, and terrain-avoidance radar. It takes a crew of five just to operate its surveillance systems. It is, in effect, a flying control tower.

Two of the Auroras, on maritime patrol, had been recalled, and were now given the task of escorting Mark Levesque and his crew north. They would watch the Labrador as carefully as if it were an enemy submarine.

A long shot, Blair thought, but at least now the poor bastards at the Pole might have a fighting chance. If the Lab doesn't break down en route. If it isn't beaten back by weather. If we can find fuel caches along the way …

CHAPTER NINE

Grounded

During the Hercules flight taking Fred Ritchie's sartechs from Edmonton to Alert, the aircraft commander, Major Jim Burger, briefed himself on the crash by eavesdropping with his high-frequency radio on communications between the rescue centres. About four hours into the flight, he learned that there were survivors on the ground. He relayed this information over the microphone to Fred Ritchie in the rear.

Raising his voice above the roar of the Herc's engines, Ritchie told his sartechs to prepare the gear for a night drop.

Even with the ample cargo space of a Hercules, quarters were cramped. Rescue equipment and flares were stored in metal cargo containers of the sort used on ships and trains. These ran the length of the cargo bay. Gear was strewn over them, and on the floors, and was hanging from the fuselage walls. Parachutes, toboggans, and cargo nets cluttered the tail section. The sartechs had placed their b-25 kits in cargo nets. Now, in preparation for a jump into the crash site, they strapped parachutes to these nets and to the 300-pound rescue toboggans.

On the ground, lighting would be a priority. The sartechs strapped strobe lights to the toboggans and to their own helmets. They taped chemical lights to everything in sight, since the extreme cold would rapidly deplete batteries. They shoved pencil

Canadian Forces CC-130 Hercules transport, tail number 322 — Box Top 22 — shown in an earlier landing. After the crash and fire, only the tail section, a small portion of fuselage, and the overturned wing remained intact. (Department of National Defence, Canada.)

An austere posting, the secret military installation at Alert has to contend with routine blizzards that prevent travel even between buildings. The gravel landing strip is visible at the top of the photograph. (DND photo.)

Canadian Forces Station Alert is the world's most northerly permanent settlement. If the rescuers had flown south instead of north to reach the survivors, the distances covered would have brought them to the Amazon basin. (DND photo.)

An arctic wolf pictured on Ellesmere Island near CFS Alert. Wolves visited the survivors and their relatives, in waking life and in dreams. The wolf that visited Sue Hillier had blue eyes and a black flash. (DND photo.)

Captain John Couch (RIGHT). The aircraft commander and Gulf War veteran died of exposure a few hours before rescue. (DND photo.)

Master Corporal Roland Pitre (BELOW). The loadmaster was thrown from the tail section on impact and died shortly after. (DND photo.)

Lieutenant Joe Bales (BELOW). The first officer endured much the same hardship as Couch, as both men were exposed to the storm while tending the two survivors buried in the snow. (DND photo.)

Lieutenant Michael Moore (LEFT). The navigator survived the crash but suffered facial burns in a fireball some hours later. (DND photo.) Sergeant Paul West (RIGHT). The flight engineer was a steadying force on the ground, and the only survivor still lucid at the time of the rescue. (DND photo.)

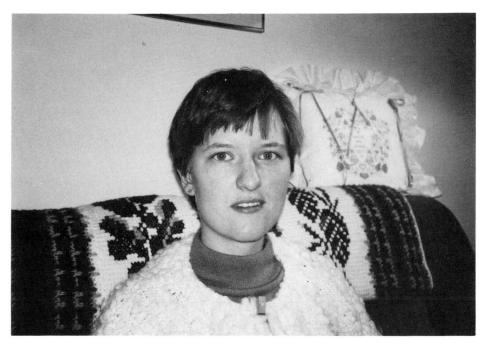

Captain Wilma de Groot, a physician and newlywed. Her forceful and logical manner was balanced by a deep spirituality, and she rallied the spirits of the survivors trapped in the tail. (Author photo.)

Sue Hillier, a hair stylist from Trenton, Ontario, was badly injured and buried in a snow cave near the paralyzed Bob Thomson. Vivacious and outgoing, she inspired Couch and Thomson before her own near-death and her experience with the wolf. (Author photo.)

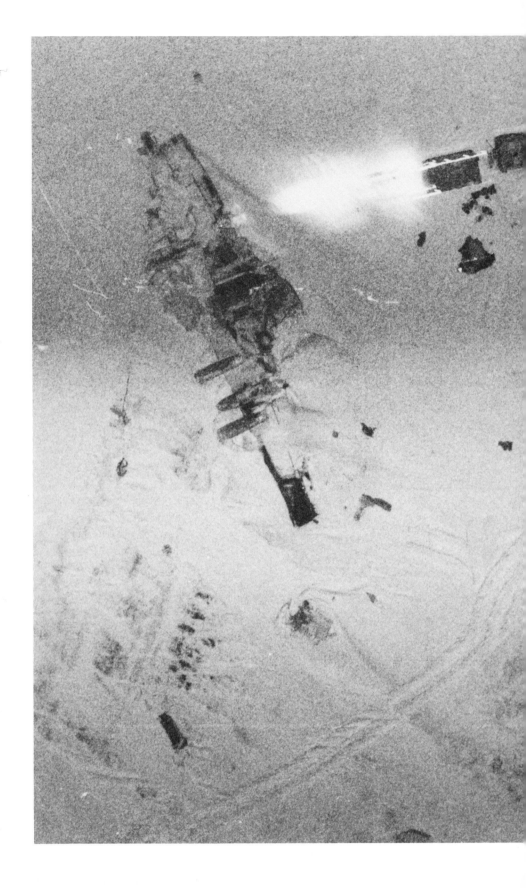

The crash site in an aerial photograph taken after the rescue. The Hercules landed in a desolate landscape of rock and ice, but in the one location where the passengers and crew had a chance of surviving the impact. Lights from rescue vehicles illuminate the scene. (DND photo.)

The tail section offered psychological refuge but gave little real protection. It only partly sheltered survivors from the fierce Arctic winds. (DND photo.)

Home. The survivors huddled in the fire-blackened tail section awaiting rescue. Their clothing froze to the floor grating and the chilled metal drew away their remaining body heat. (DND photo.)

The only shelter the rescuers carried was their parachute canopies, which they draped over the opening, protecting survivors from the cutting wind. It had an immediate effect on their revival. (DND photo.)

Captain Mark Levesque (LEFT) and Captain Pierre Bolduc, in the CH-113 Labrador. Their remarkable dash to the Pole was the stuff of aviation legend. (Author photo.)

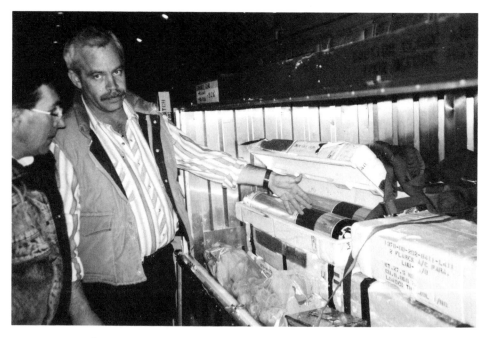

Master Corporal Jim Norris (LEFT) and Master Corporal Chuck Coutts, both loadmasters, show the LUU-2B flares in the hold of a rescue Hercules. Coutts became known as the "Mutant Ninja Loadie" for emptying an entire Herc in one pass in a desperate bid to get equipment to rescuers. (Author photo.)

Captain Wayne Todd (LEFT) and Major Don "Smokey" Blair masterminded the rescue effort from the rescue centre in Edmonton. (Author photo.)

Major Marv Macauley, Arnie's younger brother and the commander of the Greenwood rescue Hercules. Reason battled with passion in his decision to fly the sartechs to their perilous mission. (Author photo.)

Search and rescue technicians, or sartechs, are expert parachutists, mountaineers, and scuba divers. Corporal Jim Brown is shown here during an assault on Mount Logan. Note the trademark "Explosive" helmet. (DND photo.)

Corporal Steven Cann (LEFT), one of the mechanics at Alert who volunteered to drive the tracked vehicles in the overland rescue effort. (Author photo.) Sergeant Gerry Dominie, (RIGHT) jumpmaster on the Greenwood Hercules and a jumper himself in the even more hazardous deployment from the Edmonton Herc. (Author photo.)

Corporal Eric Larouche. The Greenwood SARtech's encounter with a wild thing in the darkness earned him the nickname "Bearic," and a place in folklore. (Author photo.)

Warrant Officer Arnie
Macauley, the sartech
team leader from Greenwood,
Nova Scotia. He led the first team
of parachutists, who knowingly
risked their lives to reach the
survivors in time. (DND photo.)

Warrant Officer
Fred Ritchie, the
sARtech team leader
from Edmonton, Alberta.
His treacherous overland
journey to the crash site
rescued the rescuers.
(DND photo.)

A CH-113 Labrador, of the type flown by Levesque and Bolduc on their polar odyssey. Their navigational aids were worthless, and the aircraft is especially prone to disaster from engine failure or icing.

flashlights in their pockets and clipped miner's headlamps above their visors. The pockets of their jumpsuits bulged with personal items – some carried oranges, others a flask of brandy. Jim Brown, as usual, carried a lucky bullet.

While the SARtechs made their preparations, Ritchie wrote out his operations order. His plan was to throw one survival toboggan out the tail door; four SARtechs would jump after the toboggan and retrieve it. Once those four were established on the ground, the rest of the SARtechs and survival gear would follow.

Jim Brown had been eating a boxed lunch, his "Explosive" helmet at his side, when he and some of the other SARtechs noticed that the photo technician on board was sprawled over cargo bundles, asleep.

Brown reached into his lunch bag for the pepper packet. He tore it open and carefully upended the contents into a plastic straw. Once he was sure of his ordnance, and of an audience, he stealthily approached the sleeping photographer. He placed the straw against the man's nostrils and blew. The desired effect was achieved.

Brown waited until the photographer had recovered somewhat before addressing him.

"Private," Brown said, "my name is Jim Brown. I am a SARtech. I am about to cover myself in shit and glory with the most daring rescue ever conceived. My Daddy is a rat farmer in southern Alberta. I am going to make my Daddy proud of his son. And you are here to record the event. When I sleep, you sleep. When I work, you work. Do we understand each other on that?"

The photographer nodded.

"Take no notice of him," Fred Ritchie yelled above the noise of the aircraft. "He's crazy. Jim, get your ass over here. I want you as team leader."

Brown sat down beside Ritchie, who had the rescue plan mapped out on a sheet of paper.

"Jim," Ritchie said, in a tone of remonstrance.

"Nothing wounded but his pride."

Ritchie went through his sketches and orders of deployment, half shouting to make himself heard. Brown listened carefully, his eyes bugging out, which they do when he's paying close attention.

"Our biggest problem will be darkness," said Ritchie. "We stay together. The first thing we do after the jump is get together and count heads."

"Why don't we wait for first light?"

"Because there is no light, Jim."

Brown nodded solemnly. Ritchie was reminded that Brown, for all his previous heroics, had no Arctic experience.

"When we penetrate the crash site, we'll split into pairs. Two on medical triage, two breaking out the toboggans, and two walking the perimeter of the site."

Brown gave him a quizzical look.

"I want them tramping down the snow. Once they've circled the site, nobody leaves the perimeter. I don't want anyone getting lost. And if any of the survivors have wandered off, the SARtechs on the perimeter will see their tracks in the snow."

An hour out of Alert, Major Jim Burger in the Edmonton Hercules locked onto the emergency locator beacon of the downed Hercules. He radioed back to Ritchie that they were closing on the crash site.

Burger's own Hercules had an array of radio communications but only one ultra-high-frequency radio. UHF was the type of signal used both by the emergency beacon of Box Top 22 and by the hand-held PRQ 501 radios that had been stored in the Herc's survival kits.

At the crash site below, the downed engineer, Paul West, had recovered three of these radios and was using them alternately, to preserve battery life. When the rescue aircraft came within earshot he used them again, trying to hail the Edmonton Hercules; but Burger's UHF radio was tuned to the frequency used by the locator beacon. For this reason, he couldn't hear West trying to hail him. It was a waste of precious minutes of battery life.

Burger had been vectored by Glow Worm air traffic control at Alert to the minimum safe altitude of 2,000 feet above the highest ground obstacle – a height of some 3,600 feet above sea level. As it turned out, however, the cloud ceiling over the crash site was about 1,000 feet. There would be no chance of spotting the wreckage from the minimum safe altitude.

Burger and John Couch both flew out of 435 Squadron in Edmonton. They saw each other every day, drank from the same coffee machine, attended the same funerals. Burger's crew on this flight knew Couch's crew on the ground like family. Burger didn't hesitate to add one more violation to the growing list of infractions he committed during the rescue effort. He busted the minimums.

As a tactical pilot, Burger felt comfortable flying 500 feet above the nearest obstacles, or at a circuit altitude of about 1,800 feet above sea level. This was about half the minimum altitude he should have flown on an instrument track. Glow Worm would get its knickers in a knot. Burger raised Glow Worm on the radio and solved the problem the only way he knew how. He lied.

He told Glow Worm he was converting to visual flight, even though his visual references were confined to the dark belly of cloud in which he was flying. In reality, he flew on an instrument track, closing on the crash site at a height of about 800 feet above the ground. At that altitude, he'd crash the airplane if he strayed over the higher hills five miles to the west. So he instructed Glow Worm to alert him at four miles off track. He set the radar altimeter to 700 feet and briefed his crew to call altitude and airspeed.

"If the radalt light goes on," he said, "I want to know about it."

As the rescue Hercules neared the crash site, the beeping of the locator beacon grew louder in Burger's ears. He set 50-percent flap, slowing the Herc to about 150 knots. He clicked the microphone switch and spoke to the loadmaster in the rear: "Clear to open."

The tail ramp of the Hercules lowered on its hydraulic arms, and the temperature inside the cargo bay instantly dropped about 40 degrees Celsius. The sound of rushing wind and the droning of the engines overwhelmed the SARtechs' voices.

"Open and locked," the loadmaster replied.

"Red!" Fred Ritchie shouted.

Corporal Rick Peck – known as Red for the colour of his hair, his neck, and his temper – looked up.

"Into the monkey tail!"

Peck was a broad-backed youth who weighed in the mid-200-pound range. Years of tossing hay bales to his horses in St. Albert, Alberta, had given him dorsal muscles like wooden planks, and Ritchie wanted him to toss the gear from the tail. If anyone could handle a 300-pound toboggan while buffeted by icy winds in the bucking tail of a Hercules, it was Peck.

Peck clipped on the restraining harness and made his way along the open ramp. He leaned over the edge, trying to catch a glimpse of the ground. He saw nothing but blackness. Jim Brown, meanwhile, was sprawled on the floor of the cargo bay, his head sticking into the Plexiglas bubble of the Hercules SAR door in the frigid roar of the wind. He, too, could see nothing.

Ritchie stood behind Peck, a radio marker beacon and a marker light in his hands. The marker was a battery-powered white light on a metal base; it would provide a visual target for the jumpers. The jumpers were suited and ready to go but needed a target.

At five seconds to target, Ritchie gave both markers to Peck. Then he grabbed two of the magnesium LUU-2B flares and set the ignition timer to 250 feet. Peck tossed the two markers over the tail. The white light blinked as it plummeted towards the ground, then vanished.

"Malfunction!" Brown shouted.

Ritchie passed the flares to Peck. Each metal cylinder weighed twenty-five pounds and gave 3 million candlepower of illumination. Peck threw them as if he were tossing basketballs. The flares ignited but threw no light on the ground. It was now clear to everyone that their Hercules was enveloped in dense cloud, which glowed eerily with bright orange light.

"Can't see a damn thing!" Brown called.

Desperate as the SARtechs were to reach the survivors, there was no way they could jump blind. Ritchie had to admit defeat. "Stop drop," he said into the microphone.

An air of profound dejection settled instantly over the SARtechs. Survivors or not, there was nothing to be done. The Hercules was running dangerously low on fuel. It was picking up ice on the wing, and as little as a quarter-inch of ice can bring a plane down.

"Stop drop," Burger confirmed. The tail ramp was closed, and Burger banked the Hercules for a landing at Alert.

―――――――

Alert is known, by pilots who fly there, for its saucer-shaped runway. Snow drifts into the saucer and becomes hard-packed by wind, making the runway appear level. In fact, the central segment of the runway is, at best, trickier than the button; at worst, it can rip out the nose landing gear.

As Burger prepared to land, the winds at Alert were from the north by northwest, meaning they were at right angles to the landing strip. Burger and his co-pilot, Captain Derek Stobbs, would be landing in a crosswind of thirty knots. It was probably gusting higher than that; aviators regard the weather reports from the Alert station as notoriously optimistic. The runway condition was rated at eleven. A dry and clear runway is rated at twenty-three; slick ice is rated at zero. At the weight Burger was carrying, and with a moderately slick runway, the Hercules operating manual does not recommend a landing in crosswinds higher than twenty-seven knots. It would be a white-knuckle approach.

Burger briefed his crew for a crosswind landing. Stobbs had the wheel. The wind was coming from his right, so he held the right wing down. This caused the aircraft to bank; he compensated with hard left rudder. So far, so good. The Hercules landed on the button. At this point, Stobbs transferred the flight controls to his commander.

"Your wheel," he said, and he reached for the nose-wheel steering. At the same time, he straightened the rudder. He would not be needing the rudder, he thought, since he'd be controlling his direction with the landing gear. That is the correct procedure in a landing to the south. Stobbs did not realize the nose wheel had virtually no effect on Alert's slick, snow-packed gravel runway.

As the rudder straightened, the aircraft became a giant weathervane. The Hercules achieves its flight characteristics by broad, flat control surfaces. The towering rudder caught the wind and yanked the tail 40 degrees to the left. The Hercules was still moving forward along the centre line of the runway, but it was in a 40-degree drift, skidding sideways down a short, narrow strip of frozen gravel at more than 110 knots.

In the cargo bay, the Plexiglas bubbles were still in place – despite regulations requiring that they be replaced by the steel doors before landing – and so the SARtechs had a ringside seat for the show. Fred Ritchie and his boys gazed out the bubble at the funhouse landing, wondering if they were finished.

The aircraft was caught in a roaring sideways skid. It was shuddering violently, snow and gravel were clattering against its underside, and it was lurching dangerously to one side. As it continued its skid, the right wing lifted skyward and the propellers on the left wing were driven towards the ground. To the SARtechs, it looked as if the Hercules was about to auger in on the left wing and perform a farewell cartwheel.

"C'mon, Jim," Ritchie said under his breath.

On the flight deck, Burger was gripping the controls and twisting the yoke to the right. The right wing gradually responded, falling back towards the ground, levelling the aircraft. But it was still in a skid.

"More rudder!" Burger shouted. "Differential power!"

Stobbs forced the left rudder pedal the length of its travel, while his right hand reached for the engine controls. He yanked the two left-hand engines back to ground idle position. The controls are protected by a gate at this point, to prevent the application of reverse thrust in flight. Once Stobbs had lifted the controls over the gate, the left-wing propellers would be thrusting in reverse. It was a delicate step: too much reverse thrust, and the aircraft would cartwheel to the right. Too little, and the skid would not be corrected in time.

"Easy," said Burger.

Stobbs' hands were gentle on the controls as he nudged them back. With a delicate touch, he corrected the skid, and sixty-five tons of rogue Hercules were reined into line. The aircraft coasted to a stop.

Fred Ritchie looked around the cargo bay, at the scattered equipment and white faces of the SARtechs.

"Now," he said. "Wasn't that special?"

CHAPTER TEN

Voices in the Dark

THE AMOUNT of lifesaving equipment carried on board a Hercules is impressive. The aircraft routinely flies around the world and has recently seen service on behalf of Canada in climates as diverse as Pakistan and Qatar. It is equipped with gear to help overcome the extremes of survival at sea, in the desert, in the deep woods, and in the Arctic.

Box Top 22 had been carrying a twenty-person liferaft kit with flares, a fishing rod, a solar-powered water still, desalination chemicals, a pocket knife, 200 tablets of Gravol, a whistle, a sponge, and six tubes of insect repellent. There was a snake-bite kit. There was a first-aid kit with petrolatum and surgical dressings, scissors, and splints. There were two rolls of red toilet paper, which could be used for hygiene or as a signal banner. There were safety matches, a compass, a rat-tail file, and snare wire. There was an axe. There were 500 surgical masks, sunscreen, and mirrors. There were seven red star magnesium flares. There were hand-held radios. There was a pressure cooker, a pot, three yellow plastic bowls, and three dessert spoons. There was a sewing kit, a pad and pencil, and a pack of playing cards.

They were all stored along the fuselage racks. They were all blown to hell in the crash.

In the Arctic survival kit there was an assortment of treasure.

The Canadian Forces are generous in granting their dispensations to fallen souls. What comforts, what consolation every kit brings!

All passengers would have tinted sunglasses, so they would not have to carve eye-shields of ivory, as the Inuit must, to protect their vision from white-out. They would be given a snow saw, for carving their cosy igloo from blocks of snow. They would have an ice chisel, for reaching the teeming abundance of marine life under the ice. A funnel, a whisk broom, a dozen plastic baggies. For their temporary quarters, they were given a survival tent in rugged orange sailcloth, with eight tent pegs – tent pegs, mind you – in plastic, so as not to damage unduly the sensitive Arctic permafrost.

Everyone would have a balaclava, and a wool cap to pull over their balaclava; wool mittens, with leather mittens to pull over their wool mittens; blended nylon-and-wool undersocks, with coarse wool socks to pull over their undersocks; felt booties, with rubber-and-nylon mukluks to pull over their felt booties; cotton thermal underwear, with nylon wind pants to pull over their underwear; and, as the final sign of consideration, each and every survivor was issued with twenty-four waterproof matches.

All this was stored in the overhead racks. All of it was blown to hell in the crash.

Foraging in the debris, members of the flight crew did find two torn mukluk liners, black felt and sodden with diesel. They gave them to a passenger whose boots had been blown off in the crash. They found Arctic mitts, with fleece lining and sheepskin backs, and gave those away. The sleeping bag taken from the corpse of Robert Grimsley was given to Montgomery, whose skull fracture had left him wakeful but confused. Paul West found a balaclava and pressed it against the head of Wilma de Groot.

"Want it pulled down over your face?"

Wilma shook her head no. Paul didn't have a hat. None of the working crew had hats. Now that they were less active, she noticed, Paul was beginning to shiver.

The flight crew had lace-up leather shoes, which were coated in a frozen slurry of snow and fuel. They had polycotton flight suits, which were beginning to glaze over with frost.

Don't say anything, Wilma. They're doing this sensibly. The most seriously wounded should get the most clothing. They are not being irrational.

But Paul's hands, when he'd given her the balaclava, had become icy and stiff.

West walked away. In the span of a few paces, he disappeared in the storm. She had no idea where he was going, or how he found his way back. But he kept returning with things: radios, a fuel stove, a homing beacon, clothing, flares. He became the group's finder; he had a mechanical eye for useful things half buried in snow.

After one of his scavenging trips, he returned with a stretcher. Its back was broken, and it was missing one handle, but it was a stretcher nonetheless. He set it down by the wing, and then the crew members went to prepare the tail as best they could.

There was a general and intuitive resolution to move to the tail. None of the survivors trusted fire any longer, not since the fireball, and there seemed little point in building a shelter of grainy snow, even if they'd had the strength – which, by now, they did not. In the aftermath of shock, the passengers had become apathetic, seemingly lifeless. The flight crew had spent much of their energy reserves. The metal tail was assembled, ready for them, beckoning. The tail was the largest built structure in their environment, and it was natural that they would gravitate towards it.

Experts at Arctic survival later noted this mistake. They noted that the metal skin of the tail would draw the heat of the survivors' bodies away from them, rather than reflecting it back. They noted that the tail was resting at right angles to the prevailing wind; its gaping mouth would slice the air and carry whirling eddies of ice crystals over the people inside. The crystals would melt at first, then freeze into a coating of ice as they overwhelmed the bodies' defences. They noted that it was not good shelter. But the experts who later dissected the efficiency of the shelter were not writing their reports from an arid plateau of ice, wind, and rock in a blinding storm. They had lamps to write by, and computers to write with. They had houses with porch lights awaiting their return.

The tail had travelled some distance on its own, scooping up snow, diesel, and rock like a goblet passed through greasy rime. It had itself been ablaze, and a toxic fire of aircraft debris had burned for some hours at the entrance. Inside, it stank of fuel and burnt wiring. The walls were charred black and frosted with ice. Grey insulation drooped in sheets from the ribbing; scorched wires tugged at the survivors' faces as they struggled through the opening. They could not see the mess of wires and insulation, even though it was right in front of their eyes. It was dark as pitch in the tail.

The ramp section of the tail was resting on a slight angle upwards from the opening. Much of the tail section was not useful; snow had packed itself into the rear. The habitable space measured about ten feet by ten feet. As the passengers walked over the tail section, they stumbled in the holes of the metal grating of the floor. It was made of perforated steel, for weight reduction, and in addition to the loaf-sized holes there were two larger cavities towards the rear, rather like wheel wells. These would serve as toilets, for those able to move.

The flight crew tugged at the insulation, tearing it from the walls and arranging it on the floor. They placed the insulation panels over the honeycomb of holes, but the panels were covered with a slick plastic film and slid about under their feet. They also dragged in a section of liferaft or survival tent, it was hard to tell which. It was a piece of tarpaulin material, laced with nylon cord. They laid it down near the opening, as a cover for the more seriously wounded. Then they went back to the wing with the stretcher, ready to load Mario Ellefsen.

Mario did not want to be moved into the tail. He was cold, he was scared, and he did not want his broken pelvis to be jostled about. When he'd tried to move, the bones of his pelvis had ground together loudly and the pain had been almost unbearable.

Mario looked over at Monty, beside him. It was hard to tell what had happened to Monty. There was blood spilling from his boots, he had lacerated his left arm, he had a depressed skull fracture, and there seemed to be fatty tissue exposed on his fractured skull. Mario turned his head and studied Tony Cobden. He too had some kind of head injury. His scalp looked rather as though he were wearing a bad toupee, and the cold had not closed the wound because the head and neck generate so much of the body's heat. Blood continued to ooze down his face. It had discoloured the entire front of his parka and his wind pants, an unbelievable amount of blood.

"Okay," Mario said. "Move me. But Jesus, don't drop me."

They placed him on a stretcher. He helped them as best he could, dragging himself onto the canvas with his elbows. Joe Bales tried to steady Mario's hips and felt the pelvic bone shifting. Mario screamed profanities.

It was a tough struggle to move the stretcher cases into the tail. Neither Montgomery nor Vance had screamed as loudly as Ellefsen, but the crew were in constant fear of dropping them.

As they were half lifting, half dragging the stretcher across the snow, Couch stumbled over a pair of mukluks. His feet were not cold at that point, but they were wet. He would need the mukluks later, but he couldn't stop right then. It would take twenty minutes to untangle the frozen knot of his laces, and his feet would freeze during the transfer. He had to get the remaining passengers into the tail. He set the mukluks aside, with a mental note to return to that spot and collect them later. But by then the blizzard was in full force, and the mukluks had become covered with snow. He searched for them, with one of the pencil flashlights the crew had recovered, but in vain.

As they carried Vance, he remarked: "It's getting much colder. I can feel it. The temperature is going down."

"There's a storm," West told him.

"And I can hear a plane," Vance said.

West looked down at Vance's swollen face. The eyelids were shut grotesquely tight.

"You've got good ears, buddy," he said. "You're right. There's a plane up there. You listen for us, all right? Tell us when a plane's coming. We need to know."

Vance said he would.

By the time they returned to the wing to assist the survivors who were able to walk, the crew members were again dripping with sweat. They continued to work that way for another hour, in the steadily worsening temperature and wind.

There is a little saying drilled into students at the Arctic survival school conducted by the Armed Forces each winter, a rule of thumb about the essentials of life in the cold: "Sweat and die."

The survivors were laid across the breadth of the tail like cordwood, with their feet towards the entrance and their heads in the stinking darkness. It was a tight squeeze. There was a long period of bumping and jarring as they settled themselves. The insulation kept slipping out of place; knees and feet and elbows got caught in the grating; there were moans and curses and whimpers of pain. At last, it became silent.

Wilma de Groot realized that she knew virtually no one around her. She knew Paul, and liked him. Then there was young Mike, the one whose face had been burned in the fire. And Joe, who she assumed was the pilot. And then there was John, who had been so worried about leaving Sue and Bob out in the snow.

Paul, Mike, Joe, and John.

"Who's here?" she called out. "Paul, are you here?"

From behind her came a voice. "I'm here. Mike's here. John and Joe are out with the others."

There was a scurrying sound, and she heard someone moving towards her. Someone was right there, in front of her face. It was Mike.

"Doc, can you see me?"

"Not really," she said.

"It's my balaclava, Doc. There's something wrong with it. It feels like it's stuck to my face."

She heard him scratching and tugging at it, and then the orange-white light of a flare that had been dropped from overhead lit up the tail section, and she made herself look at his face, though she had a good idea of what she'd see. The black balaclava, a wool-and-polyester knit blend, had been covering his face when the fireball exploded. The synthetic fibre had melted, and the skin of his face had melted, and the two materials had mingled together into a wet slurry. As the blood, flesh, and fibre had dried, they had all fused together into something that was neither quite a face nor a balaclava. It was impossible to tell which part of the mask was made of scabbing blood and which part was made of black material. From this awful mask, Moore's eyes shone, bright and uncomplaining. Then the light from the flare faded, and they were back in total darkness.

"Help me peel it off."

"No, Mike! Leave it. Don't touch it."

He returned to his place, and Wilma began to see that the first principle of survival was not the elevation of the wretched to the comforts enjoyed by the more fortunate, but the slow putrefaction of all, towards the lowest common denominator of misery. The strong will become weak, the first become last.

Wilma's broken ankle now gnashed, bone against bone, whenever she moved. It also gnashed when others moved, tugging at the tarpaulin that lay over top of her. The best she could do was wait for the morphia of cold. Her own body had become as helpless as Mike Moore in his black mask; the corruption had begun.

She lay quietly in the darkness for a while, listening to the others and the sound of the storm. They were, all of them, reduced to nothing now. They had no territory, no status, no meaning; their lives were nothing more than the fog of their own breath in the freezing night. They could do nothing but wait for death or deliverance.

But they all had names, and names are powerful things. The name calls into existence, and calls into being the bonds of existence. God made Adam, and named him; and Eve also. Man named all of the animals. Even God was a name.

Captain Richard Dumoulin, with the smashed cheek and dislocated eye, was the first to invoke her name. He was a mature man of forty-four; he seemed kind. He had studied psychology and history, had counselled younger recruits; he had become a logistics officer because he liked to serve people's needs.

"Hey, Doc," he said in the darkness. "Everybody calls you Doc. What's your real name?"

"My name is Wilma."

The words were exchanged in darkness; no one could see anyone else. But everyone could hear everything.

"Did you say Thelma?"

"No. Not like Thelma and Louise. Wilma. Like the Flintstones."

"Well," he said. "My name is Rick."

"Okay, Nick," she said. Why not? It would help them to remember.

"All right, Thelma."

Wilma heard some chuckles. Dear God, it was fine, to have them chuckle at her expense. It was fine.

"My name is Mario," came a frightened voice.

"Like Super Mario?" Wilma asked.

"I'm sure not feeling very super right now."

She laughed. "Okay, Super Mario. Super Mario and Rick. Who else is here?"

Suddenly the names came from all directions in the darkness. Wilma told herself to remember, the names were important. They were mortally important. To remember, she imposed meaning on the names. She knew that four of the survivors had life-threatening injuries; in military code, these are called "reds." She recited to herself the names of the reds: Bill, Dave, Mario, Monty. Then there was the four-man crew: Paul, Mike, Joe, John. That was two sets of four, she thought. The third set of four names was Tony, Marc, Rick, and me. Then there were the two outside, Sue and Bob, the ones John hadn't wanted to move. That made fourteen.

"All right," said Wilma. "Let's see if I've got this straight. Bill."

"Here."

"Dave."

"Here."

And on down the line. She saved the crew for last, and when she came to John and Joe, there was no answer.

"They're out with the others," said Paul.

The roll call had been established, voices in the dark. They were no longer fourteen individuals who'd lived through a plane crash. They were a community.

CHAPTER ELEVEN

Acceptable Risk

MAJOR Marv Macauley and his co-pilot, Captain Randy Price, had spent most of the seven-hour flight from Greenwood, Nova Scotia, scanning their high-frequency radio, trying to find out what the devil was going on in the effort to rescue the survivors of Box Top 22.

Marv's squadron was the target of a certain jealousy from other Hercules flights in Canada for its sophisticated avionics and radio systems. His airframe was the 1965 E model, the same model that was now in burning pieces on the ground. But he was equipped with the most modern navigation systems available and had a full array of radios: high-frequency, very-high-frequency, and ultra-high-frequency. Marv always knew where he was in the air and could talk to anyone he liked. In the Canadian Forces fleet, his Herc was as rare as Noah's Ark.

At one point Marv's crew had raised a military post, which connected them through a telephone patch to the Trenton headquarters of the Air Transport Group. At other times they raised Edmonton. Once in a while they picked up a stray bounce from other Canadian Forces aircraft. But nobody was able to tell Marv the one bit of information he needed to know: the crash coordinates.

The land mass covered by the rescue effort was a formidable

obstacle to command and control. The Canadian rescue centres, operating with a few squadrons of aircraft and roughly a gross of SARtechs, cover a wedge-shaped arc measuring 90 degrees longitude and 41 degrees latitude – a quarter of the hemisphere's span. If this rescue area were placed over Europe, it would begin at Tralee on the west coast of Ireland and extend east nearly as far as Moscow. Along its southern border, it would pass the cities of Dieppe, Frankfurt, Prague, Cracow, and Kiev. It would embrace all of Great Britain and Northern Ireland, Belgium, the Netherlands, Poland, Denmark, Sweden, Norway, Finland, and the newly liberated Baltic states. It would include large chunks of Czechoslovakia and Germany, and a corner of France; the Baltic Sea, the North Sea, the Norwegian Sea, the Barents Sea, and, for good measure, the island of Spitsbergen.

Rescue work costs the Canadian military about $110 million a year, less than one per cent of the Armed Forces budget. Yet it is one of the Forces' few operational units, and SARtechs are the most highly decorated group of individuals in the military. Among SARtechs still or until recently serving, there were five Stars of Courage, Canada's highest decoration. There were fourteen Medals of Bravery, eight Medals of Military Merit, two Queen's Commendations, four Orders of St. John of Jerusalem, twenty-eight Chief of Defence Staff commendations, ten Air Command commendations, thirteen Air Transport Group commendations, twelve base commander's commendations, four U.S. House of Representatives Awards, and four Airman of the Year awards. That's an impressive record for an outfit the size of four platoons with no commissioned officer, all the more so considering that the list does not include flight crews, who have their own record of decorations.

A reading of the Register of Canadian Honours gives some flavour of the character of SARtechs and of the heritage to which they aspire. But those are accounts of remarkable rescues that drew recognition; they do not give any sense of the SARtechs' daily stock-in-trade of lost, foolish, and desperate souls. Their work is nearly always done in isolation; they have no photo opportunities, and there are no dramatic re-enactments for the nightly news. Their military adventures have little to do with the roar of jet fighters or the clatter of tanks; and they are far removed from the public's appetite for politics, finance, and intrigue. Their pulse quickens to the tiny sound of a homing beacon cheeping in the woods, an arm waving a red handkerchief from the deck of a dory, a set of footprints in the snow.

SARtechs received scant public recognition even for their involvement in one of the largest peacetime marine rescues in history. In October 1980, the 400-foot Dutch cruise ship MV *Prinsendam* foundered some 150 miles offshore in the Gulf of Alaska. The vessel was ablaze and the passengers and crew were going overboard. A supertanker had reached the area, but it was impossible to transfer passengers between the ships because of forty-knot winds and high seas. Visibility was poor; the cloud ceiling was 100 feet. The U.S. Coast Guard requested Canadian SARtech assistance. The first Canadian Labrador helicopter to respond was knocked out by an electrical fire on board; it ditched over land. The second hoisted thirty-one survivors from one lifeboat, found the lost passengers of another, and landed with only minutes of fuel remaining. On shore, Canadian SARtechs treated some 300 survivors for hypothermia and shock. In all, more than 500 lives were saved; not a soul was lost.

The *Prinsendam* has entered SARtech folklore but lies outside the memory of the Canadian public. The very existence of SARtechs is scarcely known, even among the Canadian military. Search and rescue is known as a place where pilots and unaspiring soldiers go to finish their careers, devoid of glamour, recognition, or advancement. SAR is the runt of the military litter. SARbird pilots bitch about the "bombs and bullets" boys at

National Defence Headquarters in Ottawa, who have visions of CF-18 fighters dancing in their heads and want the Canadian Forces out of the rescue trade altogether.

They bitch, and they go about their business.

Marv's co-pilot, Captain Randy Price, had the easy good looks and tight blond curls of the doomed aviator in black-and-white Battle of Britain films. But he had been devoted to the work of SARtechs for over a decade, and been accepted among them. He played hockey on the same line as Arnie and Marv, and shared their gung-ho attitude. The SARtechs called him Randy, which was all the recognition he desired.

He himself had been decorated for bravery, four times. The first of these, a Chief of Defence Staff commendation, was earned in his first year on the job. A U.S. Navy Labrador had slammed into the vertical cliff face of an American mountain during a foul-weather search for a lost Canadian climber. SARtechs were called to assist. The co-pilot and a deputy sheriff had survived, although Price didn't know that. One had both arms broken and was unable to switch on his homing beacon. The other was 300 feet below him, with two broken legs. The winds were at seventy knots and the mountain was shrouded in cloud at 7,000 feet, where the survivors lay.

Price's Labrador arrived with four SARtechs on board. They had started to rappel down to a small ledge on the cliff face when the pilot became disoriented, lost control of the aircraft, and told the SARtechs to jump for their lives. They scrambled down their Sky Genie ropes, but the flight engineer said, "We're not abandoning ship," and Price calculated a safe heading. The helicopter performed a pedal turn into the wind. They were in a cut in the mountain, with a cliff face to either side, and adrift. Price thought he knew a heading to safety, but the aircraft commander disagreed. So the young co-pilot mashed over the cyclic control and performed a spiralling dive to safety.

The sartechs had meanwhile mountaineered to the survivors, but the U.S. helicopter pilots on stand-by refused to fly up the mountain in those conditions. The Canadian Labrador returned – hitting drafts that at times slammed it downwards at 2,000 feet per minute, and at other times forced it to hover ten feet from the cliff face – and pulled the survivors off the mountain ledge.

Price was on his way to becoming a respected rescue pilot. He still carried remnants of his earlier attitude. Rescue work, he believed, involved risk. In an operational military environment, casualties are expected. While younger pilots arrived with a more cautious attitude, Price thought it necessary in search and rescue to take risks; and the hardest decisions he ever made were the decisions to give up and go home.

———————

Closing on Alert, Marv's Hercules from Greenwood tried to raise Major Jim Burger's Hercules from Edmonton. Marv tried the radio every few seconds; finally, the weather office in Alert came up on frequency 126.7. Weather stations in remote outposts like Alert are not known for their strict adherence to radio procedure. A voice in Marv's headset said, "Hey, listen, you guys."

"Yeah?"

"Stop trying to call Rescue Three Four Two. It's already on the ground. Who are you guys, anyway? Rescue Three Three Eight?"

"Who's that?"

"The second Herc out of Edmonton. The MAJAID flight. Is that you?"

"No," said Marv. "We're Rescue Three Zero Five out of Green-wood."

"We don't have anything on a flight out of Greenwood. We're waiting for Rescue Three Three Eight."

"Listen to me, buddy," said Marv. "I've got fourteen SARtechs and a hundred and thirty flares on board, and it would be very frigging nice to penetrate the frigging crash site. If someone there would be kind enough to give me the frigging coordinates."

"I can give you the general vicinity. But I better patch you through to the command post."

The VHF signal from the command post was weak, and efforts to squelch the static only buried the voices. Through the static, Marv's earphones picked up another sound: the faint, undulating "ping, ping, ping" of the emergency locator beacon.

"Never mind," he said. "We've picked up the homer."

Price was flying the aircraft; Marv, although aircraft commander, was in the right seat. He preferred it that way; he could focus on the mission and leave the flying to his first officer. The pinging grew louder in his ears, until they were right over the beacon.

Their droning aircraft was shrouded in blackness; at that altitude, 4,000 feet, they were enclosed in a thick layer of cloud that extended all the way down to the 1,000-foot elevation of the crash site.

"Let's drop a flare," said Marv. "See what's down there."

The established procedure for night flare illumination of a target is straightforward. The pilot flies upwind or crosswind of target and drops the flare. Once ignited, the twenty-five pounds of magnesium burns for five minutes, casting a vast umbrella of light as it falls to the ground beneath its parachute. The pilot banks the aircraft into a descending left turn of 1,000 to 2,500 feet per minute, chasing the flare on its descent. The flare is kept on the left side of the aircraft as the pilot spirals downwards, circling the flare until he reaches minimum safe altitude. SARtechs on the left side of the aircraft scan the ground, searching for signs of wreckage.

The procedure was standard, but these conditions were not. There is normally no call for a night flare illumination through cloud; neither is it usual to follow a flare in winds gusting above thirty knots, as SARtechs never jump at such wind speeds.

"Flare clear."

"Ignition."

The clouds around the aircraft were suddenly bathed in orange light. As Price banked the aircraft 90 degrees to the left, Marv shaded his eyes, trying to peer through the surrealistic vapour; everything was orange, and uniformly bright.

"Can't make out the goddamn flare."

Price flew downwind, parallel to the imagined course of the LUU-2B canister, then banked left 90 degrees once more, throwing an aerial lariat around the descending flare.

"We don't want to wear that guy as a hood ornament," said Marv.

Magnesium will burn through the skin of a Hercules like hot coals through silk. It is an exaggeration to say that a flare can slice the aircraft in half; it is not an exaggeration to say it can sever control cables, damage hydraulics, or set the aircraft ablaze. Flare patterns are carefully planned so the dripping magnesium stays well clear of jumpers, crash sites, and the Hercules itself.

Marv and Price were both squinting through the pulsing orange glow around them when an orb suddenly gained definition in the cloud bank. The circle of light shrank in size and grew more intense as the orb drew nearer. By the time Marv realized what was happening, the flare was plainly visible as a white-hot cylinder of dripping incandescence. They'd descended into the path of the flare.

"Flare!" Marv shouted. "Twelve o'clock!"

The flare was ahead and above the nose of the aircraft, and they were closing on it at a speed of 150 knots. Price found himself in one of those moments when acceptable risk turns to imminent peril. The burning magnesium flare was drifting, he knew, at a speed of about thirty knots. Without other visual clues, it was impossible to tell in which direction it was drifting. With a pencil and a pad of paper, he could have figured it out in a few seconds; but in a few seconds, magnesium might well be scorching through the windscreen.

Price made an instinctive crank and bank to the left. The Hercules sat on its left wing, bled airspeed, and climbed. The flare streaked away to the right side of the aircraft.

"Good call," said Marv. He spoke lightly, but relief was written on his face.

"What now?"

"I'm going to be honest," said Marv. "I've got cold feet."

"Want to go home?"

"We're not doing any good here."

Because the Alert runway was already chock-a-block with Hercules aircraft from the mounting rescue operation, Rescue 305 headed for Thule to put down. After an uneventful landing, the team from Greenwood headed for the transient quarters.

Once Arnie had grabbed a bite to eat, he had a chat with his brother. It was an argument, really, a heated difference of opinion regarding acceptable risk. Normally, the two saw eye-to-eye, but the extremes of polar rescue are not normal. Arnie figured Marv had let himself become rattled by the flare. Marv thought that Arnie, frustrated by the knowledge that his good buddies were hurt and helpless, had lost his perspective on the question of acceptable risk.

SARtechs are a breed apart. They have a firm belief in their own capabilities. The commander of their branch of the Air Force, Brigadier-General Gord Diamond, was himself a respected SAR pilot of Buffalo and Labrador aircraft and developed a healthy respect for the "daily heroism" of the group. He casts a tolerant eye on their undisciplined nature, calling it a form of "necessary arrogance." But not all senior officers relish the fact that SARtechs tend to salute when they feel like it, wear uniforms when they feel like it, or call officers "Sir" and refer to them by rank when they feel like it, which is usually when they think the senior officer is a first-class dink. As a group, SARtechs lack the flattery and polish so essential to advancement in today's armed services, because they would rather be regular guys than dinks.

They have, it is true, a sentimental side. Many SARtechs are injured in the line of duty, and some are killed. These are revered in the collective memory, and the symbol of the reverence is the red beret. On the wall of every SARtech unit is a poem, written after the death of eight members of a rescue crew in an Arctic crash in 1970. It was written by the widow of one of those killed, Corporal Bill Platt. In part, it reads:

Hush, my son, don't cry.
You're too wise for your three years.
I can't tell you why he died,
I don't know how to dry your tears.

I can tell you that he loved you,
I could tell you to great length.
But we weren't the only ones
That depended on his strength.

There were many other people
With little boys like you,
That Daddy went to look for
Because it's what he had to do.

Someday you'll be a man,
And go your separate way.
But I know I'll be damned proud
If you wear a Red Beret.

The poem may be cloyingly sentimental, but there isn't a SARtech around who can recite it without pausing to clear his throat, or who doesn't believe every word – Marv and Arnie Macauley included. The poem helps explain the importance of the red beret as a symbol of their work; it helps explain the motivation of people like Marv and Arnie; and it sheds some light on their disagreement.

If the SARtechs had tried to jump in those conditions, Marv reasoned, there would almost certainly have been casualties. Then what would they have done? Thrown more jumpers after them? Added more bodies to the casualty pile?

Arnie saw it differently. Maybe there would have been casualties. Maybe the first guy out would have paid the price. So be it. And if there'd been casualties in the first group, all the more reason to send jumpers after them. You couldn't just leave them there.

At Thule, the Macauley brothers never did settle their difference, perhaps because it grew out of the thorniest question that underlies rescue work: When do you risk a life to save a life? SARtechs seldom, except in private moments and with fumbling words, articulate when and why they would do such a thing. They may all have had different definitions of acceptable risk, but they all had this baseline in common. They did not value their own lives any more than those of the suffering souls on the ground. But they did not value them any less, either.

In theory, Marv was commander of the aircraft, with authority to cancel the jump. Next time they got airborne over the crash site, the decision would be his. In practice, however, he knew it would be a difficult order to enforce.

The brothers walked away, leaving the matter unresolved. But each had made an inner resolution.

Arnie had decided he would be the first jumper out the door, and wouldn't tell Marv until he was on the ground. He thought that was pretty clever.

Marv figured Arnie would probably try to outsmart him by being the first jumper out the door. He decided to respect his brother's wishes, although he wouldn't tell him so until later.

Marv was worried sick about his older brother. He didn't tell him that, either.

CHAPTER TWELVE

Mission Impossible

C APTAIN Mark Levesque stepped from the deadhead flight from Trenton and hurried over to the waiting helicopter. The Buffalo had flown him to Wabush, near Labrador City on the border between northern Quebec and Newfoundland. Despite his French name, Levesque was an anglophone. Political boundaries meant nothing to him. His main interest was the distance to the nearest fuel dump; his main worry was sleep deprivation.

The military's normal fatigue limits and twelve-hour "bottle to throttle" rule – no flying within a half-day of taking a drink – were out the window. Levesque had slept three hours in the previous twenty-four and had something like forty hours of flying time ahead of him. He was exhausted, and the flight north would be gruelling, at best. But a Labrador helicopter was needed at Alert; someone had to fly it there, or at least make the attempt; and he happened to be the someone. He tried to push his weariness to the back of his mind, and consulted the flight charts.

The rescue centre was working one step ahead of Levesque, uncovering the remote caches of JP-40 aviation fuel stored across the High Arctic. These would be his stepping-stones to the North Pole. He would not know, from one stone to the next, what his next destination would be. Neither would he be able to raise the

Edmonton rescue centre while in flight; he would rely on radio-telephones from each isolated Inuit fishing village along the way. All in all, it struck him as a bit hare-brained. But he was a soldier. He was a rescue pilot. The crash victims were family. Besides, the notion was kind of intriguing.

Levesque spoke with his first officer and his engineer, his finger tracing the route.

"The Aurora won't pick us up until Fort Chimo," he said. "You can see the lines of magnetic variation, here. About 80 degrees – a quarter of the rose. Magnetic compass won't be much help. The directional gyro's out – it's been out of service for four years. HQ says they're working on it. We might have gyro compass in a day or two.

"The long and the short is, we'd better make use of the day-light while we've got it."

"Fuel stops?" the engineer asked.

"We find out en route. And one thing – we never shut her down. The old workhorse might get us there, but if we let the engines go down, forget it."

The crew was contemplating a flight of nearly forty hours through extreme climates. The Labrador, on average, has a minor mechanical breakdown every one and a half hours; it has a mal-function serious enough to render it incapable of performing its mission every six hours. Levesque figured the only chance of stretching its endurance was to keep the engines and blades turning. But this raised a hazard of its own.

The engineer blanched. "Hot refuel the whole way?"

Levesque nodded. Hot refuelling was an approved procedure for the Labrador but only in dire emergency. It meant the engineer would pump explosive aviation gas into the fuel sponsons – the outboard fuel tanks on both sides of the rear fuselage – located only a few feet from a burning jet engine. The tandem rotors would be spinning above his head, an added danger. He would be using an electrical pump or, where there was no electricity, hand-pumping the fuel from forty-five-gallon drums. Because of the whine of the engines, he would be unable to talk or hear shouted commands. And he would be working in darkness, with numb hands, frozen hoses, and awkward couplings. One spill, one spark, and they would all go up in flames.

"Let's get started," Levesque said. "We're burning daylight."

Levesque began the starting sequence. The twin GE turbine engines coughed to life, producing a total of 2,700 shaft horsepower.

The airframe was nearly as old as Levesque, but the Boeing-built Labrador has considerable abilities, despite its age. Still, Levesque would have to coax every ounce of effort from the machine to make the trip.

He had certain advantages. A single-rotor helicopter produces yaw from the spinning of the overhead blades, so a tail rotor is needed to keep the aircraft straight, resulting in wasted horsepower. The Labrador's fifty-foot blades chop the air in a counter-rotational direction, which means no yaw and no wasted energy; it all goes into lift.

At nearly eleven tons, the Labrador is a medium-sized aircraft, but its massive blades can carry it to a height of 10,000 feet. Long before then, however, its performance deteriorates; it becomes sloppy in thin air, a little like driving on ice. It is not unusual, especially in the Far North, to encounter weather systems rising to an altitude of 10,000 feet. Levesque would have two options. He would be flying either very low or very high.

Any advantage in aviation has a cost. The 125-knot cruising airspeed of the Labrador is impressive, but this gain is achieved at the expense of endurance. The Labrador is a short-range helicopter. A normal fuel load is 4,000 pounds, giving it a range of 440 nautical miles and an endurance of three hours and forty minutes. Pilots prefer this load, since there is less fuel to dump in case of engine failure, and the Lab is slow at dumping fuel.

Levesque elected to take the maximum fuel load of 5,000 pounds. This decision would add fifty nautical miles to his range and thirty-five minutes to his endurance, which could save his life. In the event of a breakdown, however, his decision could cost him his life. Any advantage in aviation has a cost.

A polar attempt should have been made with an air-refuellable helicopter, but the Canadian Forces had none. The trip would be planned in strides of less than 600 nautical miles. The next footfall from Wabush was Kuujjuaq, three hours' flying time and 325 nautical miles to the north, on Quebec's shore of Ungava Bay.

Accompanied by a co-pilot, a flight engineer, and two SARtechs, Levesque launched at one-thirty in the afternoon, under daylight visual conditions. Northern Quebec and Labrador is a black hole for the Omega navigational system, so it was fortunate they could follow landmarks. Perhaps this wouldn't be so bad after all.

————————

Less than halfway to Kuujjuaq, Levesque was flying about 100 feet above the impenetrable northern forest, taking advantage of the dense air at lower levels, when he noticed that the trees faded out in the distance ahead. His eyes must have been playing tricks on him. The forest extended to a range of rising hills, then seemed to stop abruptly. It seemed as though the hills were set against a solid painted mural of grey canvas.

As he drew closer, he realized the backdrop was a weather front, starting at the ground layer and rising vertically some two miles. Levesque gave a whistle of admiration for a formidable opponent.

"All right," he said to his co-pilot. "See if you can hail anyone on the HF radio. Transmit to all military stations. We've got to know what's behind that weather."

The first officer worked the radio but finally gave up. "Nothing," he said. "The HF is useless."

Levesque decided to puncture the cloud and fly blind. On his other radio, he could raise the same Buffalo aircraft that had dropped him in Wabush. The Buffalo was now above him, ferrying the second flight crew a few stepping-stones up the line.

"Raise Rescue Four Five Two and file an immediate IFR flight plan," he said. "Base it on our present lat-long." Levesque was thinking ahead: if the Labrador went down in the bush, the filed instrument flight rules plan would aid in the search for his aircraft.

The curtain drew nearer, and he steadied his hands and feet on the controls. His eyes locked onto the flight instruments, for he knew that as soon as he entered the weather system he would lose all sense of orientation. Unlike the pilot of a fixed-wing aircraft, he would have to concentrate on stabilizing the helicopter in all three dimensions. He steeled himself; the helicopter chopped ahead; the weather system hit him like a physical blow.

The Labrador disappeared from the world and entered a twilight of steel grey. Levesque experienced vertigo; he fought to restore his balance and ward off nausea by fixing his gaze on the instrument panel. His head swam; and he noticed that waves of fatigue were mixed in with his imbalance. He fell silent, hypnotic, on the controls.

He was jerked to attention by one of the SARtechs in the rear: "Mark! Ice on the stub tanks!"

The Lab had entered an ice system. Levesque had been suckered. He looked up at his windscreen; it had been converted to dimpled glass. Ice was rapidly forming on the forward surfaces of the aircraft. The aviator has many assassins – disorientation, fatigue, engine failure – but ice is the swift, silent killer.

Ice on the lifting surfaces of a fixed-wing aircraft kills by adding weight and disturbing the gentle curve of low-pressure air over the wing; the aircraft stalls, then crashes. It is no less punishing on a helicopter. Ice on the rotors can destroy lift, but the Labrador had a special vulnerability – the engine vents.

The Labrador's engines are shielded by metal screens on the forward inlets, about the same gauge as that used on car headlamps. The screens prevent foreign objects from fouling the turbines, but they are not heated, and they gather ice as a net gathers fish. When the screens ice over, the engine chokes, the blades stop turning, and the aircraft falls. There is a cruel twist to this: the ice, at the same time as it suffocates the engines, also gathers on the inboard edge of the rotors. This is the part of the blade that provides auto-rotational lift during an engine failure. If the engines die, the blades are designed to spin freely as they fall through the air and provide enough control so the Labrador can, at least, make a stable forced landing without power. But not if the rotors are iced. If the rotors are iced, the aircraft tumbles. When ice brings down a Labrador, it brings it down for good.

Levesque thought hard and fast. The outside temperature was about -5 Celsius. He brought the Labrador down to treetop level, hoping to duck underneath the weather system; but then the temperatures rose to the range between -2 and the freezing point, the worst range for ice. He had no choice but to climb and hope for drier, colder weather at higher altitude. Climbing with ice on board is counter to an aviator's reflex, with engine failure imminent; but it often works. All it takes is iron nerve and a complete poverty of options.

He put all the engine's torque into lift; the helicopter began to rise vertically through the cloud bank; already the Lab's performance was weakened. It struggled upwards past 5,000 feet, and 6,000, and 7,000. It passed through snow showers. It reached 8,000 feet, and then, sluggishly, 9,000. Levesque was near his ceiling, but the gambit had worked. The ice was still gathering on the Lab, but at a much slower rate. He'd bought himself time.

Levesque lifted the tail of his yellow SARbird and edged on. His forward speed was reduced by the power needed to maintain his altitude, and the distance to Kuujjuaq had, in real terms, doubled. He did a mental calculation of the distance remaining, and of his own endurance. He was cutting it fine, but the choice was made for him. He was past the point of no return for Wabush. He had no alternate landing field.

Three hours after leaving Wabush, deduced reckoning, based on his airspeed and direction, told him he was approaching Kuujjuaq – still known among pilots by its colonial name, Fort Chimo.

"We're coming into Chimo," Levesque told himself. "We're high, we're low on gas, we're picking up ice, we're past the point of return. We've got one shot at it."

He spotted a break in the clouds. It wasn't a clear opening, but it was the only shot he had.

"It's now or never," he said.

The Labrador descended through the broken cloud layer, clearing the base of the weather system a few hundred feet above the ground. From where they hovered, they could see the lights of Kuujjuaq.

Mark Levesque set the aircraft down, unstrapped his harness, and hurried to the aviation shed. There he would pick up the black radio-telephone and receive his orders. He would follow them. He'd follow them in spite of the fatigue crawling from his shoulders, through the tense muscles of his forearms, into the hands still tingling from the controls. The frozen tarmac swayed beneath him; he had rubber legs. He felt bleary and delirious.

Levesque had fought his way through a weather front that would have brought down many pilots. He'd been virtually lost in the air for two-thirds of the journey. He'd faced deadly ice for

200 miles, and he'd been at the very limit of the helicopter's endurance when he'd finally broken through cloud. He had been flying with no radio or navigational aids, against the storm, in a hands-on posture for two hours straight. He was spent in body and soul. He had three hours of the flight behind him, and thirty-three hours ahead of him.

He had just completed the easiest leg of his voyage.

CHAPTER THIRTEEN

Brother John

WITH SNOW packed around her thighs and chest, and a stinking rag over her face, Sue Hillier lay in the endless dark, thinking she was in a coffin. So cold, so black, so deathly quiet ...

No. Not quiet. Something had changed. It was dark and noisy. She had not noticed. The wind was loud, now that she listened to it, a huge roaring sound, consuming so much of her hearing that she hadn't even been aware of it. How did it get so strong? She imagined the wind being born at the North Pole, swirling into strength, gaining brawn as it blew south, growing into a tidal force as it swept over the frozen sea, crashing against the rocky shore.

Yes, that's what it sounded like. It sounded like the ocean. It climbed over the hills and flooded her; she was a tiny thing, insignificant.

It wasn't like the wind in Trenton at all; the wind there had been sliced and bent and spun around things. At home, you never heard the wind itself, only its footfall: the scattering of papers on the street to snap at your heels, the rustling of leaves to disturb your reading, the creaking of doors to make you start. Like so many things in life before the crash, the wind in Trenton related to her, took her into account. This wind roared right past, as unaware of Sue as a black freight passing in the night. It made her feel small and alone.

She strained to hear something, anything, besides the wind. "Bob?"

There was nothing. Oh God.

"Bob!" Her mangled tongue filled her mouth. "Bob!"

"Uhn."

"It's okay, Bob. You don't have to talk. I just want to know you're all right. Are you all right?"

"Uhn."

"Okay."

Sometimes Bob felt like talking, sometimes he didn't. That was all right. She just wanted to know she wasn't alone.

"Hear that wind, Bob?"

"Uhn."

"It sounds like the wind at my uncle's farm in Alberta. My parents went out there for their anniversary, but I couldn't go, I was too busy getting ready for this trip. Most of my family out west have these huge farms. We're the only ones on my mom's side not on the farm. I like cattle. I like outdoors stuff. Are you an outdoors person, Bob?"

There was no answer.

"Bob? ... Bob!"

"Uhn."

"Just let me know you're here. Just grunt so I know you're here."

"Uhn."

She laughed. It hurt to laugh, but it seemed so funny all of a sudden. "Just grunt, Bob. Just be a typical man and grunt so I know you're alive."

No response. Well, she'd tried to get a rise out of him. What could they talk about next?

"Bob? I like basketball and, let's see, I like horses. Do you like horses? I trained horses in high school. This man had a beautiful home, he was a Bata executive, he had this home with eight bedrooms. He had Arabians. He used to show them all over the States, Florida and everywhere. My girlfriend and I looked after them, but this is hilarious, right, we weren't allowed to ride them. All we did was exercise them and he'd come down on the weekend and ride them. That's the way he did things, that was fine.

"Anyway, this one time – like, we used to go down to the barn every day, and this one time there were wolves. I know what they look like, wolves, and these were great big timber wolves. I was surprised, because we had seven dogs down there as well. He had two big hounds, a German shepherd, an Afghan, and some small dogs. The dogs went crazy and started barking. So anyway we were stuck in the barn overnight, my girlfriend and me and the dogs barking like crazy. We were some scared. And the next day I got a gun, I got a .308 and I know how to use it. I was going to shoot them. But I didn't. I just scared them away. They were just wolves....

"Bob? Are you still there? Bob!"

"Uhn."

"I have a dog, too. She's a husky. Do you have any pets, Bob?"

Sue was interrupted by the beam of a flashlight being played over the rag covering her face.

"Who's there?"

"John."

John was nice, he kept checking on them, letting them know they weren't alone. Sue sprinkled him with questions, as she always did. Was there any news? Had they reached anyone on the radio? Was rescue on the way? There was really only one question – will I have my life back? – and John couldn't answer that, so he didn't answer any of them. He let her talk.

Sue moved from questions to observations. "It's colder, it must be the middle of the night. I know it all feels the same to you, John, but I'm like a thermometer stuck here in the snow. And an airplane went away and I haven't heard another one yet, except the wind is so strong it could even be an airplane. Have you heard an airplane, John, have you heard the wind?"

"Help's on the way," he said. "Everybody's doing their best. You just hang in there."

And then she moved from observations to despair. Talking made her pain easier to bear, and I wish Bob would talk a bit more, it would do him good. But I'm really scared up here, I'm afraid you're going to leave me. And I know it's silly but I think you'll all leave, and the rescuers will come and you'll forget about us, and you'll all go away and leave us here.

"We wouldn't do that, Sue. I'm going to stay right here beside you, so that won't happen."

"And … I know nobody can tell me this, I already told Joe about it, but I really don't think I can handle being in a wheelchair for the rest of my life. I mean, Adrian and I were going to buy a house, and I'm thirty and I don't even have children yet. And I know some people in wheelchairs and they do all right, but it's not the same, not when you're thirty and not even married yet and don't have any children. And I'm so alone, John, I'm so scared. Why is this happening to me?"

She stopped talking then, because she was crying and her moans expressed what her words could not. She sobbed, and her sobs rose as fog to the shroud over her face, and her wet breath mingled with her hopeless tears.

John gently lifted the rag away, and they looked at each other, face to face. His face was dirty and soiled, and behind the charcoal his skin appeared grey. He had dark flaps under his eyes, and stubble on his cheeks, and grey skin was hanging from his jowls. He had aged terribly with the cold. He was suffering.

"I've got something," he said. "For you."

He fished a plastic-wrapped cube out of his pocket. It took

151

some doing. His hands were trembling and nearly useless with cold. He scraped at the wrapper with nails that were blackened and fingers that were raw. It was as though he had some kind of palsy. He managed to get most of the plastic off.

"Open your mouth," he said.

"What is it?"

"Just open."

He pressed the cube against her lips. His fingertips were ice, and her lips trembled at the touch. She felt the frozen cube enter her mouth. It was hard and cold, but began to melt. She had not realized how hungry she had become. Greedily she worked the sweet cube between her teeth.

"Don't chew it. It's a survival candy. Let it melt slowly."

Sue nodded, studying the ancient face of this young man. He waited in silence while she ate, squatting beside her, back to the wind. He met her eyes for a moment, then tucked his head between his knees. He seemed impossibly chilled, and he was bald. God, you don't even have a hat. You shouldn't be outside. But don't leave me....

Couch got to his feet. Sue watched with alarm, and he reassured her: "I've just got to check on Bob."

He disappeared from her view, and she heard a low mumbling of voices. After a few moments he returned and again squatted beside her. He put his face close to hers and said in a low tone, speaking to the ground, "He's pretty bad."

Sue nodded. She wanted to tell him that she was doing her best to keep Bob awake, that she was grateful for his company in the wind and snow, but the candy was so good she just sucked it greedily, like a baby at the breast, watching his face.

"We didn't see it, you know."

She stopped sucking. She looked puzzled.

"We didn't see the hills. We didn't know a thing was wrong. We just ... crashed."

Sue wanted him to meet her eyes but he was in his own world. He looked up, turning his face to the storm and the darkness; then he dropped his head between his knees. She could no longer see his face, but he seemed to be shivering uncontrollably. His shoulders and back were heaving so violently that someone who didn't know better might have thought he was weeping.

Sue sucked the candy. She would finish it and then tell John to go back inside. He needed a rest, he needed to take shelter from the cold, but first she would finish the candy with him beside her.

They said nothing as the storm raged. They remained in silence for perhaps half an hour, until another flashlight lit the darkness. It was Joe. John always came first, then Joe followed. Sue imagined he was checking on John as much as on Bob and herself. The beam of light jerked across the snow as he made his unsteady way, picking out old footprints, fighting the bitter wind.

"How's it going, Sue?"

"Okay."

Joe sat with Bob. Sue could hear them talking but couldn't make out the words. Then she saw the sweep of his flashlight as he stood. It caught ice crystals in its beam, small barbs of ice driven horizontally across the ground. The light swung down as Joe made his way back to the tail.

Sue finished the candy. It went like the last sliver of soap, getting smaller and smaller without ever quite disappearing. Finally it was no more than a dot of sweetness on the roof of her mouth.

"I don't blame him, you know."

John looked up, startled.

"Joe, I mean. I don't blame him. I don't blame the pilot. I know what it's like to fly an airplane. I was an Air Cadet, I learned to fly gliders. Once we went to Ottawa in a Hercules, they let us into the cockpit and I even got to fly it."

John said nothing.

"I know he must be feeling awful, but he's a good pilot. Until we crashed I thought it was the best flight I'd ever been on. All sorts of things happen at night."

"Yes," he said. "They do."

"I mean, people make mistakes, but they're accidents. That's why they call them accidents. Nobody crashes an airplane on purpose. He was doing his best. He probably feels awful, seeing us out here. But we don't blame him."

John was as still as a stone. His expression hadn't changed, but water had formed in the circles under his eyes.

"John?"

"You don't know, do you?"

"Know what?"

"My name is John Couch."

"I know," Sue laughed. "I'm Sue Hillier."

"I'm the pilot," said John, and wept.

His shoulders heaved and he sobbed loudly, and rocked slowly towards her. Grief had sapped his strength, and when he spoke again it was with a different voice, frail and barely audible: "I'm sorry, I'm so very sorry, sorry, sorry."

She wanted desperately to comfort him but she couldn't move. She was losing sensation in parts of her body, and her exposed face had become so numb she felt foolish trying to speak, as she did after a visit to the dentist, all goofy lips and rubber cheeks.

"Are you listening, John?"

His head moved, he was nodding yes.

"There's nothing to be sorry for. There's nothing to forgive."

He met her eye for a moment.

"It was an accident," she said. "Nobody blames you. I don't blame you, and look at me."

But he couldn't look at her. He lifted his head again, gazing into the teeth of the storm. His eyes were closed. He drew a shaky breath.

Me and my big mouth. I never know when to shut up. After all he's done for me, and now look what I've done. I really hurt him.

"Go now," said Sue. "Go back inside. It'll work out. They're going to come for us."

John draped the cloth over Sue's face, arranging it just so. It wasn't easy, with his frozen hands. He got to his feet. "I'll come back to see you, but I do have to go now. I'll be no good to anybody if I freeze to death."

In the tail of the wreckage, Wilma was also listening to the wind. It doesn't howl, she thought, doesn't moan. It's just a pure sound of rushing air. She heard it ebb and flow, but there was no music to it; it wasn't like the wind passing richly through the bellows of the organ at the Church of the Brethren in Christ. It was a dry sound. Dry and empty.

It didn't sound of this world at all; it sounded like it came from the netherworld. It would die down, and she would catch her breath; then it would rise again. It had a mind; it was evil. It always seemed to rise when a rescue plane approached. She fancied that the Hercules brought the wind; that its propellers angered the Arctic spirits and stirred up the storm in their frenzy.

Huddled in the tail, a reeking den of blackness and injury and grief, Wilma understood the elements as a personal enemy. The survivors were in the grip of some malevolent spirit. Why else would the storm rage at the approach of rescue aircraft? Who else would want to drown out their voices? What other purpose was there in snatching their weak radio signals and blasting them away in the storm?

"A plane," said Vance.

Yes, it was there all right. Wilma, too, could make out the engines' approach. Paul West scrambled for the tail opening, reaching in his pocket for the hand radio he kept close to the warmth of his skin. With numb fingers he managed to pull out the aerial and scan the emergency frequencies.

"… Rescue Three Four Two," a voice said. "Can you read me?"

"Loud and clear!" he shouted. "This is Sergeant Paul West! I read you guys!"

"This is Rescue Three Four Two. We have you located, Paul. What is the number and condition of survivors, over."

"Get in here as quick as you can."

"We read you, Paul. We can't get the jumpers in right now. The weather's too bad. A ground party of SARtechs are on their way. What is the number and condition of survivors, over."

"Fourteen," West said. "Six red. Six green. Two yellow." Six critically wounded, in need of immediate treatment. Six stable. Two in need of early treatment and evacuation.

"You're breaking up, Paul. Please repeat."

"The sooner you get in here, the better!"

"We've lost you, Paul. Can't hear you. Click your transmit button once for affirmative, twice for negative. Do you copy? Over."

Dispirited, West clicked the transmit button.

"Okay. Is there is more than one survivor? Over."

Click.

"More than five?"

Click.

The voice on the radio sounded incredulous. "More than ten?"

Click.

"More than fifteen?"

Click, click.

"Fourteen?"

Click.

"Okay, Paul. Fourteen souls. That's great. We're going now to assist the ground party. Rescue Three Four Two over and out."

Paul raised his voice into the useless microphone: "We really need you guys! We need you!"

No response; his batteries had died. He returned to the row of survivors, feeling their questions, wondering if he had got through. When would help arrive? He had no idea. What had he actually learned? Nothing.

"Relax," he said. "I know these guys. They'll be here as quick as they can."

He lay down beside Wilma, pressed against her back. In the few minutes outside, he had chilled considerably. He began to shiver uncontrollably.

"Are you okay?" she asked.

"We've lost the radio," he said quietly. "There's a ground party on the way. Storm's too bad to jump."

The darkened tail fell into silence; West had attempted to reassure everyone but had been short on specifics. They knew he had made contact, but they knew that already; the flares were a constant reminder. But West could not tell them what they wanted to know. How much longer must they endure?

Not knowing was a weight, one that some of the survivors almost couldn't bear. Wilma had an inspiration, the instinctive response of the Christian through the ages; she would sing in the face of adversity. Maybe the others would like to sing. It might cheer everybody up. What would people know? She began to hum the opening bars of "I'll Be Home for Christmas."

"Not that," someone said.

Right, something happier. She began to sing, in a tiny, thin, solitary voice:

It's a long way to Tipperary,
It's a long way to go!
It's a long, long way to Tipperary,

My heart tells me so.
So hmm-hmm dee, dee dee dee dum dum,
Dee dum-dum, dee dum,
It's a long way to Tipperary,
It's a long waaay
To go!

She forgot the rest of the words, and stopped. Echoes of the tune resounded in the air. Others were singing! Okay, she could keep this going. This time, her voice was robust:

I'm looking over
A four-leaf clover
That I've overlooked before!

A figure appeared in the opening of the tail section, darker black against the blackness. It was Joe.

"What's this? A singsong?"

He picked his way carefully through the bodies, then took his place beside Mario. He moved as gently as he could, but Mario had to shift to make room. They all heard the grinding of Mario's broken hips, the helpless, agonized moan.

"How are the others?" Wilma asked.

The two outside had become "the others," and those in the tail felt a shared guilt at having left them in the snow. They realized it was necessary but still felt remorse. To some extent, Joe and John had become their surrogates. They all felt better when Joe and John were out there with them, even though they knew the two crewmen suffered more with every trip.

There was no choice leading to less remorse or less pain; even the singing increased the rate of dehydration through their lungs and sped up the onset of hypothermia. Wilma knew this, but she also knew that depression would take an even greater toll. She decided to add the singing to her roll call.

"Monty."

"Here."

Thank God. Monty was having a lucid moment. Because of his head injuries, he drifted in and out.

"Where you from, Monty?"

"Can't you tell?" he said. "Newfoundland."

"Who knows a Newfoundland song?"

Someone began to sing, "This land is your land, this land is my land," believing there was something about Newfoundland in there somewhere. It was a good, rousing song, and most of them knew the words.

"What about Nova Scotia?" someone called.

Wilma began to sing "Farewell to Nova Scotia," and nearly everyone joined in.

"How about you, Super Mario?" she asked. "Where are you from?"

"Quebec," he said. "Born and raised in Bagotville. Dad worked in the paper mill. Didn't speak a word of English till I joined the Forces."

"Hey," said another passenger, Marc Tremblay. "Same as me. I was born in Saint-Félicien. Nine kids in our family. Dad was a lumberjack, died when I was eight."

"Five in mine," said Mario. "You got kids?"

"Two. Trevor, the boy, is nineteen. Sigrid, the girl, she's fourteen. Two's enough. We stopped at two."

"I've got two, too," said Mario. "Girls. Kelsy and Kayla. My two little sweethearts. They're four and two."

"Little ones. That's a good age. That's the best time. You going to stop at two?"

"I don't know."

"We did. But you know, we were happy with nine in our family. My mother, she was poor moneywise, but she was rich in things you can't replace with money. We pulled together then. A family was something. All we had was each other."

The tail was silent for a time.

"I'm afraid I don't know many songs from Quebec," said Wilma, "but I think everyone knows 'Frère Jacques.'"

Mario led the version in French, then Wilma sang a chorus in Dutch, her voice standing alone. Then, while everyone was joining in a final chorus in English, another figure darkened the lighter darkness of the tail opening.

John's back was frozen solid with frost and ice; hunched and slow-moving, he made his way in the darkness and lay down heavily, but not among them, for there was no room. He tucked himself as closely as he could to their feet. He had stayed too long in the cold this time; he would have to be more careful. Perhaps he could warm himself by singing. He joined in "Frère Jacques."

Their joined voices were wafted on the wind to the burial site in the snow. Sue was alone again – she and Bob were alone again – and she comforted herself by listening to the voices. The other survivors didn't seem so far away when they sang. When the voices faded out, Sue shouted at them to sing more, but the cloth was covering her face and the wind was blowing towards her and they couldn't hear her voice. She was left with nothing but the howling of the wind and the echo of the final roundelay:

Are you sleeping,
Are you sleeping,
Brother John?
Brother John?

CHAPTER FOURTEEN

Thin Ice

A FTER THE SKIDDING, hair-raising landing of the rescue Hercules from Edmonton, Fred Ritchie had noticed his SARtechs studying the terrain at Alert with unusual concentration. They kicked at the rock and shale under the thin coating of snow, gauged the bite of the wind. Ritchie could not command his men to jump; unlike most military personnel, SARtechs work on mutual consent, not on orders. They were sizing up their chances in a jump.

At the command post Ritchie had found Major Don Hanson, who had asked for a report.

"It's zero-zero visibility out there," Ritchie had explained. "We couldn't establish ground contact. What happened to the search party?"

Ritchie was told that the ground party had been turned back by mechanical breakdowns and weather. Reports from the circling Box Top Hercules had indicated the presence of survivors, fire on the ground, and what could have been the rudimentary makings of a camp. But the meteorological office could not forecast when the storm would blow over. For the moment, the crash site was locked tight.

Ritchie decided to split his team of SARtechs in two. Half would get some rest; the other six would go back up in the Herc with Burger to circle the crash site, in case the weather cleared. He explained the new plan to Jim Brown, his team leader.

"Why don't we mount a ground search party?" said Brown.

"The vehicles are broken down, apparently. They told us they had no serviceable vehicles at the station."

"Then what are those, Fred? Dinky toys?"

Two of the yellow Go-Tracks were parked inside the vehicle shed.

"Well, I'll be damned."

The two SARtechs hurried back to the command post. Ritchie told Hanson he wanted to organize his own ground search. He needed volunteer drivers who knew the surrounding terrain.

The defeated ground search party had returned less than an hour earlier. Steven Cann, the mechanic, hadn't even bothered to change out of his Arctic kit; he'd headed straight for the Igloo Gardens base canteen to make up for his missed supper. It was now two o'clock in the morning, and he hadn't had a meal since breakfast. By the time he joined the others at the command post, Fred Ritchie was studying a copy of the station's 1:50,000 topographical survey of the area.

Another volunteer driver, Corporal Gilles Grégoire, said, "You'll never make it across the Sheridan River. We were out there. We know."

Ritchie asked about heading for the coast and then following the pack ice.

"Can't do that either," Cann said. "The Go-Tracks weigh nine tons apiece. There's air pockets under the ice this time of year, and pressure ridges always. Go through the ice, you're a dead man."

"All right," said Ritchie. "We'll follow the coastline to here" – he indicated an inlet just north of Cape Rawson, east of the crash site – "then head inland. We have a portable homer for the crash beacon. When we get within range, we can follow the beacon to the site."

Ritchie's vehicle, Go-Track Six, took a toboggan kit with sleeping bags, stoves, lanterns, tents, and fuel. Ritchie sat in the front seat, with Grégoire driving, and two SARtechs on a bench in the rear. Cann drove the other Go-Track, Bluebell, with three more SARtechs.

By the time they set off, the storm was, if anything, worse. The Go-Tracks had not gone 200 yards when the base disappeared behind them in a fog of ice. Had it not been pitch black, these would have been white-out conditions. As it was, snow and ice pellets whipped around the headlamps of the Go-Tracks; Ritchie could not see five feet ahead of him or twenty feet to the side.

"Okay, take us to the coast!" Ritchie yelled over the roar of the storm and the machine.

"How?" Grégoire asked.

Nincompoop! Imagine, driving the lead vehicle with no idea where you're going. Fred was ready to crawl down the man's gullet and ream him clean through to the other end. He knew how to do it, too: he'd been well taught by his father, the regimental sergeant major.

"You don't know where we are?"

"I'm sorry, sir. They don't allow us to use this road in winter. Nobody on station knows this road."

"Why the hell did you volunteer, for Christ's – "

What am I doing? I have nothing against this man; he volunteered while others stood back. What would the regimental sergeant major do in a situation like this? Of course, the regimental sergeant major would never have got himself into a jam like this in the first place. Only his idiot son would do something like that.

"I know where we're going," Ritchie yelled.

"Yes, sir?"

"The crash site. That's where we're going." He smiled at the man, and at his own little joke. "The only thing I don't know is how the hell to get there."

"I know," said Ron Burke, one of the sARtechs in back.

"How?" said Fred.

"By Hercules. Definitely the way to get there."

"I sometimes forget," Ritchie told Grégoire, "how lucky I am to be working with a bunch of frigging comics."

"The communications towers are east of here," said the driver. "They have a flashing strobe on the top. If we can get around the first inlet, I think we could follow those to the coast."

Fred consulted the map; Grégoire was right. The route would take them off the road, but even through the raging storm they ought to be able to pick up the lights. After that, well, they'd worry about it later. Ritchie used his handset to talk with the Go-Track in the rear, and the two-vehicle convoy turned blindly off the packed surface of the road. The searchlight bounced erratically, and the jarring progress overland registered in Fred's spine. The ride was so brutally rough that Fred wondered whether the shale would slice through their Kevlar-reinforced treads. Ah well, they'd find out soon enough.

———————

The damned old regimental sergeant major, rest his soul. Bursting through the doors on Friday night, all starch and polish, even after a week on exercise. A week humping across the bush, and his boots were clean; a man needs a shine on his boots and a razor across his face each morning. Not for the ladies, son, for the morale. The infantrymen of the Queen's Own Rifles, if common sense or a good Christian upbringing hadn't taught them, learned such lessons quickly enough under the all-seeing gaze of the regimental sergeant major.

Load the rucksacks and duffel bags into the station wagon,

rain or shine, summer or winter, day or night, didn't matter, then burn that highway from Calgary to Banff. Sometimes Fred wondered if the regimental sergeant major ever slept in a bed. What's this, a cold? Mountain air will clean those sinuses. Tummy trouble? All that city food. Raining? Won't have to rig up a camp shower, will we? Bugs? Let 'em bite.

Every weekend, year round. A man and his boy. A man and his little man. A sergeant major and his troop. Fred humped the rucksacks, climbed up the mountain trails, let the bugs bite and the shoulders burn until he hit the dizzying emancipation of the tree line, and all God's country spilled out before him like a drink of sweet alpine water. He loved the woods and the mountains despite the old man. And how many boys were lucky enough to spend every goddamn weekend in the mountains with their fathers?

And then he hit sixteen, and neither the law nor the regimental sergeant major could keep him in school. Fred became dust on the trail, kicking around here and there. As long as there is drunkenness and youth, there will always be tattoo parlours and recruitment centres, and Fred woke up one morning and found himself an able seaman in the Royal Canadian Navy.

The navy, for Christ's sake.

Fred went to sea on Her Majesty's Canadian Ship *Cape Scott,* but the regimental sergeant major caught up with him every mail call, letting him know it wasn't good enough to be mucking about on boats, he was bigger than that, he had infantry in his bloodline. The regimental sergeant major had such high ambition for the boy that Fred felt slothful and unimportant, even thought of lying for a while, maybe let the old man think he was doing something worthy, like naval battery.

But the regimental sergeant major would know, so Fred wrote back, summoning every ounce of respect he could into the title of naval storesman. It fell several grains short on the old man's balance. A storesman? A clerk? Had the regimental sergeant major raised him to be a pen-scratcher? Oh, the fatherly concern. Here, son. Here's some fingerless gloves, in case the stores are damp. Remember to bend your knees when you lift. And whatever you do, don't cut yourself on a quill....

"Light, Fred! Up there!"

Ritchie peered out, rubbing condensation off the window. It was pitch black and the shrieking wind was fierce, driving slivers of ice almost horizontally through the lights of the Go-Tracks. Faintly, through the storm, he could see the red glow of a flashing beacon.

"Bingo!"

Grégoire nodded, grinning, and pulled the right tiller bar; the Go-Track jerked around on its tread and headed off in the direction of the light. "She won't be far, not in this weather! Probably just a hundred yards, by the height of her."

"Then we're a hundred yards off course," said Fred. "And those towers aren't more than a few hundred yards from the sea ice."

"Yes, sir. Sorry, sir."

"Well, thank Christ you've got a sense of direction. I'd have put us in the ocean by now."

"Thanks, sir."

"Fred. The name is Fred."

Grégoire used the throttle pedal, and the Go-Track, following the series of lights, made its bone-jarring way down a gradual slope to the coastline. The jolting diminished as chunks of shale gave way to finer stones and powder near the shore.

They had reached Sickle Point, Fred reckoned, a spit of land jutting into the west side of Ravine Bay. The bay was shaped like a lagoon, with Sickle Point on the west side, extending across the mouth of the bay. It came within a mile of Mushroom Point, shaped as its name suggested, which lay to the east. These two points nearly close the mouth of the bay. Okay. From Mushroom

Point they'd follow the coastline east around the right shoulder of Ellesmere Island and down to the unmistakable gorge of the Sheridan River estuary. From there, they'd wing it.

In the blackness, the convoy traced the southern shore of the bay, relying on the smoother surface to tell them they were on course. From time to time, rocks jolted the vehicle and Grégoire nudged the tiller bar to the left, correcting their route. In this manner, navigating blindly, they rounded the inside of Mushroom Point and changed direction. The cap of the mushroom curves west, towards the mouth of the bay; they followed this course. Then the point turns sharply back on itself and veers right, to the east.

Fred kept waiting for Mushroom Point to show up. The Go-Track's heater sent a blast of warmed air over his feet. It had been more than twenty-four hours since he had last slept. His dreamy eyes drooped; perhaps he nodded off. When he next focused his gaze out the windscreen he thought: Good. There's Mushroom Point straight ahead.

There was a form rather like a mushroom, about the size of an iceberg, taking shape in the white-out ahead of them.

Just a minute! Mushroom Point looks like a mushroom when viewed on a map, not when viewed out the window. Ritchie's mind raced as the white object materialized in the gloom. That was a pressure ridge formed by the grinding collision of two sheets of pack ice. It was about a half-mile long and 200 feet high, and formed entirely of frozen water.

They must be headed vaguely in the direction of the North Pole, driving over the ice pack. Concerned with correcting their travel to the left, they must have shot off the end of Mushroom Point, unaware they were passing over the frozen surface of Ravine Bay. The convoy was unwittingly proceeding at top speed in a direction exactly opposite to the crash site, over the open waters of the Lincoln Sea.

167

"We're on the ice!" Fred shouted. "Get us out of here!"

Grégoire, veering right, swung the Go-Track around. Fred, reaching for the handset, noticed a dark patch looming large directly ahead of the vehicle. They weren't more than a few feet from it when Fred recognized the black streak.

"Open water! Turn left!"

Grégoire swung back, doing a 180-degree turn over the ice. "This way?"

"I don't know! Just go back! Back!"

Black clouds of diesel exhaust belched out the overhead stacks of the Go-Track. Grégoire pushed the clanking vehicle to top speed.

Steven Cann, driving the second vehicle, saw the lead truck kick up a bow wave, which rippled towards him on the salt ice. They were on a frozen trampoline. The ice was resilient enough to take their combined weight of eighteen tons. He cut throttle and pulled his Go-Track back and to the left, spreading their weight over the surface.

It was suddenly quiet in the land vehicle. Fred felt a pang of remorse. The SARtechs in the rear scraped the ice condensation from the windshields and pressed their faces against the glass, looking for signs of land or, worse, openings in the ice. Visibility was about twenty-five feet, which would not provide much warning either way.

Damn fool he was, with three sons of his own not yet raised. Poor Pam. What the hell was he trying to prove? At least it'll be quick, he thought. When the ice buckles, it'll be over in one cold, black explosion.

Pam was auburn-haired and lovely, a strong woman, but gentle with him, and it was a hot summer, and he was a father by age twenty. The regimental sergeant major conveyed his congratulations. Reference: Your decision to raise a family. You're all set now to raise children, aren't you, now that you have a naval career? Now that you have a future as a storesman.

Fred had been at sea the first years, then had taken a posting at Downsview; and the regimental sergeant major had conveyed his delight that his son had found a mariner's trade in the famous port city of Toronto.

And the night he'd lain in Pam's arms, and told her he was going to be a SARtech, and she didn't know the word. He explained: the mountain climbing, the parachuting, the outdoors. They pay you for it, Pammie.

And what else, Fred?

Well, with my education I'll never be a brain surgeon, you know that, I'll never be a doctor; but what they teach you, Pammie, it's pretty damn close. I'll be helping people. I never dreamed in my life I'd be able to help people like that.

And what else, Fred?

And I'm ashamed, Pam. I'm ashamed of my life.

Oh, how the regimental sergeant major had flung wide his arms to welcome the prodigal son! They were reconciled; well, he was reconciled to his son. All was forgiven, all the regimental sergeant major's work had paid dividends. See this young fellow? Mark that boy. He's a search and rescue technician. Know what that means? He's a para-rescue specialist. He saves lives. He'd crawl through fire to save your pretty bottom, my sweet. Know what else? He's my son.

And then the regimental sergeant major had passed away, proud of his son; and the son was proud of his father, and respectful of the memories. Those who knew him noticed how alternately impatient and respectful he was with the small people, and how insubordinate with the commissioned ranks. He was his father's son, all right, and a SARtech made.

"Lights, Fred! Ahead!"

Sure enough, the red strobes of the communication towers cut through the storm. The two Go-Tracks had hit the coastline south of Sickle Point, travelling in the opposite direction to what Fred had imagined. He radioed the Go-Track in the rear; they were down to half fuel. There was little choice but to follow the lights and make for the polar station.

Fred checked his watch. By the time they returned to base, they would have wasted more than seven hours. Good buddies out there, injured and freezing. Christ, was it only two weeks ago he and Couch had flown a rescue mission? Seven hours of stumbling around like blind mice. There had to be a better way.

Fred's watch was not the regulation army watch: SARtechs, when they graduate from training, are issued an expensive oyster-shell Rolex. Most wear it only to formal occasions at the mess. For fieldwork, the only thing it has going for it is water resistance. Most SARtechs find their own watches, compete with one another to score the Japanese gadget with the greatest number of bells and whistles. Fred had picked up an inexpensive Casio in a jewellery store in Edmonton. It was magic. It was shock-resistant and waterproof to several atmospheres. It had a tachymeter, lap timer, time zone function, and alarm. It also had a barometric altimeter. He could use it skydiving, scuba diving, or mountaineering; it was accurate to within fifty feet.

In the humid racket of the Go-Track, he consulted his topographic survey. The contour intervals on the map marked altitude in gradations of fifty feet. If he compared his watch's reading with the map, he could determine his location within two contour lines. At the least, he would know whether they were moving inland or over the ocean.

That gave him location, more or less. What about bearing? The Go-Track bumped and jerked over the rocky terrain. Fred peered out the steamy side window. The snow had been whipped into regular ridges by the wind, much as a desert storm ripples the sand. The ridges would be at right angles to the wind direction. By radioing the weather office at Alert, he could find out the bearing of the prevailing wind; the ridges would give him a rough idea of his relation to that course.

The Go-Tracks were within a half-mile of Alert but could not find the station. Keeping the tower lights to their rear, they edged around the coastline of Parr Inlet, the last landmark between themselves and the base. Then the terrain became flat, and they lost any guiding contours. More than once they crossed their old tracks at right angles.

Give it up, Fred. You think you're going to navigate ten nautical miles through white-out by reading a cheapjack Casio watch and the spoor of the wind? A dozen souls out there in the snow, and you're going to find them when you can't even find a polar station with a fully lit airfield a half-mile away? You're going to get these people killed, Fred.

"You're awful quiet," said Ron Burke, a ginger-haired SARtech from Cape Breton and one of Fred's closest friends.

"Frustrated."

"We gave 'er our best shot."

Fred nodded. They were following their own track now; there was a 50-per-cent chance it would take them towards the station, not away from it. Ron was a good man, smart-ass though he was. By Hercules, Fred. Definitely the way to get there.

Hercules! Christ, why hadn't he thought of it? He snatched the radio and hailed the rescue centre at the base.

"Don, can you get us a Herc?"

"What do you have in mind?" said Hanson.

"I think I've figured out a way to get there, if I can see where I'm going. Get me some top cover and get me some flares. I don't need illumination, I need a target. We can spot the flares and get a bearing."

"You got it. I'll coordinate with Rescue Three Zero Five and Three Four Two."

"If we can spot the flares, we'll get a bearing."

"Just like the three wise men, huh?"

"No," said Fred. "Just like one wise man."

In truth, the regimental sergeant major would never have got into a jam like this. But he'd bequeathed his son the savvy and grit to find a way out.

CHAPTER FIFTEEN

Legs

Bob thomson heard music. He heard singing, sweetly raised voices. He was in a beer garden. Elaine was with him. The sun was shining off her golden hair; she was tanned and smiling. They'd been on their bikes. Legs. She had on the blue spandex biking shorts he liked so much, and the pale blue halter top. Her skin glistened, and there was a sheen of sweat on her shoulders. It formed a little pool in the dimple of her collarbone. He wanted to press his mouth against its wetness. The sun was shining. They were in Germany.

"Bob."

No! Shut up!

He was in Germany, and he wanted to press his mouth against her wetness....

"Bob!"

Not this woman. He did not want this woman he could not see, could not touch, could not drink the wetness from.

"Uhn."

"Just grunt, Bob. Grunt so I know you're here."

Here. Why would he want to be here in the frigid dark? He was in the dark, an intruder, a spy, tucked away in the back tables of clubs like the Lion d'Or and the Top Hat in Montreal, watching his father play the lounge piano. His father's legs reached down to the pedals, but how they pitched the sound of the jazz he couldn't tell. He was tone deaf, he'd never follow in his father's footsteps – legs – but his dad had shown him how to keep time, with his feet.

He'd left college on account of his legs, on account of how they felt dancing over the ski slopes of the Laurentians. He'd humped groceries at Loblaws on the midnight-to-morning shift and skied all day. He and Bob Tait bought a ski cottage together. He liked the bachelor life, liked being a ski bum. And he'd worked his way up from stacking shelves to designing the displays, and the next thing he was renovating old stores, then opening new ones. The grocery business was changing fast, and Loblaws was blazing the trail. Bob was becoming a cog in the food distribution machine; he found himself working with a calculator, while his waist thickened and his legs atrophied. Then Tait had gone and joined the Forces and got posted to Lahr. He'd sent back post-cards: Zermatt, Grindelwald, Gstaad. Having a great time. Wish you were here. Bob was jealous as hell. He quit Loblaws and joined CANEX.

It took him four years, but he'd finally got the job running the CANEX in Lahr. And Elaine had gripped his arm as the airplane descended over the Alps, and told him he was wonderful, it would be the honeymoon they'd never had; and he thought, Eat your heart out, Bob Tait, I'm living my dreams. They'd taken their belated honeymoon that March, in Grindelwald on account of the skiing, on account of his legs. They had stayed at the Hotel Belvedere, and Elaine had stepped out on the balcony in the mornings with the sun streaming through her gown; and she was loveliness, and he had told her it was warm under the duvet: Come. And Andermatt on the St. Gotthard Pass, Christmas with the shutters open at night, the moon shining from the snow and through their open window. The blue nights, with the stars watching in delight. Legs.

The last summer they had bicycled through Provence. Legs. They drank wine and inhaled the heady air of the cheese shops, broke baguettes and uncorked bottles and spent long afternoons in the sun. The trysting-place by the river, where he had described the course of her cheek, her jaw, and her bare collar with a twig; she rose above him, and he embraced her.

Legs.

His left heel was pressed against his shoulder, just under the ear.

"Bob, can you talk?"

"Uhn?"

"I'm scared."

It was painful to talk; the effort brought a gripping pain to his lower back. He had to speak against the wind, nearly shouting so that Sue could hear him, although they were only a body length apart.

"What of?"

"They've gone. I can't hear them any more."

"Don't be stupid."

"I am not stupid."

It had only been …

Bob didn't know how long it had been. Half an hour? Maybe a few hours. Three or four hours, tops. Six? You're losing your mind, Thomson.

"They were just here."

"It was last night. Now they've gone, I can feel it."

Joe had stayed with him the first hours, maybe the first day. Then he had gone away and come back. Away and back. And again. Again. Again?

"They're gone. They've left us here."

"They're not gone."

"I read about it once, in the papers," Sue said, her swollen tongue and the freezing cold making it ludicrously difficult.

"They left a guy in Arizona. The Army had left this guy at an intersection and he was left there, and he died. It happens."

Bob remembered the story. It was the National Guard, not the Army; and it was in New Mexico. And the Gulf War, there were lots of stories of lost platoons in the Gulf War, weren't there? He could see how it happened. The arrival of the rescuers, everyone ecstatic, bundled up and away they went. Then, maybe tomorrow, they'd remember the two civilians....

"They've abandoned us. Oh my God I can't breathe. They've abandoned us, Bob, we're abandoned and we're going to die."

"It's okay to die."

"Okay, but I don't want to go out like some crazy woman, I'm suffocating in here, they've buried us alive and forgotten us, and now I'm going to die. I'd rather die than go crazy like this."

Bob listened to the wind, picked out the drone of a Hercules through the rasping howl. The others were being taken to Alert, he realized, given blankets and hot chocolate and warmth on the Hercules, which was, at that moment, flying over his shrouded face.

Get a grip on yourself, Thomson.

Sue was screaming. "The planes! That's them, that's them!"

This is the military, Thomson. They'd never do anything like that. Leave civilians in the snow to die.

"They've gone, I know it, we're going to die!"

"Oh, for Christ's sake! Will you just shut up?"

"Shut up, why shut up? They've gone, Bob, we're abandoned, we're going to die, we're buried alive. They won't find our bodies till spring, and my mother, it'll kill my mother when they find our bodies, and the animals will have eaten us because they've gone and abandoned – "

"Deal with it, all right?"

"Bob?"

"Look, lady, I've got enough on my plate without having to

deal with you. They're trying to get to us. We're either going to make it or we're not. Deal with it, all right? Just fucking deal with it and shut the fuck up!"

Bob's head swam with the exertion. Something was sending hot daggers into places he did not know pain could reach. Panting like an animal, he felt his head sink back deeper into the icy grip of the snow.

Cold is cruel; it only becomes kind at the edge of death. At first it is a great amplifier of pain. People with minor wounds become incapacitated when the pain is combined with cold; severe cold drops them in their tracks. Cold paralyzes its victims and then, like a venomous hunter, anaesthetizes them. In deep cold, the body pulls the heat away from the extremities and into the vital organs of heart, lungs, and brain. The exposed limbs succumb to cold.

Freezing is much like burning; the sensations are similar, but the effects on the body are different. Cold kills one cell at a time. The water inside the cell expands as it freezes, and bursts the cell walls; the flesh, the connective tissue, the nerve bundles, all explode at the freezing point under the bursting shells of cold. This is called frostbite: the Arctic kiss. With the death of the nerves comes the death of pain, the precursor of death itself.

Bob was not yet numbed by the cold. It consumed him, or rather pain consumed him, and the cold made him unaware of anything but his pain. He felt no remorse at his outburst; he had withdrawn into himself and his pain. Pain marked the boundaries of his consciousness and his desire. Pain was his morality and his will.

His breathing did not subside; he breathed hard, and his shoulders rose away from the ice and heaved into the pain. It was dripping wet inside his shroud; the condensation was building. He had a relationship, other than one of pain, with only one part of his body: his right hand. It rested near his right cheek, and he could move it about six inches in either direction. His breath had kept the fingers from freezing. They were wet. He was breathing fog. He was suffocating.

He inched the hand up to the edge of the tarpaulin and tugged it. Drafts of cold air swept over him, and he gulped. Soon he felt better; the air inside the tent was drier. He felt better for a time, and then he thought he heard the sound of scratching.

It was not the scratching of the wind over the dry crust of ice but a methodical, animated pawing. An animal was at work. Legs. He heard himself breathing, and then he heard a breathing that was not his own. He was alone and then he was no longer alone. There was a beast in the blackness.

He pulled the tarpaulin shroud closed, barely daring to breathe. Maybe it won't see me. Maybe it won't know we're here.

"Bob. Bob? Hear that?"

"Uhn?"

"There's an animal outside."

"Just the wind."

"No, it's an animal, a wolf or a bear or something. Oh my God, we're going to get eaten alive."

"Quiet."

He heard her whimpering, but she said no more. He listened to the pawing sound. The sound was working its way along the piled snow the length of Bob's body; it paused at his head.

Stay calm, Thomson. You've got the tarp over your face. Probably just an arctic fox ...

The animal had stopped moving. Bob could hear it breathe on the other side of the tarpaulin, inches from his face. It was panting lightly. He was panting.

If he comes through the tarp, Thomson, he's going to go for

your face. You'll feel his fangs slice into your face. You'll feel his saliva and the rasp of his tongue as he tears off your face. Can you live with that, Thomson? He moved his right hand, furtively, to the snow around his head. His fingers probed the snow, looking for some object. They fell upon a cold piece of metal. It felt like a sharp bar, about the size of a candy bar. One end was twisted and ragged.

Polar bears don't often come this far north. Hey, Thomson, it's probably an arctic hare! You're shit-scared over an arctic hare. A bunny rabbit.

The beast pawed at the tarpaulin over Bob's face, then began to scratch away at it. Bob felt a heavy paw against his face, and the dragging of claws against the heavy fabric.

A wolf! It's an arctic wolf and it's going for your face. Way to go, Thomson. Your back is broken, you're paralyzed and freezing to death, and a wolf is going to chew off your face.

He tightened his grip on the metal bar.

The paw pressed heavily against his face. The beast was now stepping over him, towards Sue. He heard her panicked whimpering, and the scratching noise of the wolf pawing at the snow.

Which was worse? To be eaten alive, or to listen, paralyzed, as she was being eaten alive? The question was beyond answering; beyond comprehension.

"Bob," she cried. "Oh …"

There was quiet.

"Sue!"

She was blubbering, her voice the voice of an anguished child, hurt beyond understanding, beyond hope, beyond caring, a voice naked and nearly drowned by tears.

"It's gone away. Ohhh."

"Uhn."

"Don't leave me, Bob. I need you. Talk to me. Just talk to me."

And so Bob told her about Elaine, and her beauty; and about

his work, and Germany, and his bike, and skiing, and what the Alps looked like in winter. And he told Sue that she was the most irritating woman he had ever met, and that she had kept him going back then, when he was about to pack it in. And he told her that he needed her, too. And when she had stopped crying they both fell silent, and contemplated the darkness, and listened for sounds in the storm. They no longer clung to concepts of time, or of distance, or even of rescue. The time was night. Their place was an ice coffin. The end would arrive through death or deliverance.

Bob no longer thought of his home, or the south, or the shoulders of Elaine. His mind simply kept track of his own body, in the most simple terms. You're still awake, Thomson. You're not asleep. You can breathe. The hand works. You're still awake, Thomson.

If it were to be death, so be it. He would go if it came time to go. But he would not let it happen by itself. He knew he could turn off a switch at any time – that's how he thought of it, a simple switch – and he would go. But he wouldn't do that, because there didn't seem to be any point. He would watch instead, wait and see which form his salvation would take.

"Bob?"

"What?"

"I hear wolves. I hear them baying."

CHAPTER SIXTEEN

SAR*birds*

THE SMOKING SHED by Five Hangar at the Edmonton base resembles the interrogation rooms of Eastern Europe. A naked light bulb swings overhead. There are metal folding chairs, an ashcan, and a rotating fan. To Major Don Blair, the setting was appropriate; he felt as though he'd been worked over for days. He took a long drag on his Player's, burning it down to his knuckles. Then he lit another.

Blair held a sheaf of teletype and telephone messages that charted the emotional upheavals of the past twenty-four hours. Yes, it had been a shock in the beginning, but at least there had been a sense of purpose and a feeling of progress. Then the rescue centre had learned of souls still alive, and there had been a quiet euphoria, even a light-headedness. Then the souls began to suffer in the storm, and the rescue centre suffered with them. Now all of Blair's efforts had turned to sand in his fingers. He felt like crying as he leafed through the papers:

Crash plus thirteen hours: Discovery. "Command Post Alert advises Rescue 342 has made contact with crash site on 282.8 UHF via a series of clicks, indicating at least 10 survivors."

Crash plus thirteen thirty: Astonishment. "Command Post Alert advises Resc 342 reports at least 14 survivors."

Crash plus fifteen thirty: Anxiety. "Command Post Alert

181

advises Resc 342 re-established voice contact with survivors who advised there are multiple injuries and frostbite setting in."

Crash plus seventeen hours: Dread. "Command Post Alert updates that as of 311140Z survivors have taken refuge in fuselage and some are in critical condition."

And there were all the rebuffed advances:

"Thule Bell 212 returned to Thule due bad weather."

"Ground search party stranded between Mann Bay and Cape Sheridan due whiteout conditions."

"Helo resources Elmendorf AFB may take 2 days arrive at scene."

"Twin Otter diverted to Eureka due weather."

"Rescue 301 CH113 Labrador origin Gander forced landing position 5655N 6635W stranded due bad weather."

"Rescue 452 CC115 Buffalo returning to Kuujjuaq unserviceable and non-repairable."

"Second attempt ground search party with 435 Sqn SARtechs returned to station due whiteout conditions."

Such a promising start. At first the wall chart of the rescue centre had barely been able to hold all the air resources tasked to the rescue. The wall map had been marked with black lines, all inching their way up the board. Then the air resources had been crossed out with blue lines, striking out aircraft that had been stood down. Damn weather. The weather seemed to have taken a personal and vindictive interest in the rescue.

By the latest weather report, the ceiling at Alert was 700 feet, or some 300 feet lower than the crash site. The survivors were socked in, and SARtechs needed a 2,000-foot ceiling above ground for a night parachute jump. The winds were twenty-five to thirty-five knots, above operational limits for takeoff and landing, let alone for the SARtechs. In blowing snow, they couldn't jump in wind speeds of more than ten knots.

The temperature was steady at -22 Celsius. As a rule of thumb,

Blair knew, wind chill temperature is calculated by doubling the temperature and adding the wind. Must be down around -70 degrees. At that temperature, which meteorologists classify as "extremely cold," skin freezes within thirty seconds of exposure to the air. Heat is drawn from the body at an alarming rate; an exposed person moves rapidly from shivering to stupor to death. The survivors had been out there twenty-four hours. They certainly wouldn't last another day. They wouldn't last many more hours.

Blair had arranged for a field surgery to be established at Alert. He made a note to arrange for a coroner and a morgue as well. Hope for the best, plan for the worst.

His nicotine addiction satisfied for the moment, Blair returned to the base rescue centre. There was a small crowd of people outside the door; they all turned to him. Many were the duty officers assigned to assist the families of crash victims; some were family members themselves. He knew the names of some of the wives. People crowded around as he reached the locked door to the rescue centre. He mumbled an apology and gently shouldered his way through. Sorry. Nothing new to report. We're trying our best. Excuse me.

He used his pass key to enter the room. After the hubbub outside, the rescue centre was oddly silent. Half-empty cups of coffee had been left here and there. People tapped pencils on desktops, rubbed their tired faces. It was a dispirited place. The sense of impotence and frustration had banished all optimism from the room.

The base commander, Colonel Mike Wansink, was standing at the wall charts.

"What did I forget?" Blair asked. "What can we do that we haven't done?"

"Nothing more to be done," said Wansink. "Except pray for a break in the weather."

When a technician brought over the latest bulletin, Blair imagined more bad news. Another plane grounded? But no: on the wall chart the technician extended one of the black lines a few inches farther up the map. This line, unlike all the others, was continuing to move north. The technician placed a stick pin at the top of the line, with a paper flag on the pin. The flag read: "Resc 315."

––––––––––

At Kuujjuaq, on Quebec's northern coastline, the yellow tail of Rescue 315 rose off the flight deck. After a quick hot refuelling of the aircraft and a radio call to the Edmonton rescue centre, Captain Mark Levesque was back at the controls with instructions to proceed in his Labrador helicopter to the fuel dump at Iqaluit, 400 miles further north. The flight would take him over the icy waters of Ungava Bay, to the high black cliffs of the Meta Incognita Peninsula on the southeast shore of Baffin Island, over the peninsula to Frobisher Bay, then up the channel to Iqaluit.

Levesque was taking off without top cover. The Buffalo aircraft that had flown top cover on his first leg had broken down, and a Hercules had been diverted to deadhead the spare crew for the Labrador up the line; Iqaluit was the last airfield on his flight path before Alert. Levesque cursed every extra minute on the ground, knowing it would store up against his fatigue in flight. But the down time had paid off: he'd managed to contact one of the Aurora surveillance aircraft from Greenwood. The Aurora crew had agreed to intersect the Labrador's flight path. Levesque would begin to get navigational assistance from the Aurora somewhere en route; he risked flying blind until then.

Levesque had filed a routine flight plan, but that was a mere formality. There would be no need to mount a rescue effort if they made a forced landing over Ungava Bay. The Labrador's inability to maintain flight on a single engine poses an unacceptable risk, but it's a risk that has become commonplace. Levesque took the helicopter to 500 feet and set off northward. The northern shore of the continental land mass fell away beneath him.

The nose of the Labrador had barely touched the humid air over Ungava Bay when ice began to form on the windscreen and a SARtech in the rear called, "Ice on the sponsons!" Ice on the sponsons meant there was also ice on the engine vents. Levesque felt as though the elements were maliciously seeking him out, as though something was determined to coat his aircraft in ice and bring down all hands.

His instinct was to climb again, but he recalled his experience of maritime flight when he'd been posted with the rescue unit in Gander. The pilots there often spoke of a thermal layer just at the ocean's surface. You had to dig down to find it, but it made sense. It all depended on the temperature of the bay; salt water turns to ice a few degrees below the freezing point. There was no guarantee, but he decided it was the better risk.

Levesque and his crew had enough light to see the surface of the water, but it is difficult to estimate height over water, so he kept his eyes on the dials. He decided to lose altitude, all the way down to surface level if necessary. If the thermal layer did not exist, he'd at least be in a better position to ditch.

At eighty feet, the ice was still gaining mass and the temperature was unchanged. No change at seventy feet, or sixty. The Labrador was down to fifty feet – the length of one rotor blade – before it found the thermal layer. The outside temperature abruptly rose four degrees, and the dimpled ice on the windscreen began to melt away. He checked with his flight engineer: the engines were breathing easily. So was Levesque.

He continued the dash northward, skipping above the surface of Ungava Bay and entering the Hudson Strait. When he crossed the 60th parallel the light began to fail; the aircraft was soon flying in utter darkness. It would not see daylight again. The magnetic deviation increased; so did the distance from navigational aids. This went unnoticed by the flight crew until they turned to their instruments when approaching the cliffs of Baffin Island in the falling dark.

To clear the cliffs Levesque began a climb to 6,000 feet. Even his instruments seemed to confirm the conspiracy against him. The Omega navigational system senses radio signals sent skyward from ground stations at fixed locations around the world and uses them to triangulate a position. The Omega told Levesque that Iqaluit was 90 degrees to his right. The automatic direction finder, which was homing in on the Iqaluit radar beacon, pointed in the opposite direction, 90 degrees to his left. Levesque's own gut feeling told him to plow straight ahead.

The navigational aids were worthless. The Labrador could have avoided the confusion by setting its compass to work from the directional gyroscope. But there was a ban on using the gyro in northern latitudes, because it was known to be unreliable.

As it turned out, the gyro in the Labrador had been installed with its polarity reversed. Had Levesque reached behind the unit and switched the polarity, the machine would have behaved as if it were flying towards the South Pole and given a reliable bearing. No one thought of such a solution; it was too simple.

Because they were flying through darkness without navigational aids, the crew members were unaware that they were being pushed by winds of seventy-five knots on their left beam. Their forward air speed was registering at ninety knots, but their progress had been reduced to a crawl. They were flying crab-like to the right – past the eastern tip of Baffin Island and out over the Labrador Sea. There was no landfall ahead of them until Greenland, which was well beyond the helicopter's endurance.

Levesque flew on in darkness, using his own sense of direction rather than the instruments. When he peered out the windscreen, he saw only the reflection of his own instrument panel. When he looked at the panel, the only instrument of any use was the altimeter. His internal compass had given him the most accurate reading of any instrument on board; the nose of the Labrador was on target. But the wind-blown aircraft was drifting 45 degrees off course.

Levesque was intent on this course, waiting to catch sight of cliffs that would never appear, when a voice came over his headset.

"Rescue Three One Five, this is your Aurora top cover. Just where the hell you going, buddy?"

"Aurora, we have no navaids and I'm not picking up Frobisher. Can you give us some steers out of here?"

"Will cooperate. Stand by."

The radar operators used the Aurora's sensors to paint an image of the Labrador over terrain, then used this image to calculate a bearing.

"Rescue Three One Five, set course two niner true."

"Aurora, you don't understand. Don't give me magnetic steering, because my compass is spinning around. Don't give me a course, because I have no gyro. Give me a steer."

"Okay. Turn left about forty-five degrees."

Forty-five degrees? Was it possible they were so far off course? Levesque drew a slow breath at the near miss; without the Aurora, they would have died in the frigid waters below.

At least now we've got top cover, he thought. Now we've got it licked. In the midst of his exhilaration, the windscreen began to whiten with wet, sticking snow. The new course was taking them back into a snow shower. Back into the ice. Suckered again.

By now the strain of flying in a continual hands-on posture for more than three hours was showing. Levesque's shoulders were in knots, his neck was stiff, his hands were aching. He had to think through the fatigue. The snow was glazing into ice on the windscreen. He couldn't descend, not with the cliffs hovering in

187

the distance. He would have to climb again, and hope …

He could use the Aurora!

"Aurora, we're picking up ice at six thousand. Think you can do some pathfinding for us? Find us some dry air?"

The Aurora climbed and dove ahead of the Labrador, its sensors sampling the air: "Three One Five, you'll find it nice and cosy at nine thousand."

Levesque climbed. He knew he was reaching altitude by the dials and by the growing sloppiness of the aircraft. In the soggy handling at 9,000 feet, and crosswinds that nearly matched the aircraft's forward airspeed, the Labrador was swimming around the air current like a speeding car on ice. Levesque fought the fog in his mind as he struggled to stay cognizant. He was stretching his body's limits, and he knew it.

We'll change crew in Iqaluit. Just have to make Iqaluit. Soon we'll lock onto the beacon. I'll follow the wire, put her down, get some rest. What happens when you crack? Does the body go first, or the mind?

Levesque was flying visually in pitch blackness; there may as well have been a black hood over the cockpit. The aircraft was on instrument flight, and he was the instrument. Like the compass needle, he was starting to spin. His balance and sense of direction were holding the Labrador on course, and he was losing both. He felt vertigo; waves of exhaustion rippled through him, cramps developed in his back, and the stiffness in his hands became almost paralytic. He was losing control.

And he'd long ago passed bingo fuel, the point of no return, the minimum amount of fuel needed to reach an alternate airfield. They would reach Iqaluit or they'd ditch.

Levesque was jerked back to alertness by a glowing yellow light on the instrument panel. "Warning: Fuel low." He had less than thirty minutes remaining. His forward speed had been cut in half. There was 9,000 feet of snowstorm between the helicopter and the ground. He doubted they could cover the distance before the last drop of fuel was drained from the sponsons. He doubted they could find Iqaluit, even if they got there. He had a sense of winding down; soon he'd be released.

It was clear to every member of the flight crew what would happen. The sponsons would be drained, and the engines would cough, shudder, and fail. Levesque would attempt to maintain control, and the Labrador would auto-rotate through the cloud. Then they would pick up ice, and the ice would cost the auto-rotational control. The Labrador would pitch, and tumble, and turn. It would take a long while to hit the water from 9,000 feet. They would have about ten minutes to make their peace.

He'd tried. They'd all tried.

"Rescue Three One Five, this is your top cover. We're low on fuel and making our final approach into Iqaluit. See you on the ground, good buddy."

"Aurora, I'm requesting you cancel final approach. Overshoot. I am declaring a mayday. Low fuel lights are lit and we can't acquire the Iqaluit beacon. I'm going to need you in the air."

"We'll overshoot, Three One Five. But we're past bingo fuel ourselves. What do you need?"

"I want you to make a max effort climb to level nine thousand and circle the townsite. Turn on all your lights. What I need is a lighthouse."

"See you upstairs."

Levesque dimmed his cockpit lights, cutting his own reflection in the glass. He waited a few minutes, burning precious fuel.

Finally the Aurora came up on his headset. "We're on our way, buddy. We've acquired you on radar. You were off course. There's some nice big hills dead ahead of you. Turn left ninety degrees and you'll see us."

Levesque turned and saw the blinking lights of the Aurora burst out of the cloud cover. The aircraft wheeled to the left and began to circle. He had a beacon. No mariner was ever more pleased to see the lights of port.

"Acquired you visually. Looks real good."

Levesque pointed the nose of the Labrador in the direction of his lighthouse, estimating his distance at about twelve miles. It would be close. The Labrador passed over the peninsula and through the humid air over Frobisher Bay, and began to pick up ice again. To hell with it.

"Aurora, can you see Frobisher from your position?"

"Roger, Three One Five. Can see the lights from here. They're right below us."

It was deathly quiet in the cockpit. All ears were tuned to the whine of the turbines; everyone was waiting for the sudden cough, the death-rattle, the silence, the whistling air, then the dead beating of the rotors during the slow tumble to the ground.

Levesque reached the circling Aurora. Peering directly down through the glass chin bubble of the Labrador, he saw nothing but nimbus. Then, a wink. He saw lights. The lights flickered off and on, as the broken clouds passed over them. Levesque was reminded of the opening scenes of clouds passing over the lights of London in a Disney film.

"I've got Iqaluit. Thanks, Aurora."

The Aurora banked away, peeling off towards its approach pattern. It too was dangerously low on fuel.

Levesque did not want to lose sight of the airfield, not for a moment. He plummeted the nose of the Labrador through a spiralling dive towards the airfield lights. This was it: one kick at the cat. He struggled to keep the spinning aircraft level, so the pumps could drain the last drops of fuel from the sponsons. Dimples appeared on the windscreen, as ice formed on the plunging nose.

The Labrador broke the cloud a few hundred feet above the airfield; Levesque took his bearings and managed to put the helicopter down next to the fuel dump.

The engineer unbuckled his harness and scrambled out the door; he would have to hot refuel immediately, before the sponsons went dry. If that happened and the engines starved, they might never start again.

When the refuelling was completed, and Levesque had got over the willies enough to feel sure on his feet, he got out to check the fuel load. They'd been down to 100 pounds a side. Maybe five minutes.

"I'm going in the hangar to meet the Aurora crew," he told the engineer. "I'd like to talk to them."

They had lots to talk about. Levesque wanted to say thanks, and he wanted to discuss the next leg of the voyage. There were no more airfields between here and Alert, it was pitch dark, and they would have to grope their way around Baffin Island. The journey so far had been unlike anything Levesque had ever experienced. The next leg might well be tougher still.

After Marv Macauley and his crew from Greenwood had landed at the Thule air base, they'd phoned Alert for instructions and been told to get some rest. They had bedded down in the North Star Hotel, the base transient quarters. Marv, still in his flight suit, hunkered down like the bear he resembled. His mind was clear and untroubled. Someone else would surely reach the survivors in hours. By the time he awoke, the rescue would be over. Might as well grab some shut-eye before firing up the SARbird for the flight back to Greenwood and home.

He slept four hours, awoke refreshed, and switched on the television set. The Americans, of course, had CNN; the Canadians at Alert watched canned tape. CNN had a live news flash: a military transport had gone down near the North Pole. A massive rescue effort had been mounted but was facing incredible odds.

Reporters. Talk about old news. Operation Arctic Storm was history. Marv picked up the phone and called the Alert command post.

"Hey, I was just going to phone you," said the duty officer, an old friend of Marv's. "The ground party got turned back, the weather's a bitch. But Hanson's cooked up some scheme for you guys to fly top cover."

"When?"

"Now. You guys are back in the breach."

Marv ran down the corridor of the transient quarters, banging on the doors of his crew.

"Rise and shine! Showtime!"

At the Thule operations centre, Marv's flight crew laid out air navigation charts and planned their course and minimum altitudes. The navigator was a sharp-eyed youth from Longueuil named Marc Favre, and Marv liked him. The kid was quick on the uptake. He'd already photocopied a map of northern Ellesmere Island in a 1:50,000 scale. The map was itself a photocopy; the image was faint. But it was five times more precise than the charts on board the Hercules, and Favre thought it might just come in handy.

When Marv and the crew bundled out to the Hercules, Arnie and his SARtechs were already on board, waiting.

Marv's co-pilot, the cool-headed Randy Price, got the latest conditions. Not good; in fact, aircraft had been grounded at Thule. The winds were at right angles to the runway, thirty-five knots gusting to forty. The turbulence warning on the navigation charts was in full effect. Severe turbulence was reported off the departure end of the runway.

Price looked at Marv. Marv knew the disdain with which Price viewed the basket-weavers who flew SAR straight and level. Price had no problem with the wild weather. He'd go at the drop of a hat.

Arnie would, too. But Arnie was sitting in the back. He didn't have responsibility for eighteen souls and a $21-million piece of military hardware. Marv did, and he felt the full weight of responsibility of the aircraft commander.

Ordinarily, Marv would blow his top and curse the goddamn weather and storm out of the cockpit and raise hell in the operations room and get Alert on the line and raise hell there, too. He'd rack up one more screw-up.

Arnie'd simply fly the airplane out of there.

Marv was the one who blew his top, the one with the temper. Arnie was the quiet type, but the passionate one. He came through, while Marv reasoned himself into a corner. Goddamn big brother.

The wind was howling across the runway; snow was drifting over the white pavement and piling up against the runway lights. The book said the plane should be grounded. But there were fourteen souls stranded out there. Marv thought of his good buddies entombed by that snow and bitten by that wind. Was passion so out of place? What is rescue but an act of love?

"So what are we going to do?" he said to Price. "Sit here all day?"

They were busting the limits; the takeoff was going to be dicey. Marv reckoned they were about five knots over maximum crosswind speed, but he didn't look it up. He could have; there was a book on board, the aircraft operating instructions, with a table giving crosswind maximums. If he'd opened it to that page, he would have found that under those runway conditions and his payload, the maximum allowable crosswind speed was twenty-six knots. Not thirty-five, gusting to forty. He was fourteen knots over the limit, and Thule is a slippery strip to begin with.

Marv had briefed for a crosswind departure. Price would fly the wings while Marv handled the engine controls, nose wheel, and rudder. Between them, they would keep the aircraft level through their rising speed as the crosswind sought to push them aside. The four engines came up and the Hercules – eighty tons of metal, thirty tons of aviation fuel, and 3,300 pounds of incendiary magnesium flares – began its hurtling course down the runway.

The takeoff roll would be about 4,000 feet, less than half the Thule runway. The wind was striking them from the left. Marv gave hard right rudder and edged the nose wheel into the wind. He selected full power. Price held down the left wing by turning the control yoke towards the wind; the wing lifted, resisting him. Steadily, he pressed the wheel to the left. It reached the end of its travel; the aircraft had full left aileron and full right rudder. At about seventy knots – decision speed – Marv dropped the nose-wheel steering and grabbed the yoke.

"My wheel," he said.

"Your wheel," Price confirmed.

Marv now had hands-and-feet control of the Hercules. The aircraft was turned full crank into the crosswind, but it wasn't enough. The wind blew the high tail of the Hercules and pushed it like a weathervane. The aircraft began drifting perilously to the right. They were past the point of no return, and the rudder and wings didn't have enough authority against the wind.

Arnie, in the cargo bay, felt the aircraft drift and grabbed an intercom headset. He wanted to hear what was going on in the cockpit. He wanted to hear the big, booming, reassuring voice of his little brother, laughing at some minor slip-up.

He heard Marv say: "Fuck."

They couldn't abort now, not without causing a world of hurt. They had one chance: shut down power on one outboard engine. Marv hoped there was enough runway remaining for a three-engine departure. He hoped the differential power would steer the Herc into the wind. He pulled the throttle lever back.

The engineer saw the falling gauge: "Low torque on number one!"

"Number one's down," Price said. "Abort?"

"I'm doing it!" Marv shouted. "I'm doing it!"

The Hercules strained towards rotation speed on its remaining three engines, but the gambit had worked. The Herc followed the centre line of the runway as Marv counted off the yards, feeling the nose cone lighten its weight on the runway as the Hercules prepared to become a creature of the air.

Then they hit a snowdrift. The cockpit banged loudly, the cargo bay shuddered. The Herc was not under control; it was in transition between ground and sky, and if it chose sky, the collision with the drift wouldn't matter. If it chose ground ... well, that would be another story.

The nose lifted; the landing gear left the ground. Marv restored full power and the Hercules climbed steeply to clear high terrain on the departure end of the runway. Then, at 600 feet, they hit severe turbulence. The Herc dropped 100 feet through an air pocket, slamming as it regained its traction against the wind. Finally, they were away.

In the cargo bay, Arnie turned to his SARtechs, most of whom were green-faced and white-knuckled: "That's my little brother."

CHAPTER SEVENTEEN

Misery

THE SINGING had long since ended. It had ended and been forgotten like the vapours of a dream, like the dreams of warmth, of family, of love, all forgotten now. None of the survivors any longer remembered reasons for living; they were living without reason, without memory. They were nearing death; they were living.

They did not lie there, coated in ice, and warm themselves with the memory of a child, of a curving waist, of parents. This would have been too painful to bear. While the cold exploded the cells of their hands and feet, they mourned the loss of trivial things. One of them realized, as the pain became a pleasant numbness, that he would miss his morning jog. That is what lost legs would mean; missing the fresh stillness of morning, his warmed body moving through the dawn. Another would miss woodworking with his hands, creating things simple but durable: a lawn chair, a table, a child's swing.

They had spoken among themselves earlier, of other things. Through lips numb and increasingly useless they had shared their lives and remembered the things worth living. They had named their children, their jobs, their towns. Then they had stopped speaking of such things, by silent accord, just as they had stopped singing.

The inner walls of the tail were encrusted in ice; ice crystals spun about them as the wind howlingly probed the tail. Ice crystals came to rest on their clothing. They were becoming ice. Their diminishing heat melted the ice and turned it to water to mix with the diesel fuel on their clothing, and then their skin had become cold. Cold as ice; dead, pale, hard flesh, exploded cells and frozen fluids. The slurry on their clothing had also turned to hard ice.

The metal grate burned them. Comfort was nothing more than the vapour of a dream; but they attempted to relieve the pain anyway. They would lie still, until the cold metal burned into a shoulder, a hip, or a knee, and the wounded cried out in pain. They would all have to move at once; it was too crowded for only the one suffering the most to move. They shared their suffering, in a real sense; it was painful to turn over. It took a long time – about twenty minutes. Their clothes had frozen to the metal grate, and it took all their strength to break their clothing free; they jostled one another as they did so. An icy elbow would dig into the burnt flesh of a face; a hand would press against a broken hip, grinding the bones; a leg would become tangled in the nylon rope, twisting the fractured bones. Each move was a chorus of groans, apologies, curses, screams.

Monty, whose mind was never clear – he could tell you his name and unit with perfect clarity one moment, and believe the plane was landing the next – had decided to go home. "I'm tired of waiting," he said. He'd got out of his sleeping bag. His hands had frozen into mallets and he could not pull off the bag; he pushed and pounded at it, twisting and thrusting his body. This caused hurt all down the line. Somehow he got out of the bag and stood on his frozen feet. "I'm going to walk to Alert."

"Don't be stupid, you'll never make it. You'll be dead inside twenty minutes."

"All right," he said. "I'll walk to Edmonton."

They had struggled with him, grabbed his coat and held him.

197

He got back into the sleeping bag, and the others made him lie crosswise behind them, so he would have to step over their bodies if he decided to wander off again. They had no strength to hold him, but used their own broken bodies as a protective barrier.

"Home," he said, then slipped under.

———————

Something had beeped once, back when they had still thought of rescue. An electronic beep was a familiar sound, as a whistling kettle once was; it was the sound of answering machines and alarm clocks and microwave units heating coffee. It arrested them, because it took them back to the world.

But it was only Mario's watch; the beep was his wake-up call to catch the flight. It told them that twenty-four hours had passed since they'd started this journey. They had resented it quite a bit. But that had been a long while before.

The wind rushed against the tail, a demonic roaring of wind that never gathered enough voice for a howl. It hissed, as particles of ice scratched against the metal shelter.

Wilma tried not to listen, even though the wind filled her brain and made her angry, weak, insane. Paul had told her she would be able to hear the parachutes of the sartechs; they will flutter and pop, he said, and we will know of our deliverance.

I'll hear nothing, Wilma thought. I'll hear nothing but the wind.

She had no idea how long they had been like this. She thought Mario's beeping watch, her last bearing in time, had been twelve or perhaps twenty hours ago. She knew they were into their second day on the ground. The second day – she'd forgotten. Time for the last of the candy.

My hands, where are my hands? Oh, in the sleeve. I put them in my sleeve. There they are. Imagine, Wilma, losing your hands like that. The candies are on your chest, nestled on your breast, for warmth. There. They are cold. Your skin is cold.

Why do they put them in these plastic wrappers? It's hard to get the wrappers off. Don't drop them, Wilma. Use your teeth. You are shaking. Shaking is good. Stop shaking and you die.

Maybe if I eat a candy I will warm up. Maybe my foot will thaw. Then it will hurt again. Should I eat a candy? There, it's done. The wrapper is off. There's a body. There's its head. Its face is cold. Find the lips. Push the candy through the lips.

"Thuck. Don't shew." Dear God, now even her mouth was ceasing to function properly.

Another body, another face, another open mouth. So many mouths. Like little birds, like Communion. Have you been good little birds?

One more. I can do three at a time. I counted; so now I know. That's something. Three at a time. Three is a holy number; which one? After three days, he rolled aside the rock. He must have been cold, dead for three days. Three, and then my hands don't work. I can't find them. When I do find them I can't move them.

"Open." Push the candy through. Oh, I hurt this one. This one has the broken jaw.

"Can't thuck."

"Tongue," Wilma said. "Melt."

Next is Paul. No candy, Paul. Have to wait until Wilma gets her hands again. She pushed against Paul's back. He had been very wet, from the exertion, and now he was ice. His back was cold and solid. He felt like the woods in winter; hard, frosted.

Poor Paul. Because he was the engineer, everyone expected him to make things work. Paul had fired the flares. Paul had worked the radios. Then they had found the fuel stove and brought it to him. They had plenty of fuel, diesel fuel, and the primus stove could be switched over to burn diesel. But Paul's hands were too cold to work the valve; he needed a small wrench, or some kind of tool. They remembered the knife, the one that had fallen through Rick's pocket.

Such a tiny mistake.

John and Joe must be freezing out there. No hats. They shouldn't go outside without a hat, not in this weather. At least Joe has plenty of hair. John is bald. You lose most of your heat through your head. What was it, 60 per cent? That's a number. That's something.

What do I think they should do, take Bob's hat? They are being logical. They gave out the clothes when they were warm and didn't need them. Now they are cold and need them more than we do, but if we give them our hats then we'll be the ones who need them. When there is one less of us, there will be one more hat for the others.

The others. Sue and Bob. I must remember. Sue. Fractures: both lower legs, ribs, right shoulder, elbow, maybe neck. Internal bleeding. Legs lacerated and burned. Bob. Horribly broken back. Right leg fractured in two places.

Remember. I must remember. For the rescuers.

———————

Every now and then there was an outburst. Someone would lose heart. Bill, blinded, would tuck Monty's hands away. A few minutes later he would hear the hands beating against the icy metal of the tail, an odd pinging thump. Bill would tuck them away again. Shuffle, thump, tuck. Shuffle, ping, tuck.

"When those mastards get here I'm going to give them a piece of my mind. Where are they? What's taking so long? They'll hear from me, those mastards."

"That's the spirit. That's what I like to hear."

The others let the tired heart speak. No one interrupted. Someone would confirm what had been said, for the benefit of the others. Then no more was said.

There was movement at the mouth of the tail. A dark figure. Wilma started. I didn't hear them. I didn't hear their parachutes, because of the crazy wind; but I knew they would come. Remember to tell them about Sue and Bob.

It was only Joe. His cotton flight suit was frosted over with ice, but his body heat had melted through the vital places. His back, his underarms, and his groin were wet. There is no more efficient way to drain off heat than through cold water. Walking through the storm was like placing a candle in the wind. Outside, in the raging howl, it was -66 Celsius, -92 Fahrenheit. The cold was almost inconceivable.

Joe had been shivering for as long as he could remember. He couldn't make the shivering stop, even when the muscles of his back and legs had cramped solid. He had thought the cramp would at least stop the shivering. He found that cramped muscles also shiver. He found a whole new level of pain.

Joe crawled into his place, directly behind Richard Dumoulin. Richard felt the man press against him, shivering.

"How are they?"

"Alive."

Richard thought he was as cold as he could get, but Joe's body pressing against his back made him feel even colder. Then he felt Joe pounding against his back. Joe was hitting him, hard.

"What are you doing?"

"Knock the ice off."

Dumoulin allowed him to pound, felt Joe tugging at the shards of ice as they broke apart but clung to the fibres of his parka. Joe's tugging, like every movement, caused pain down the line. Mario's hips ground sickeningly as the bones shifted. He twitched involuntarily, and his foot slipped through the grate. His leg was trapped.

Mario cried. He was huddled under the tarpaulin and sounded

201

far away. He was crying, and he apologized: "It's just me talking."

They took pity on Mario and somehow managed to move him away from their company. Some of the men pulled their own clothes free of the ice and dragged the whimpering Mario down by their feet. They placed him there, in his sleeping bag, so their exertions would not hurt him. When John came in, he could lie with him. John was in and out all the time, and now he could huddle with Mario and now –

Someone was hammering on the tail! It sounded like a penny hammer being struck against the frigid metal, or like blocks of wood being struck against each other. Clang. Clang. Clang. It was a hammer. Wilma's heart filled with joy. It was them! *I didn't hear them, because of the crazy wind. But I knew they would come.*

"You're here!" Wilma called. "Who is it?"

"Me," said Monty. "Straightening out my hands."

His frozen hands struck the metal of the tail. Clang. Ping. Clang.

Wilma imagined the flesh being chipped away like marble on the hard metal. "Monty," she called. "If you do that any more, I'll kill you."

"Okay, Doc. No more."

Clang! Clang! Clang!

"Somebody stop him!"

Richard Dumoulin somehow managed to drag himself backwards until his face struck a frozen boot. He crawled over Monty and found the poor man's hands. He held the shattered hands in his own, pressing them against his own broken face. He held them until, mercifully, Monty went under again.

———

Mario cracked.

"I can't take it any more! Get a gun. Bust have a gun here. Get a gun and shoot me. Okay, then. Get a gun, I'll shoot byself!"

The others listened to his sobs. Mario, with such a beautiful family. It wasn't something extra to live for, now, just something to think about. His beautiful family were vapours. He felt all the more desolate without them.

"Get a stick! Somebody get a stick. Get a stick and hit be with it. Hit be in the head until I'm dead."

Wilma said to Marc, "Maybe you should talk to him in French."

"I don't want goddamn French. I want a stick! I don't want it to hurt any more. Blease I need a stick, blease!"

Is this how it will go? Is this what we will become, one by one?

Who is that now? John. Stumbling in. He is walking like a zombie, a drunk. He should have a hat.

"Alive," he said.

"Good."

No one spoke. A few minutes passed. John lay down beside Mario – it seemed to take forever – and then spoke again.

"Isn't going to work. They're not coming. Aren't going to make it. Never going to come."

He was in the garden of Gethsemane, Wilma realized. He was on the cross of doubt, asking after his father.

"They won't come now."

The others did not know what to say. John had never before had a moment of doubt.

Paul said: "Caw row."

Did I forget to call the roll? I'm forgetting so many things; the roll, the names, my hands. Let's see, then. The reds.

"Mario." Mario has a fractured hip. Mario hurts. He cries a lot. He sounds far away. He wants to die.

"Here."

"Dave." Dave is burned. He has a bruised spine, like mine but lower down. His kneecaps are broken, and his left arm.

"Yuh."

"Bill." Third-degree burns on his face and chest, burns on his thighs and groin. I rolled Bill in the snow. Bill rested his head in my lap. I never looked at his eyes.

"Here."

"Monty." Monty has a low level of consciousness. Monty isn't speaking to me.

"Bill, is Monty there?"

Bill reached out his hand.

"He's here."

"Hands in the bag?"

Bill traced the outline of Monty's frigid body, found the hands. They were outside the bag, hard as metal. He tucked them in, like putting dumb-bells in a gym bag.

"They're in."

Monty won't stay in his bag. Paradoxology. No. Paradoxical. Paradoxical undressing. Monty's brain is burning up, all the heat is in his brain. Monty's freezing to death and he feels hot.

Where was I? Yellow?

"Rick."

Rick, not Nick, Rick with the torn face, the eyeball like a raw egg yolk. The smashed face and bruised back.

"Tony."

Tony who couldn't talk right. Cut-up Tony, with the broken jaw.

"Uhn."

And me. Wilma. I'm here. All of me, even my hands. Wilma has a bruised spine and broken ankle. I'm the doctor. Doc.

"Marc."

"Yeah."

"Mike."

Mike who looked out through something that was neither quite a face nor a balaclava. Please don't touch it, Mike. Please don't pull off your face.

"Here."

"Paul."

"Here."

"Joe."

"Here."

"John."

Nothing.

Joe's flight suit was bonded to the frozen grate, like a child's tongue to an iron fence. He worked it unstuck and then, on hands and knees, like a baby learning to crawl, he negotiated the grate. His hands slipped on the ice, the shreds of insulation, the blackened jumble of char and ice. He made his way in the frozen reek of fuel and cinders and urine. There he was. There was John. He put his cheek to John's lips.

"John," Wilma said again.

"No."

"John?"

"Wilma," said Joe. "Don't."

CHAPTER EIGHTEEN

Stop Drop

THE MOUNTIE in Iqaluit had run his snowmobile out to the hangar to tell Mark Levesque and his crew they were nuts if they thought they could fly a helicopter inland up the length of Baffin Island in this weather. The constable knew the area by air and warned of fjords that would trap them. Their only possible route would be along the eastern shoreline to Cape Dyer, the Mountie said, and they'd be crazy to try even that.

They decided to try it. There were people dying out there.

They took off in the Labrador, hugging the coastline, using the radar "paint" of the Aurora flying above them to ride a very thin line. Too close to the coast and they risked slamming into the cliffs; too far out and it would be fatal to ditch the aircraft.

Mark Levesque was in the back seat. He'd been relieved at the controls by Captain Pierre Bolduc and his flight crew; they had been awake as many hours as Levesque, but as passengers on the deadhead flights. They flew without incident to Cape Dyer, an Inuit fishing village with a usable fuel cache. Levesque got out to see if the weather was breaking at all, and saw a fifty-foot white Frisbee spinning above his head – the whirling rotors were solidly coated with ice.

Bolduc got out, too, and the men considered the problem. There was finely pebbled ice on the aircraft's leading surfaces and fuel sponsons. There must also have been pebble ice on the whirling rotors, which would destroy their lift.

They didn't want to shut the engines down; if they did, the engines might never start again. They decided to idle them; then, with the blades spinning freely, they would apply the rotor brake just long enough to shake the ice free. Bolduc allowed the engines to whine down, then hit the brake. The Lab shuddered as the chop of the rotors came to a halt. Ice shot from the rotors, spraying the tarmac.

The Frisbee was now only four feet in diameter. They could fly, but they could not control the aircraft in the event of engine failure. Levesque and Bolduc discussed whether to continue. The engines were long overdue for a mechanical breakdown, and now, with the ice, they didn't stand a chance of surviving an engine failure.

They decided to press on to Clyde River.

Bolduc set his altitude by the cloud cover. He hugged the base of the weather system, flying between 100 and 500 feet above the water. It was pitch dark, and the Labrador was following a course set by the Aurora.

A SARtech in the rear of the Labrador spotted the first iceberg. It towered some 400 feet above the waterline of Home Bay. He watched its dark, steely, luminescent shadow pass beneath the belly of the Labrador.

"We're in a pack of icebergs," he said.

Everybody was remarkably calm; it was as though the twists of the voyage had exhausted their store of alarm. Bolduc rose to 500 feet. There was some discussion about how close they had come to actually striking the iceberg: perhaps no more than fifty feet. The Lab was now flying in a thin vertical corridor, 100 feet deep at most. That corridor was the only safe passage between the mist of ice above and the mountains of ice below.

All the passengers and crew kept their eyes peeled out the

round portholes of the Labrador. Neither the Lab nor the Aurora overhead could detect the bergs on the radar; eyes were their last defence. Most fell into a kind of anxious reverie.

"I've been thinking," the SARtech said, after a time.

"So have I," said Levesque. "What it would be like to ditch in that water."

"What I've been thinking," said the SARtech, "is, who rescues us?"

———————

On his second foray from the Alert station on the Go-Tracks, Fred Ritchie and his SARtechs had followed the convoy's old tracks as far as Mushroom Point. They had made good time over the first few miles. They strayed out over the ice a few times, heard it cracking in the darkness beneath them. It scared Ritchie half to death. He could never tell whether the crackling noise was simply the treads chewing the ice, or the ice itself breaking up. Each time they'd made it back onto solid ground.

They had loaded up the back of the Go-Track with five gallons of hot coffee in an urn, a crate full of Magic Pantry dinners, a pallet of Coca-Cola, a box of Hershey chocolate bars, a 300-pound survival toboggan, and five SARtechs. With a twenty-five-knot tailwind at 340 degrees true, they found themselves going downhill with a stiff breeze at their back. They were smoking along.

In the frigid, stormy darkness, they rumbled along the coast-line and then veered inland. They climbed over hills and through low valleys. Each time they approached a ravine, Fred hopped out and ran ahead to check it out. The bitter wind instantly sucked the air from his lungs. It was frigging cold. Those poor bastards out there.

They moved inland, climbing gradually through the storm.

According to the direction of the ridges, they were heading south, zeroing in on the crash site. They hit a steep ravine, and the drivers of the Go-Tracks – who were not hairy-forearmed SARtechs but vehicle techs – told their passengers to get the hell out because they didn't know if the Go-Tracks would make it. In the howling wind, the SARtechs formed a chain of flashlights across the ravine; the drivers roared the Go-Tracks ahead, tipping over the edge, slipping and sliding down the slope. Then everyone got back in and the vehicles clambered up the other side.

A few minutes later a couple of the other SARtechs got out – Fred was getting cold – to guide the Go-Tracks along the edge of a ravine. They were supposed to keep the tractors away from the brink, but they got separated from each other by about twenty feet. They could see the Go-Track lights, but they couldn't see each other. Each thought the other had fallen into the ravine. It should have been a warning. But the SARtechs climbed back in, and the Go-Tracks roared along at full throttle, hell for leather and protected by God's patience with fools and a Casio watch. They were at top throttle, tiller bars pressed against the metal dashboard, Fred peering out. The lights picked up the white blindness of snow hurtling out of the darkness at them.

The whiteness turned to ink.

"Stop!"

The driver cut throttle and yanked back the tiller bars. Fred reached for the radio transmitter. Inches ahead of the flat pane of their windscreen, the snow seemed to run out. Beyond the white edge was a dark void. Good Lord – it was a sheer ravine. Visibility ahead was reduced to a few feet, and Fred could see no more than four body lengths to the side. He strained to find a way out to the right.

"That was lucky," he said.

A jagged line of blackness came creeping through the snow crust towards the Go-Track. They were on a cornice of snow overhanging the edge of the ravine. It was breaking away.

"Holy shit!"

The black crack crossed behind Fred's line of vision; the nose of the Go-Track pitched forward; they were looking straight down. "Turn left!" Fred shouted to the Go-Track behind, bracing himself as his own Go-Track plunged, nose down, and smashed into a rock ledge thirty feet below. Fred was buffeted left and right before snow sprayed over the windscreen. He believed he would die, of spraying glass, rocks, and mangled metal; or of the impact of the 300-pound toboggan behind him. In the white heat of panic, he felt remorse. The other SARtechs, meanwhile, were grabbing their seats and one another, faces tight with fear; the impact had thrust the toboggan forward, all right, but it had caught on the engine compartment between the two front seats. SARtechs crashed into it. The compartment was awash in hot coffee and Magic Pantry dinners.

The driver had been thrown forward onto the tiller bars, driving his feet into the throttle pedals, and this is what saved them. Rather than tumbling over and continuing its plunge, the Go-Track clutched at the ledge, ground away at it with full power. The treads gained purchase, carrying the machine forward. It found its feet and lurched down to the canyon floor. There, the driver pulled the tillers back. The engine idled, and the shaken SARtechs gathered their wits.

"My ass is so puckered up you'd need a Sledge-o-Matic to drive a nail up there."

The laughter was manic with relief.

The Go-Track headed towards the frozen sea, thumping and grinding along in the darkness. The second tractor followed along the top of the ravine; they would meet at sea level.

Fred pondered. If that cliff had been any deeper, you'd have killed five people. Some hero. What's with you, man? Are the risks really worth it?

As they rumbled down the ravine bed to the shoreline, Fred called up Alert for word on survivors. The latest – and it would be their last word, the radios having died – was that fourteen souls were still alive. Their spirits were failing. They were critically cold and had critical injuries. Frostbite and hypothermia were setting in. They were suffering as no creature ought to suffer.

Fred calculated his chances at about fifty-fifty. No contest: he would press on. He was no longer doing it for the regimental sergeant major. He was doing it for them. He was acting not from obligation but from desire. He was doing it because it was his job to save lost souls.

The Go-Tracks met at the shoreline and turned south. At the estuary of the Sheridan River they were again forced to head out over open water. The vehicles creaked ominously on top of the ice – everybody held their breath – but did not break through. Once past the Sheridan, Fred reckoned, they were home free.

They turned inland. As they gained altitude, they entered a thick cloud bank. The wind and ice pellets were even worse than they had been, but Fred was exhilarated. They had finally entered the Arctic storm that hung over Box Top 22 like a shroud.

Marv Macauley and his Hercules arrived above the crash site in time to make out the roof lights of Fred's convoy as it entered the heart of the storm. Freaky, this weather. The flight from Thule had been clear as a bell. Even the coastline of Ellesmere Island had been perfectly clear. A few miles inland, over the crash site, it was socked in down to the ground. Marv called up the Alert station.

"Alert, this is Rescue Three Zero Five out of Greenwood. We're flying top cover for the ground search party. Give us their frequency so we can establish ground comms."

"No way, Three Zero Five. You relay through us, we get them on the VHF-FM radio. We talk to you, you talk to us, we talk back to them. You don't have VHF-FM on the CC-130."

"My Herc is equipped with VHF-FM, Alert. Give me the frequency."

"We're supposed to coordinate with the command post."

"Now listen, buddy."

"How will command keep track of you?"

"Give me that goddamn frequency, you little puke."

And so, circumventing the textbook command, control and communications procedure established by the Canadian military, Marv bypassed Alert and spoke directly to the ground party. Fred's first words to the circling Herc were, "Good old Marv."

"Turn ninety degrees to the right, buddy. You're approaching a ravine."

Sometimes the ground party's roof lights were lost to the Hercules; Fred would tell Marv when he could hear the Hercules overhead. Other times, Marv could see the ground party clearly even though ground visibility was zero. At these moments the Hercules navigator, working from his radar scope and from the chart he had photocopied in Thule, was able to supply precise, immediate directions for the blinded ground party. Not that Fred always followed them.

"Okay, Fred, you're in a ravine. Turn right fifty degrees and you'll find an easy way out in about a hundred yards."

"That'll take us out on the ice. We've got to turn left."

"Negative, good buddy. You're heading out to sea now. Turn right."

"You're ass-backwards, Marv. We're turning left."

Marv instructed his loadmaster to drop a flare.

"Okay, Fred, see that flare?"

"Drop it any time, good buddy."

"It's behind you, Fred."

There was no reply, but Marv could see the headlights swing away from the pack ice.

Every quarter-hour, the Hercules peeled off to check weather conditions over the crash site. They'd made innumerable passes when the weather broke temporarily and Arnie's SARtechs were able to spot the tail section of Box Top 22 in a clear, snowbound field about a mile long and a half-mile wide. There were no signs of life.

Marv left Fred's ground party to its own devices; it was time to concentrate on a parachute attempt. In the back of the Hercules, Arnie's SARtechs suited up in an atmosphere of keen anticipation. They'd been waiting for this chance for nearly thirty hours, ever since leaving Greenwood. They were primed and ready.

Marv circled the crash site, flying a box pattern, but by the third pass the exhaust from his turboprop engines had created cloud cover. He was flying through the condensation of his own contrail, and the jumpers lost sight of the ground. The jump had to be called off.

Meanwhile, the U.S. Air National Guard arrived on the scene. The Americans had dispatched two Hercules aircraft to the area. The first, from Keflavik in Iceland, had flown to Thule to act as an air-to-air refueller for the Pavehawk helicopters winging their way to the U.S. air base in the belly of a c-5 Galaxy Transport. The second Hercules, from the Elmendorf air base at Anchorage, had a load of para-rescue jumpers on board. It flew directly to Alert and began circling above Marv.

Marv asked the Americans to drop some flares; perhaps they could provide enough illumination that he would need only one pass over the crash site. That would solve the exhaust problem without sacrificing light. The American Hercules was a few thousand feet higher than Marv, however, and its flares disappeared in the cloud cover above him. The clouds pulsed overhead with an eerie orange glow, but not much light filtered through.

Marv continued to fly a box pattern, dropping flares. He was flying on the gyro compass, putting the aircraft through a series of tight manoeuvres while maintaining an altitude of 2,500 feet above sea level. That give him 1,500 feet of clearance over the crash site. On each pass, the pilot gave a five-second warning, then spoke over the intercom: "Flare, release ... now!"

"Flare clear."

The flare fell 250 feet before the abrupt jerk of its parachute ignited the magnesium core: "Ignition. Flare burn."

Marv followed the procedure again and again. After one release, the voice in his headset said, "Malfunction!" The flare had ignited, but its dazzling core seemed to be bouncing across the sky. Marv watched the light skip along.

"That's no malfunction. It's hit the ground."

Somehow they had flown, unwittingly, within 250 feet of the rocky terrain. Marv lifted the nose, as the flight engineer cross-checked the altimeters – "Altitude's okay" – and the co-pilot, Randy Price, cross-checked the compasses.

"Christ, Marv," said Price, "there's a thirty-degree variance."

The violent manoeuvring of the aircraft had thrown the gyros out of whack. They had travelled a few degrees from true with each turn of the aircraft, so gradually that nobody on the flight deck had noticed. Marv was 30 degrees west of where he thought he was. The terrain elevation in his quadrant was 2,200 feet, not 1,000 feet as he had imagined. "We're outta here," he said, and began to climb above the cloud cover.

Arnie came over the microphone. "Marv, what the hell are you doing?"

"Compasses are out. We have to reset them."

When the circling U.S. Hercules saw the Canadian SARtechs bank away from the crash site, it moved in. "Rescue Three Zero Five, this is 56th Air Rescue. Since you're leaving, we'll see if we can get our guys in."

Arnie heard the exchange on his headset: "Marv, you can't!"
"Have to."

"My boys are going nuts back here. You've got to get us over the site. Those bastards are going to waltz in and beat us to it."

"We have to do this. Keep your shirt on."

Arnie was nearly blind with rage at his own impotence, inadequate gear, and lousy luck. But his little brother was in command of the aircraft. He had to defer to Marv.

Frigging Americans! Arnie could just see the U.S. parajumpers with their $1,000 Robocop jumpsuits (he wore kapok padding and cotton); their night vision goggles (he had a miner's lamp); their global positioning units (he used bush sense); their state-of-the-art square canopies that would tame any wind (he had a vintage round canopy). Of course the Americans would get in. They had the technology. They'd pull off the most daring rescue in Canadian history, and his SARtechs would be bystanders.

Goddamn! Arnie ripped off his headset and fired it at the bench.

CHAPTER NINETEEN

A Big White Room

IT'S MY BIRTHDAY. I'm twenty-six. I was born on the first of November and married on the fourteenth of September. I've been married six weeks. I'm twenty-six years old. Precisely.

Clang. Clang. Clang.

"Mondy!"

"Straighten my fingers."

"Why?"

"Mathroom."

Kidneys still working. That's good.

No, bad. Heat loss through the groin. Freezing urine, groin, thighs. Bad.

Good or bad. What am I deciding? Oh, yes. "Try to hold it, Mondy."

Good to want to. Good to hold it. Come back, Joe. Don't stay outside. Come back inside.

"I'll help him."

Who's that? Marc. Trying to get up. Stuck to the tail. Frozen stuck. All stuck. Just have to pass water in his bag.

Going to see if there's bags outside. That's what he said. He meant, going to see if they're dead.

We have three bags. The others have four. If they are dead, we should take their bags.

I don't want a bag. Twenty-six. Six. Little numbers, too little. No, it's good. Good for George. Don't think of George.

Joe. I hear him. He's back. He's at the opening. I can see him.

Empty-handed. Great news. They're alive. Lie beside me, Joe. You're so cold. You're cold as stone.

"How are they?"

"Afraid. Leave them."

"We won't."

Oh, Joe. You're wet again. Shivering so. Paul, too. Paul is so cold. Cold and still. He said, "Waw." I asked what he was thinking and he said, "Waw, ghosts and colours."

My bladder is full, too. How will I do this? Easier for the men. They used the hole in the back. When they could still move. Now they empty the bladder where they are. Sometimes the zipper is frozen, or their hands, they go in their pants. Sometimes they get the zipper down. They try to put it through the grates. The urine is wet, it freezes to the metal. I hear them crying, tearing skin.

It's not easier for them.

I don't want to wet everyone. Sometimes the men wet everyone. The urine steams, you smell it. It flows around the grates and then freezes, and all the clothes are frozen to the metal. Pants stuck to the metal with frozen urine.

Roll over. On my knees. I can do this. I can pull my pants down so they won't get wet.

Didn't work. Wet from thighs to knees. Warm, then cold. Then stiff.

The flow has started. It was … Tuesday night. Wednesday, Thursday, is this Friday? I've started.

They'll smell it. A polar bear. A wolf. They'll smell it on the air. They'll follow the hormones, stalk the trail of pheromones. The rescuers won't find us but the animals will. They'll follow my scent to this tail. They'll eat us before we're dead.

My fault.

My body's fault. My body.

George. Six weeks.

Pull up my pants. Pull down the balaclava. At least Joe has stopped shivering. That's good.

Good or bad?

Twenty-six. Six. Precisely.

Honey, I am here. In this room. A big white room. That's where I am, honey. I was somewhere else before. I went to see the bags.

They were worried I would go away and leave them so I covered them with snow.

I covered them with snow because the bags were burning and one of them had a punctured lung. Tom. His name was Tom. The other one was named Glow Worm. They died in my arms. Have you seen Glow Worm? He was shivering. The bags had a sore back from shivering.

Honey, do you know where I left those bags? Did I leave them with the baby? You prayed for me? And the baby? I have to go. I have to find some bags. I said I wouldn't leave them.

They fell down in the snow. The bags tried to walk through old footsteps, but the snow grabbed at them and they fell down. They stood up and fell down. Flat on their faces. It hurt their faces.

Honey, get Karen to help find the bags. Get the whole crew together, help me find the bags. I think we put the bags down for a minute, but when we came back the bags had drifted over.

Did the wind blow the bags away? I think they're gone. Tell the others to help me find the bags. I promised I wouldn't leave them. I want them to come back.

They didn't answer the roll call. John didn't answer and I said Wilma don't.

———————

Bob remembered hearing the footsteps. He had seen the beam of light.

"Joe."

"Ogay?"

"Hey, I can' dalk. Godda go. Godda get back o'r people."

Hours ago.

Bob marked time in fractions of an inch. When he was first buried in the snow, the tarpaulin had been about three inches from his face. His right hand, the only movable part of his body, could travel about six inches, from his nose, across his cheek, past his right ear. He had been able to lift his head and swat at the soggy goose feathers. As time went on, his cavity grew smaller. Snow piled up on the tarpaulin. It was packed down by the wind.

Bob now had less than an inch in front of his face – he could touch the tarpaulin with his tongue – and about three inches of movement with his right hand. It was pitch black. A one-inch by three-inch black cavity. Time had moved two inches.

Bob had a raging thirst. Being marooned in snow is rather like being lost at sea; you're surrounded by undrinkable water. Snow will not slake a thirst, and Bob knew better than to eat it – it would drain his body of precious calories and cool his body core. But he was dying of thirst. Severe cold rapidly increases the body's rate of dehydration through the lungs. Even at rest inside a snow shelter, with the humidity approaching 100 per cent, Bob was losing a litre of water every twelve hours through the mere act of breathing. He had lost nearly three litres, without replenishment.

He decided to have a drink. With his free hand, he worked the frozen snow behind his ear. The right ear – his heel was behind the left one. His fingers were stiff, devoid of feeling. Still, he had his little metal spar. He poked at the snow. The heat thrown from the back of his neck – where the body sheds most of its heat – had melted the snow. It had then frozen again, into a solid headrest of ice. This was hard for Bob to break up. He chipped at the ice behind his ear. His hand and forearm were exhausted by the effort. But he was being driven mad by thirst. Just as he had never known such pain, he had never felt such need.

He had a plan. He would hold the chips of frozen snow in the palm of his hand. The hand would melt them, and he would drink.

It was not easy. He got enough chips to fit in his palm, and closed frozen fingers around them. He worked the hand between the tarpaulin and his face, until the edge of his hand was against the corner of his lips. Then he squeezed.

Even though his hands were cold, the ice would melt under pressure. He waited, squeezing, feeling his hand cramp. Then he felt a few drops forming on his knuckles. They pooled, then coursed down his fingers to his lips. Drink!

His mouth filled with the noxious taste of diesel fuel. You idiot, Thomson.

He tried to relax the hand. He tried, a few times, to reach his fingers across his face and dig away the feathers blocking his mouth and nostrils, but the fingers were too cold and stiff, and the space too tight.

He lay still, feeling the venom of the cold deaden him. A snake of morphine. It entered the stomach, worked its way through his bowels towards his chest. It entered his fingers, moved into his hands and up through his arms. It got as far as the backs of his shoulders. His arms were gone, his stomach was gone. In those parts he had no warmth. They were numb and asleep and had no life in them. He could feel the core of his chest begin to cool.

This is it, Thomson. You're going to be a brain. A brain and nothing else.

Then the cold began to retreat. Bob felt it had something to do with his breath. His breath seemed to get warmer. The freezing snake withdrew; where it retreated, he was racked with agony. The thawing flesh burned as if it were on fire. The sensation of burning did not go away as his stomach and arms warmed up; they warmed only to the point of unfreezing. The so-called hunter reflex. As the body cools towards freezing, the smooth muscle tissues around the veins tighten, cutting off blood to the extremities. The limbs freeze. The same muscle tissues that cut off the blood then lose their ability to contract, because they are so cold. They relax, and a trickle of blood returns, giving the muscles the strength to contract again. And so on, in an excruciating ebb and flow. So much for the gentle morphia of nature.

When his hand thawed, came back to him, it was on fire. Bob brought it to his face. He did not know why he did this. It seemed important to feel his hand close to him. It was his remaining friend.

The pain went away with the return of the snake. Back and forth it went; freezing and thawing, ice and fire. A battle waged along his rack of flesh.

Bob did not pick sides, particularly, but he admired his body's performance. When he viewed himself from afar, he was astonished at the strength and endurance of his own body.

The snake returned, slithered up his arms and belly. It moved into his chest and coiled around his shoulders and neck.

This is it, Thomson.

He became deathly tired and felt himself about to drop off.

I'm going to sleep now. This is the end of it.

Someone was curled up behind him, his front pressed against Bob's back. A man. Bob felt the man's heat and strength. His face was pressed against Bob's left ear, where the heel used to be. His arm was Bob's left arm. His arm was strong. Bob felt it embrace him, hugging him.

Hey, bud.

The man's voice was deeper than Bob's, and husky.

Who are you?

I'm Buddy. What's up?

I'm tired, Buddy. I'm scared.

What are you scared of?

Scared I'm going to suffocate. Scared the tarp will get heavier and push against my face. It's right there, Buddy. I can't breathe. I can't breathe any more.

Hey, no problem.

Bob felt Buddy's arm fishing around in the cavity.

Don't you have a piece of metal or something?

Here. Hey Buddy, if you can break us out of here, we're both going to be all right. We'll be free.

With his strong left arm, Buddy slit the tarpaulin open.

Bob was blinded. He closed his eyes against the light. Sunlight streamed through the vent. Sunlight, heat, fresh air. He felt the sweet air fill his lungs. The feathers were gone, he breathed freely. He opened his eyes and saw a measureless expanse of blue. Summertime blue. Dawn! He'd slept right through spring. The air smelled sweet, of cut grass and warm afternoons.

This is great, Buddy! We can get out now!

Bob rose towards the light. He soared through the opening towards the blue sky.

There was no Buddy.

He was alone. It was dark.

Thomson, you're an idiot. How could you have done that?

His problems had vanished. He had experienced joy. Then it had been taken from him. He began to cry. He had not, until now, cried. Wetness flowed from his eyes and mouth and nostrils, matting the feathers, and his desperation compounded itself on the choking feathers and the dark. He gasped, heaving with sobs; and as he cried, he drew a draft of cool, dry air.

He poked his tongue out, exploring the canvas. There was a small slit, cut by his metal spar. Fresh air was flowing through it. The air rejuvenated him. He felt his strength return. His body pushed back the snake; fire returned to his arms and belly.

He was suffering. He would live.

Thanks, Buddy.

———————

Sue had heard someone through the wind, had seen the beam of light.

"Guys ogay?"

He sounded so cold; his voice was shaking, his words half formed.

"Okay."

"Godda go."

She was alone again. Bob no longer talked to her. He said he was tired. She imagined he had gone to sleep.

She was on her back, and the snow came in from the sides of her shelter. It drifted over her face. She waited until it was several inches thick before brushing it away. She didn't have the strength. She let it pile up until she could no longer breathe. Then she found the strength and brushed it, as high as she could, to either side. Snow drifted back down the sides and covered her face again. She didn't have the strength.

She decided to get up. She brushed the snow away, removed the diesel-soaked rag. She worked her elbows up her side, and actually levered herself into a semi-upright position. This was achieved at great expense in pain. She fought the nausea and the fainting. She believed her neck to be broken; it was too painful to support her head. She leaned on one elbow, grabbed her collar with the free hand, trying to support the neck. She heaved on the collar and managed to poke her head above the shelter.

Blackness. The wind blasted her face, and ice spicules pricked her skin. It hurt, and then her face was numb.

She sank back down. She couldn't move for quite a while. She thought about her pain for a long time. It felt as if someone had cut off her head with a guillotine.

She worked the rag back over her face. The smell made her feel sick. She wondered if she could still make her legs move. She reached down and tugged at one leg, trying to make it respond. She felt the flesh tearing, her hand being soaked in new blood. Then she lay still.

She had, until now, made a routine of raising her back off the ice, to save her kidneys and vital organs. She did this by arching her hips and raising herself on the points of her shoulder blades. But her shoulders had frozen and been rubbed raw against the ice. She had felt the frostbite enter them, felt the flesh being rubbed off the bones. She no longer arched her back.

She let the snake invade her. It worked its way up her thighs, through her groin, into her waist. It entered her fingers and made its way up her arms. The back of her neck was her greatest pain; it did not go numb. She was reduced to the parts of her that were going numb, leaving her, and the parts that remained, tormenting her.

The snow drifted over her mask, piling several inches high. She let it.

She felt a flow of warmth and wetness between her thighs. The urine turned to ice; it was barely out of her body when it froze, sucking what little heat remained from her groin area.

This is it. My kidneys are shutting down. That's one of the last signs.

She imagined her future, saw herself frozen in her ice coffin until spring, when the thaw would reveal her body. Perhaps the animals would get to her body first; in any case, she would not be returned to her parents until spring. She thought of the grief this would cause them, felt their grief, and she cried, and heard the baying of wolves.

I'm not going out a nut case. I'm going to be calm.

Sue prepared her list, including everyone who was important to her. She was a gregarious woman, and the list was long. Her primary relationships were at the top of the list. She spent a long time talking with her mother, and let her go. Then she dealt with Adrian. She had many things to say to them, private things.

She went to her father, and her sisters, visited with them. Then her relatives and her friends, her clients, everyone she was leaving behind. She did not mind so much the going, but she wanted more than anything to go on peaceful terms. She made her peace, and she heard the snuffling of an animal by her ear.

A polar bear?

It padded around the outline of her body. She felt the weight of it on the packed snow. It walked the length of her, rounded her feet, and came up the other side.

Maybe it will go away.

It stopped at her hips. It began to dig. She felt it digging towards her hips and thighs, where the flesh was laid open to the bone.

It's the blood. It's the same leg I was digging at. It smells fresh blood. It would start there; it would start by gnawing at her hip bone.

Its snout entered the cavity it had dug, and snuffled for the blood. She felt its breath on her skin.

It withdrew.

Nothing happened for a while. Then it crept up her belly and chest. She felt its paws. It stopped, with its weight on her chest. She heard it panting.

Not without seeing my face.

225

She summoned the last of her will. This was not courage but a type of stubbornness. She moved her hands, pulled the rag from her face. Snow fell into her eyes and mouth. She lunged almost upright, ignoring the stabbing protest from her neck. Snow fell from her face. She let out a scream.

She opened her eyes, looked directly into his. He blinked, once, and pulled his head back; then he moved his nose towards her face. Sue pulled her head back in astonishment. They considered each other.

A white arctic wolf, the most beautiful animal she had ever seen. His face was radiant, seeming to glow in the darkness. His fur was long and spiky, and there was soft white down underneath. There was a black flash running from his forehead down his nose. His tongue was pink, and white vapours marked his panting.

His eyes were striking – as striking as Sue's own. A pale, iridescent blue. They shone. They stared into Sue's eyes, neither malicious nor curious. They simply regarded her.

Sue screamed again.

The wolf cocked his head. He turned, not hurriedly, and stepped off her chest. He padded away, stopping once for a final look back. Then he disappeared into the darkness.

Sue sank back.

I'm not dying here. And I'm not getting eaten by some wolf. I'm not freezing to death. If I have to, I'll crawl to Alert.

Sue went back to the people on her list, starting from the top. She told them she'd be coming home.

CHAPTER TWENTY

Riders on the Storm

IT WAS SOMEHOW comforting, Captain Marc Favre thought, to be using the same technology used by Magellan. Favre stood on the crew bunk of the Hercules flight deck, sextant in hand. It was the first instrument he had learned to use, and his favourite. His poked his head into the ceiling bubble of the cockpit. As Marv Macauley took the Hercules up through the cloud cover, Favre found himself in a sea of stars. It was a brilliant night – he never would have guessed it from the suffocating storm below.

Favre set his sights on Vega. He took the reading and consulted the ancient logs and almanacs. Fifteen minutes later, the Herc's compasses had been trued. Marv descended back through the clouds, down to 2,500 feet, and raised the American Hercules on the radio.

"We're coming down to your altitude."

"All yours, Rescue Three Zero Five," said the U.S. aircraft commander. "There's no way we're going to jump into that. You go ahead and be crazy, if you want."

When the U.S. Herc banked away, Marv dove in to take its place. This would have to be fast; he was worried. He was fast approaching bingo fuel for Thule, which would mean no other airfield but Alert.

In the rear, Arnie's sArtechs pulled on their white balaclavas, snugged their helmets, and snapped down the visors. They checked their parachutes and rigging. Some put an orange in a pocket, for the survivors, or a flask of whisky. One carried his lucky mittens, knitted for him by his mother.

The weather had completely socked in during their quarter-hour absence. The crash site was again enveloped by cloud, rising to 4,500 feet. Marv ordered a light and flare drop from the aircraft, hoping to pinpoint the site. Both were blown away by the wind and never seen again. To hell with it; they'd thrown over ninety flares by now and knew the wind speed and drift by heart.

Marv could find the site by homing beacon, but the jumpers needed light. He decided on an untried method: he would drop the flare at 5,500 feet, three-quarters of a mile upwind of the crash site and above the cloud layer. Then he would bring the aircraft around and dive into the cloud, keeping the flare on his left. Then he'd race ahead of the flare, flying downwind to the crash site. Once he got a fix on the wreckage, he'd double back and drop his jumpers with the flare still in the air, but out of harm's way.

Marv had dropped and circled a flare in cloud once before, with nearly disastrous results. This time he would set himself a vector to give himself plenty of clearance. The real problem was time. The flare burns for five minutes, but the drop is cancelled if the jumpers aren't out the door within three. Otherwise the flares will burn out before the jumpers hit the ground, and it is perilous to land in total darkness.

At the moment of ignition, the navigator began a count. Marv had precious little time to get the Herc in position.

In the rear, the SARtechs had a countdown of their own. As they doubled back over the crash site, the jumpmaster began counting the number of seconds before the first six jumpers would leave the door.

The Hercules dived and banked, raced the flare, and doubled

228

back as the navigator called the time on the cockpit intercom: "Two fifteen. Two thirty. Two forty-five."

In the tail, the jumpmaster counted down over the roaring wind: "Ten. Niner. Eight. Seven. Six ..."

At five seconds to drop, the navigator called three minutes. "Stop drop!"

The jumpmaster stretched his arm across the open door: "Stop drop!"

Arnie tore off his helmet in a rage and asked what the hell had happened. "Three minutes," said the jumpmaster. "No flares." After a quick conference with his SARtechs, Arnie grabbed the intercom mike to the flight deck: "We're doing it again, Marv. We've talked it over back here. We are not, under any circumstances, calling a stop drop again."

Marv knew that tone of voice, knew there was no point arguing with his older brother, even if it was practically a suicide mission they were contemplating.

"All right," he said, and began the climb back to 5,500 feet. He felt oddly calm, except that his upper lip was twitching uncontrollably.

———

Addressing his men, Arnie had to make himself heard above the droning engines, the rushing wind, and the cockpit commands coming over the intercom.

"Okay, guys, you know the situation. The winds are pretty stiff. They've blown away all our marker lights. The count is thirty seconds from one thousand feet. The drop zone is about a half-mile wide. It looks like a snowfield down there, but ground conditions are unknown. We'll be landing at a good clip. We'll try for flare illumination but I can't promise you anything.

"One more thing. Once we're down there, we're down for

good. Marv will try for a supply drop, but we can expect the survival gear to be blown away. We'll have no way of extracting ourselves or the survivors."

A thirty-second count at 1,000 feet meant the SARtechs would drift one and a half miles horizontally for 1,000 feet of vertical travel. They would have an eight-to-one glide slope, a slope angle of 11 degrees. They would be travelling nearly parallel to the ground when they hit it.

The winds were more than three times greater than operational limits. Depending on whether their canopies were running with the wind or against it, they would strike the ground at between thirty-five and forty-five knots. It would be like leaping from a moving car at a speed of between forty and fifty-two miles an hour.

The SARtech rulebook forbids jumping in wind speeds above ten knots. It also forbids night jumps without illumination. It also forbids any jump below 2,000 feet.

They would be hitting the ground at highway speed, with a visibility of ten to twenty feet in blowing snow. They would not be able to see the ground or adjust their direction before they hit. There would be no time to use the reserve chute if the main canopy failed or tore in the wind. The jump would be conducted at airspeeds of up to 150 knots. Stepping out of the aircraft, they would be plunged into darkness and the unimaginably icy blast of the slipstream. The temperature on the ground, with wind chill, was -66 Celsius. They would be hurled into the wind's fury and dropped into a frozen hell. If the count were off by seconds, or if Marv's aim were off by degrees, they would miss the snowfield altogether and be dashed against the surrounding rocks and boulders.

"That's the situation, men. We can expect casualties. I have to inform you that the jump involves a knowing risk of life. I can't ask any of you to do this."

Some of the SARtechs studied their boots, others looked out the open door into the howling void. One by one, they looked back at him. "Arnie," one said. "You know how we feel."

Good guys, Arnie thought. I hope like hell I'm doing the right thing.

Arnie checked the closures on his padded orange jumpsuit and the fasteners of his parachute harness. He pulled on his gloves. The jumpmaster clipped their static lines to the overhead cable, and the men crowded around the open door. There were six of them. They squeezed into the opening and grabbed one another by the legs, arms, waist. They would go together.

On the flight deck, Marv was struggling with his face. It was a funny feeling; he'd never had a nervous twitch. His upper lip had started to quiver so much he thought everyone in the cockpit must have noticed it.

He briefed the flight crew on headings, altitudes, and times. The co-pilot, Randy Price, would call the headings. The flight engineer, Sergeant Bill Sura, would call altitude and airspeed. The navigator, Favre, would check ground clearances and follow terrain and flares. Marv would fly the plane.

The homing beacon on the ground was dying out. Price had the UHF receiver turned to full volume, and Marv had to speak over its undulating distress call. It sounded like the sonar return of a submarine; it was growing more smeared and faint: "Ping. Ping. Ping."

"Turn that thing off," Marv said. "Stop using the homer."

Price cut the volume to the pilot's headset. But he did not flip the power toggle; the direction finder was left on, and its track bar still pointed towards the crash site. Price reached for another dial and boosted the sensitivity of the needle. He didn't fully trust his tacan instrument, he told himself; he wanted a second opinion. But he also wanted contact with the survivors. His way of reaching for them was through a small needle on the instrument panel.

Marv broke cloud cover at 4,500 feet, and they dropped the flares from the tail.

"Flare away."

"Clear."

"Ignition."

The navigator began the three-minute count. Marv dropped the left wing and began racing the flare through cloud. Price called vectors. Favre called clearances from the flare and the crash site. The flight engineer called airspeed and altitude. Marv's eyes were fixed on the dials, his hands on the yoke. His tongue was reaching out and grabbing his moustache. He figured he could stop the lip from quivering by pulling on the moustache.

At 2,500 feet, they broke through the bottom of the cloud layer. Marv was surprised; it had been socked in down to the ground when they'd gone up. The flares pulsed their fountains of orange light over the rocks and snow below.

Sergeant Gerry Dominie, jumpmaster of the Greenwood SARtechs, was lying on the floor of the Herc, his head poking out the SAR door, watching the frozen waste pass beneath him. The outline of the crashed tail section hove clearly into view.

"Acquired crash site. Five seconds to target. Over target … now!" He began his thirty-second count.

"Won't make it," the navigator said. "We're only fifteen seconds to stop drop."

Marv had to decide. He was low on fuel. But the conditions were the best he had yet experienced. Arnie had said no more stop drops. But to drop in darkness, after the flares had gone out? Madness.

"Prepare two flares to send after the jumpers," said Marv.

"Deploy flares fifteen seconds after jumpers away. There will be no stop drop. Repeat: No stop drop."

This procedure wasn't in the books. Bill Sura leaned over towards Marv. "Level and two," he said. "Airspeed one fifty. Good old Marv."

Marv's head filled with voices on the headset: checklist, bearings, flaps fifty per cent, SAR doors open, deflector doors open, fifteen seconds, level and two, speed one fifty, vector two niner.

Suddenly, the steady drone of the engines ceased and the flight deck reverberated with a rising and rolling "wow*wow*-wow"from the number one engine. The aircraft felt all right in Marv's hands, but something was wrong. "My God! No RPM on number one!"

The four propellers of the Hercules are electronically phased to be kept in synchronized rotation. The tach generator for the number one engine had failed, so the phaser no longer knew the speed of its propeller, or its angle in relation to the masters. The propellers lost their harmony and reverberated; the gauge indicated the engine was dead. The effect is noisy and unsettling, but it does not affect the flight performance of the aircraft. Marv thought he'd been suckered, but he was wrong.

Flight engineer Sura scanned the dials and rested a reassuring hand on Marv's shoulder. "We just lost the tach genny. It's okay, the engine's good."

"Five seconds to drop," Dominie said over the headset.

Marv's twitch was lifting his entire lip, baring his upper teeth. He held the aircraft straight and level.

"Steady," Dominie said. "Three. Two. One ... "

Of the many ways a pilot orients his aircraft, one involves, literally, seat-of-the-pants flying. From his years in a Labrador helicopter, Randy Price was particularly sensitive to the messages sent by his seat: pitch, roll, yaw. In the Hercules, he could feel the exit of a single pair of jumpers. The plane told him when the jumpers left the aircraft; he felt it as a twitch in his buttocks. This time, as six jumpers left at once, he felt the Hercules sigh.

———

Arnie could see nothing from the open doorway. He felt the arms of his comrades being ripped away and felt the static line yank his chute open. He was torn by the roaring wind for a second, then became a part of the wind. He felt no cold. He saw nothing on the ground. He turned this way and that, but there was nothing in the eerie gloom. He was bathed in orange light from the fading flare. Ice crystals and fog streaked past his eyes.

He was down to 300 feet when he saw it heading his way through the icy mist. It was solid and dark. It rushed towards him; he fell towards it.

It was the tail of the Herc. They were on a collision course. Arnie pulled on his right toggle to steer his way past the flat of the tail.

The tail flashed past. Man, near miss. Arnie was reflecting on his good fortune and grabbing his capewell releases, to pop his parachute as soon as he landed, when his helmet was driven, as if by sledgehammer, into his face. He bounced; his parachute lifted him back up into the air as his body twisted behind the shroud lines. The first bounce carried him thirty yards, then he bounced again. He popped a capewell, and rolled to a stop. The parachute sighed, fluttering noisily in the gale.

Arnie lay spread-eagled on the snow. After a time he was able to draw air into his lungs, fighting the pain in his ribs. The survivors, for all he knew, were dead. His team was still in the air. For a moment, it felt as if he was the only human being at the Pole.

Then he looked up and saw the most beautiful sight. The second set of flares was pulsing against the base of the cloud. The outline of the Hercules was starkly drawn. Other jumpers, still airborne, were lined up in a row. He wished for a camera.

The jumpers passed a few feet overhead, then bounced. He heard their sudden anguish as the wind was knocked out of them. They were dragged at a terrific rate across the snow; the ground barely slowed them. Their parachutes sagged, and one by one they got to their feet.

Arnie looked towards the crash site behind him. Where was the downed airplane? He saw the overturned wing and thought it must have been the remains of the fuselage. The severed tail loomed in the orange murk. It was still; no one came out to greet them. With a sinking heart, Arnie realized they were all dead.

Marv, meanwhile, was putting distance between the jumpers and the coming flares. The more height and distance he could put between them, the safer they would be from burning magnesium. He thrust the four throttle levers full forward, reefed back the control yoke, and began a climb to the left. The Hercules heeled over at a 45-degree angle, and its nose heaved upwards.

The loadmasters in the back were not prepared for the manoeuvre. They knew Marv could really yank the Hercules around, but this was a muscular move even so. The loadmasters, Master Corporal Chuck Coutts and Master Corporal James Norris, were being helped with the gear by one of Arnie's SARtechs, Corporal Keith McKellar.

McKellar's nose was out of joint. He had trained as a medical assistant, but tired of pushing laundry carts; SARtech work gave him the satisfaction he'd sought in medicine. Now, though, at a time when he could have been saving souls, Dominie had awkwardly placed an arm around his shoulder: "Keith, I need somebody to stick around and help with the flares and kit. What do you think about that?"

"Goddamn you, Gerry," McKellar had told his higher rank. "You know damn well I want out of this airplane. But if you're looking for someone to stick around, I'll do it."

McKellar had been chosen for his physical conditioning and knowledge of the Hercules. Together with the heavyset Coutts, he was responsible for retrieving the deployment bags, which envelop the parachutes until the actual jump tears the bags off. There is a motorized cable for retrieving the static lines and bags; but the loadmasters wanted the cable available for the next jump, in case one of the parachutists got hung up. On this jump, they had to retrieve the six bags manually, yarding them in against the tremendous pull of the slipstream. In a normal procedure, the pilot waits for the loadmaster to say, "Bags in." Then, with the doors closed, he follows up by saying, "Clear to turn."

This was not a night for normal procedure.

Coutts had his hands on the static line when Marv banked the airplane sharply; McKellar was braced against the door. Behind them, Norris held a magnesium flare in his arms. He'd set the timer; the flare was armed. The cabin became a funhouse, the floor banking and the nose pitching up. McKellar had a foothold by the open door. The icy wind blasted him. He grabbed the lines, and heaved. He had one leg on either side of the open door of a pitching Hercules and he was yarding in cable with all his strength. Coutts, struggling to keep his balance, wrapped his arms around McKellar, grabbed the lines, and heaved also.

The bags were out the side of the aircraft, and had become wrapped around the high lobster tail of the Hercules. The climbing bank was working against them. Finally they got the bags through the doorway in a sudden rush, and McKellar and Coutts fell in a tangled heap to the floor. Norris stepped over them, the live flare tube in his arms, trying to brace himself.

McKellar was in Norris's way. He imagined Norris tripping over him, the timer winding down, the flare chute firing, the lanyard pulled, the spray of magnesium. He scrambled out of the way, ending up on top of Coutts.

Coutts grabbed McKellar by the hair, drawing him close and looking in his eyes. "Keith," he said tenderly. "I didn't know you felt this way."

Once the flares were out the door and ignited, Marv began flying a pattern for the delivery of the second stick of sARtechs, while waiting for word from the ground. They were less than thirty minutes from bingo fuel.

Marv recalled his argument with Arnie at Thule. Arnie had probably been among the first set of jumpers. Whatever had happened, had already happened. If Arnie was lying in a heap, his brains bashed out on a chunk of shale, well, he'd done his best for his big brother. He hadn't called a stop drop.

The radio was quiet. How it was quiet. Marv waited five agonizing minutes before he finally heard his brother's voice on the headset: "Rescue Three Zero Five."

Marv's nervous twitch ceased as abruptly as it had started.

"Nice soft landing," said Arnie. "Plenty of snow on the ground. Send down another five jumpers."

The cockpit crew looked at one another and started shouting and cheering like sophomores. Marv caught himself yelling, "Yahoo! Goddamn!"

Price transmitted the reply: "Good work, Arnie. Second stick on the way."

The sARtechs on the ground, all injured but none debilitated, watched the second stick of jumpers sail down towards them.

There were more minor injuries, but everybody was able to gather their chutes and join the first group of sartechs.

"Spread out," Arnie told them. "Get ready to receive the gear." He spoke into his hand radio: "Ready to receive supplies, Marv."

Marv was now less than twenty minutes from bingo fuel, and the weather conditions at Alert were iffy. He had less than twenty minutes to drop the supplies and attempt a landing in the heavy crosswinds at Alert. If he missed the approach, he might have enough fuel for one approach at Thule. He called over the intercom to the loadies and sartechs in the rear: "One pass. You've got thirty seconds to get everything out. Drop it all."

There was well over a ton of equipment in the back, tied down with restraining straps. Jim Norris went over the bundles, checking parachutes. Chuck Coutts grabbed a thick, razor-sharp cutaway knife; the other men heaved, and they emptied the guts of the Hercules in record time. Everything went out the tail: SAR toboggans, B-25 personal survival bundles, chainsaws, stretchers, penetration kits, camp kitchens, tents, stoves, heaters, food, water, blankets, fuel, medical toboggans. In a moment of unrestrained, Santa-like generosity, Coutts even slashed the straps of the SKAD kits – Sea Kits, Air Droppable – for saving ships in distress. He thought they might come in handy.

———————

On the ground, in the howling darkness, Arnie radioed the flight deck: "We're ready, Marv. Drop the supplies any time."

The weather had closed again. The sartechs on the ground hadn't seen a single bundle fall from the sky.

When told that the loads were already down, Arnie shouted at his men to fan out downwind. They needed a survival toboggan, but the canopy release mechanism on the SAR toboggans was a bad piece of kit; it released the canopy only when there was slack in the shroud lines. In this gale, the parachutes would not cut away; the toboggans would be pulled across the frozen ground at wind speed – forty knots.

Arnie squinted into the storm and caught the faint blinking of a strobe light. It was a survival toboggan, all right, but it was too far off, and travelling too fast, for him to reach. He shouted at one of the SARtechs who was closer: "Errr-ic! Toboggan!"

Corporal Eric Larouche sprinted in the direction his team leader had indicated. Larouche was twenty-eight years old, formerly an infantryman of the 22nd Regiment, and weighed 165 pounds. Despite whiplash and a sprained back from the jump, he was fit in body and possessed an intrepid spirit; but he did not have any firm idea of how he was going to stop a 300-pound steel toboggan being towed towards him by a thirty-two-foot canopy across snow and ice at highway speed in the dark.

Perhaps he could get in front of it and grab the canopy by its nose. As the toboggan sailed past, the canopy would point into the wind and deflate. That was the theory, anyway. On the other hand, the parachute might rip from his hands, or he might not be able to grab it in time, or he might approach it from the side. In that case, Larouche thought he might leap onto the toboggan, rather like trying to mount a runaway horse. He had no idea what he would do after that. He would ride the toboggan and see what came next.

The strobe light had died, the flares had died, and Eric Larouche found himself running blind in a storm after a rogue toboggan. He heard the sound of panting above his own. He saw the white flank come heaving out of darkness, saw the flank rise and fall with its panting breath. Terrified, he spun on his heels and took off in the opposite direction.

"Bear!" he shouted.

Arnie noticed the beam from Larouche's miner's lamp bobbing towards him.

"What?"

"Polar bear! It's after me!"

Shit, Arnie thought. The rifles are all in the rescue toboggans. He took off with Eric. They ran for their lives, side by side, past the other SARtechs, who looked on in astonishment.

"Bear! Run!"

The SARtechs all sprinted away from the crash site, away from the bear. But they didn't run fast enough. Arnie saw it first, heard steel hissing against snow, saw the white nylon canopy swell and fall in the wind. The toboggan raced past and disappeared into the darkness, never to be seen again. Larouche collapsed, catching his breath.

Arnie stopped, too, panting. We're shit out of luck, he thought. We've got nothing but the clothes on our backs. Our personal medical kits are frozen. We've become eleven more survivors somebody has to bail out.

"Way to go, Eric," said Arnie.

The other SARtechs realized what had happened. Eric had thought the billowing chute of the toboggan was a polar bear.

"Right. Way to go, Bearic!"

"Yo, Bearic!"

The SARtechs waved their arms and pretended they were bears rampant. They lumbered menacingly towards Larouche. They growled and romped on the snow in a howling storm, dancing bears in orange jumpsuits.

"Hey, Bearic! Run!"

"I'm going to eat you, Bearic!"

"Woof, woof! Roaaar!"

It was 66 below and they were a bunch of guys on top of the world.

240

CHAPTER TWENTY-ONE

The Nick of Time

B LACK," said one of the SARtechs. Code for dead. "Another one. Another black."

The tail, Arnie thought. The others must have gone inside the tail and died there. He made for the tail section, hunched against the storm, calling: "Hello? Hello?"

The wind was in his face; there were no voices on the wind. He reached the entrance of the tail and shouted: "Anybody in there?"

Aw, shit. After all this.

"Hey! Anybody hear me?"

"Ahhss."

Was that a noise? It sounded like something between a hiss and a moan.

"Anybody here?"

The voice, struggling with the word "Yes," would have alarmed a less composed man. It was an old voice, thickened almost beyond recognition by pain and cold.

"How many? How many are you?"

"Leven."

Eleven. That's what he'd said. Hot dog! Arnie felt something marvellous. He tried to focus on the feeling, pin it down. It was joy.

"In here, boys! Let's go!"

Arnie told his men to rig chutes over the opening. He stepped inside. He stepped on someone, who moaned in agony. He cast the beam from his headlamp around the tail, lighting walls thick with ice and a huddled mass of humanity, filthy and black. They looked like rats in a stinking hold. The tail smelled of burnt things, fuel, and urine. It smelled like a crash site. It smelled wonderful.

One of Arnie's SARtechs stepped in beside him.

"Careful," Arnie said. "The floor's alive."

There was a shuffling movement. Someone said something. "Who's that?"

One of the figures lifted its head. Arnie shone his light. The man's face was streaked and grimy, the skin beneath the smudges white as snow. The lips were grey, or blue. The man looked like the risen dead.

"Smee."

"Jesus. I know you."

Paul West's ghastly face blinked in the beam of light. "Whos air?"

"I'm Arnie Macauley. I'm the SARtech leader from Green-wood. And these are my boys."

Other survivors were beginning to come around; cutting the wind from the tail was already having an effect. So was the human presence. The SARtechs heard curious, nonsensical mumbles. They moved carefully about the tail and went gently to work. They spoke to the survivors and listened to them babble on, in voices thick and slow.

One of the SARtechs pulled a pair of mittens over the hands of a survivor. "It would be a privilege for me to give you these," he said, with odd formality. "My mother made them for me."

Many of the survivors, returning to themselves, began to cry uncontrollably. Many of the SARtechs, without ceasing to work, cried with them, wrapping them in parachutes. Every survivor was in the severe, final stage of hypothermia, perched on the thin ledge between stupor and death. Methodically, expertly, the sARtechs went about the delicate task of helping them off that ledge.

Joe had met so many nice people in the white room, people he had longed to see. Sometimes a person would come into the room that he didn't want to see, and Joe could make the person go away. Then a man came into the room dressed in an orange coverall, with a bright eye in the middle of his forehead. Joe wished him to go away, but the man remained.

The man was tucking something around him. Joe resisted, but then something shifted in his mind and he recognized the orange jumpsuit as that of a sARtech, the glowing eye as a lamp. So that was it. He had been rescued.

He received his deliverance with the same detached interest he'd had in his imminent death.

There were hands on her, soft fabric being tucked around her chin. Wilma felt she was being cared for, and nothing else mattered. Of all the balm to follow – the warmth, the morphine, the hot water, the Magic Pantry dinner or the Hershey chocolate bars – none was worth as much as that first human touch.

sARtechs are well aware of the importance of this touch and are as gentle in their way as lovers. They know the profound release that follows on rescue, and describe it as rescue shock; many souls have been lost at this point. Like all matters of desolation and love, rescue is a delicate business.

Wilma could not relax; there was something on her mind, struggling to get out: the others.

"The others. In the snow."

More voices joined in, slurred voices that sounded drugged and surreal: Yes. The others. Get the others.

Arnie worked his way over to Paul West's feet, then slid up beside him. Paul seemed to be the only lucid one.

"There's two blacks out there," Arnie said quietly. "Is that who they mean?"

"Smore. Twomore."

West gave directions as best he could, and Arnie sent a detail to search the snow.

"You did good, Paul."

West tried to smile, but couldn't. He tried to shake his head, but couldn't. He tried to whistle, but couldn't. He tried to speak, and what came out might have been, "Nick of time, boys. Nick of time."

———————————

Smokey Blair was at home in Edmonton, sleeping, when the phone rang. It was Friday night. He had last slept on Tuesday night.

"RCC, sir," said the duty officer.

"Yeah?" said Blair groggily. "What is it?"

"Message from the command post at Alert, sir. Alert advises at zero five fifty-five Zulu that six SARtechs from Rescue Three Zero Five have penetrated crash site."

Someone in the bedroom was making a lot of noise. Blair realized he was making the noise. He was screaming. He took a moment to get a grip.

Five fifty-five Zulu was five minutes to one in the morning at Alert. The survivors had been on the ground thirty-two hours and thirty minutes.

"Sir?" the duty officer asked.

"What's the status of our helo resources?"

The duty officer explained that Rescue 315, the 424 Squadron Labrador helicopter, had reached Ellesmere Island from Trenton. It was en route from Grise Fjord to Eureka. The American c-5 Galaxy had unloaded the two Pavehawk helicopters at Thule, and they were preparing for departure to Alert in a few hours. The Edmonton Twin Huey helicopter had just arrived at Alert, in the belly of the Hercules, and they would start assembly any minute.

"Get a helicopter in there," Blair said. "Keep the MAJAID Herc on stand-by. Find out the status of the ground search party. And see if we can get more jumpers down."

Blair dressed and headed back to work. Wonderful news, better than he could have hoped for. But they weren't out of the woods yet.

After dropping Arnie's SARtechs and the supplies, Marv made Alert on his first approach and landed on bingo fuel. The propellers of his Hercules had not wound down when the SAR doors opened and the three remaining SARtechs on board sprinted across the tarmac through the storm, carrying their parachutes. They were running towards the Edmonton Hercules under the command of Major Jim Burger.

Burger was warming up for takeoff, with the other half of Fred Ritchie's SARtechs on board. They were under the stern command of – well, Jim Brown was the team leader. The Greenwood SARtechs piled in with the Edmonton team.

"Thought you might need a hand," said Gerry Dominie. "We did a thirty-second count from a thousand feet. The boys damn near hit the tail."

The Edmonton Hercules took off and set up an orbit around

245

the crash site. The jumpmaster led the same recital Arnie had given his men.

Jim Brown could see the man's lips moving. Earphone cords snaked up underneath his "Explosive" helmet and into his ears. If you got close enough, you could hear the tinny beat, even over the racket of the Hercules. He had a Walkman in his pocket.

It was clear what the man was saying. He was saying this is the end. He was saying desperately in need of some stranger's hand, in a desperate land. He was saying riders on the storm. He was saying the snake is old, its skin is cold.

He said ride the snake.

Brown clicked off the cassette, ending the Doors concert. He said to the jumpmaster, "Let's do some work."

There was some dispute, later on, as to how low the Hercules was to the ground when Jim Brown led his men out the door. Certainly lower than Arnie's jump had been. The most experienced SARtech on the deployment estimated their height at 500 feet; consulting maps, Arnie later calculated 400 feet. One-fifth the minimum for a night jump. There is also some dispute as to where they landed. It was somewhere far from the crash site.

The men left the door in such a tight bundle that Gerry Dominie nearly collided with another SARtech, Keith McKellar. He was close enough to shout, "Turn off!" Despite the roaring wind, McKellar heard him. Dominie was close enough that he could see McKellar's face. Dominie turned into the wind; McKellar ran with it.

Both men thought they had collided with each other when they hit the ground. McKellar, who whacked the frozen terrain at forty-five knots, thought he had collided with Dominie because he never felt his feet touch the ground. He felt only the emergency chute on his chest cracking his ribs, and his helmet being driven into the bridge of his nose. Then he felt himself take off across the snow. He had no idea how long he'd been dragged along when he finally managed to pop his capewells.

He didn't get up right away. Dominie came over to him.

"Hey, buddy, you all right?"

McKellar rolled over on his back, groaning. "Fuck," he said through the pain of broken ribs. "Isn't this exciting?"

Getting to his feet, McKellar said he thought his ribs were cracked. Dominie said that was too bad. As they carried the parachute bundles between them, McKellar nearly fainted. He asked Dominie to switch sides. He felt better after that.

Everybody was banged up. The team got together and agreed they had no idea where they were. Jim Brown had an idea. He used musk-ox logic.

"Everybody stand in a circle, facing out," he said. "I'll call down a flare."

He reached the Hercules on his radio, and the aircraft dropped a flare.

"I see it!" said a SARtech on one side of the circle.

"I see it!" said a SARtech on the other side.

Some weird kind of polar illusion? What had happened, in fact, was that Fred Ritchie's ground party had sent up a flare at the same time that the Hercules had dropped one. Brown was stumped.

"Let's forget that happened," he said, and called for another flare.

The team broke into twos and began to leapfrog their way towards the crash site. The first pair would get about twenty paces ahead of the others, and be lost from sight. The third pair would then overtake the first, and so on. The system was hopeless. They asked constantly for flare correction. When a flare was dropped, they tried to get in a straight line. Dominie peered ahead at Brown.

"Okay!" he shouted. "Stop moving!"

"I'm not moving," said Brown.

One of the SARtechs saw a flash of white at the edge of the gloom. It scared him.

"Jesus Christ! A polar bear!"

Too small for a bear. But something.

Joe Bales had recovered enough to sit up. He had a parachute bundled around him. Arnie kneeled beside him, pressing his ear to Bales' lips, and followed Bales' pointing finger. The poor man was white as a ghost. He was desperate. You could tell he was being as purposeful as he could be.

"Air," Bales said. "By him."

"That one?" asked Arnie, pointing to a headlamp.

"Him. His right."

Arnie left Joe to rest and went over to the SARtech. "The co-pilot says they're around here somewhere. He says they were alive a few hours ago."

The SARtech looked at him sceptically. "I've been over this stretch a hundred times, hollering."

"Go over it a hundred more," said Arnie.

Bob and Sue were shouting in their tombs. Both had heard strange voices and started to call out at once. Each was surprised to realize that the other was alive.

"Here!" they called. "We're aliiii!"

One of the search party thought he heard something. He walked downwind.

"Where are you?" he hollered into the wind.

"Here! We're here!"

The SARtech walked about in the storm, seeing nothing but

crusted snow and rock. He passed within a few feet of them more than once.

"I can't see you! Where are you?"

Bob still had his one good hand. He closed it around his little metal spar. He still had one good hand and a metal spar. He tried to poke at the tarpaulin.

The SARtech thought he saw something move under the snow.

―――――――

Arnie saw the lights of Fred's Go-Track rising up the hill towards them. He sent a SARtech over to stop them at the perimeter. "Walk them in here. We don't want them driving over any bodies."

Arnie was deeply satisfied. Now they'd have heat, light, and shelter. Fred had rescued him.

When the tractors were still about a hundred yards away, Arnie ran over at a trot. Fred piled out the passenger door of the Go-Track.

They regarded each other.

Arnie had this loopy smile, but he didn't know what to say. He turned and waved towards the tail.

"We could use a windbreak, Fred."

"Arnie."

Fred held out his hand. Arnie shook it. Then they wrapped their arms around each other.

"Hell of a place for old friends to meet."

―――――――

Mike Kobayashi, one of Fred's SARtechs, scrambled out of the Go-Track; he wanted to walk in on his own. He let the vehicles pull away, then started towards the crash site.

He could see the tail rising above him, in stark silhouette against the pulsing backdrop of orange light. Figures moved about busily, methodically, eerily lit. It was silent, except for the rush of the wind.

He caught a shimmer out the corner of his eye; he turned slowly, not knowing what to expect. He'd thought he was alone.

The wolf regarded him for a few moments. Then it turned, trotting, and vanished.

———

At the station in Alert, the airframe crew from 408 Squadron guided the stripped-down Twin Huey from the tail ramp of the Hercules that had flown it up from Edmonton. They pushed it, on its rickety trolley, to the battery maintenance shed. It was a tight fit. They had four inches clearance on either side.

The shed was equipped with a single overhead crane and a furnace. Everything else needed to assemble an aircraft they had brought with them. When the doors of the shed opened, it took thirty seconds for flesh to freeze to metal. It took a half-hour to warm the place up again. The door had to be opened frequently, to move the helicopter around.

They were five men and one woman. The lead airframe technician, Sergeant Terry Sheppard, asked the crew if they wanted to start work right away or sleep first. Corporal Dave Gunn spoke for them all: "They're out there in the cold, and they're hurt. We're in here, warm and fine. Let's do it, boss."

They started to build the aircraft at two o'clock in the morning. In Edmonton, it had taken a crew of sixteen people with heavy equipment eight hours to take it apart. In a battery shed in Alert, it took a team of six, poorly equipped, five hours to put it back together.

They worked like fiends. They installed the right and left

cyclic control tubes. They replaced the cowlings over the transmission and both engine inlets. They rewired three sets of antennae. They installed the right and left elevators. They attached the tail rotor. They dropped the main motor mast into the transmission. They placed the two rotor blades back into the hub assembly, lifted the main rotor on top of the mast, rebuilt the main rotor assembly. They replaced the stabilizer bars. When they had rebuilt the helicopter from the engine up, they tightened the rotor to the mast. The blades of a helicopter are attached to the rotor hub with a single lock pin. The hub, in turn, is fastened to the transmission – to the airframe, in fact – with a single, crucial nut. It is called the Jesus nut, for various reasons.

They improvised. They didn't have the precision jig for dropping the blades into the hub, so they put the hub on a mattress and manhandled the blades into place. Each blade is sixteen feet long and weighs 230 pounds. The blade is held in place with a restraining bolt tooled to a fine tolerance. The alignment is difficult, even with a precision jig. They got it right, first time, on both blades.

They worked up a sweat. The hub and rotor assembly weighs 760 pounds, and the overhead crane didn't move from side to side. They couldn't line the Huey up underneath it, so they muscled the rotor. They filled it with fuel and called over the test pilot. They were ready for another sixteen hours' work, because a Huey never flies right the first time after a re-assembly. It needs to be fine-tuned, flown hard, and fine-tuned again. Never in Sheppard's experience had it flown right the first time.

The test pilot gave it a shake-down flight around the airfield. He took it out over the bay. He came back and reported, "Smooth as silk." It was within the vibration tolerances. They could start the evacuation of survivors as soon as the helicopter was loaded with flares and aircrew.

Sheppard was floored. It had never happened before, let alone with an airframe exposed to that kind of vibration, knocking about, and temperature changes. It had been rush-loaded and flown through turbulence. It had been pulled out of the Hercules on a rickety trolley pulled by a four-by-four truck with a cantankerous clutch. It had been slammed together. They had put the blades together on a mattress.

One of Sheppard's mechanics came over, grinning. "What was it, boss? Was it the extreme cold? How the hell could it fly like that, first time out?"

Sheppard looked at the young fellow. A man doesn't easily speak of such things, but Sheppard didn't hesitate. "I have no doubt what it was. In my personal opinion, it was a higher power."

————————

From the Labrador helicopter that had not been shut down since leaving Trenton, 3,600 miles and thirty-seven hours earlier, Mark Levesque spotted the lights of Eureka. Last stop before Alert.

The latest leg had contained no more than the usual store of horrors. The top-cover Aurora had left them in Grise Fjord, to fly south for fuel. The Labrador's crew had tired of waiting and decided to strike off on their own.

They were going to zigzag up the island in two final strides. From Grise Fjord to Eureka was 180 miles; from Eureka to Alert was another 240 miles. They looked at the charts. Southern Ellesmere Island was all fjords and mountains. Fine. They'd bound over mountains and dive through fjords.

They got a little lost. The wind blew them seventy nautical miles off course, and they didn't know it. Right about when their calculations told them they were in a sea-level fjord, somebody saw a 6,700-foot mountain peak looming like a shadow. They climbed hastily to 7,700 feet and kept the peak on their right side.

The Aurora returned and picked them up forty miles out of Eureka, giving them a steer. They landed at the small weather station, which had a fuel cache but no pump. The flight engineer broke out the hand pump and started pumping from the barrels with the engine still firing. Levesque got out and walked around. His legs were wobbly. The Labrador had been airborne for thirty-seven hours, and he'd been at the controls for too many of them.

He watched the engineer work. The manual pump was spraying aviation fuel over his hands, chest, and face. The man worked on regardless. Figure it out, Levesque thought. They've got more energy now than when we left. They're happy when they should be miserable, happier than they would be at home in their beds. Figure it out.

Levesque wobbled into the Eureka weather station and raised rescue control. He was now three hours away from Alert. He was advised that sartechs had penetrated the crash site, that the Twin Huey was flightworthy, and that he and his crew would not be needed for the rescue.

Levesque replaced the handset. He felt tired. He felt happy and sad, in a goofy sort of way.

———

Jim Brown poked around the crash site, looking at all the stuff. The snow was littered with stuff, mostly burnt stuff. He went over to a big drum and looked inside. A few hundred gallons of diesel fuel were in there. Hadn't they built a fire?

Brown was getting cold, waiting for the helicopter to come and take them out. He threw a match in the drum. It didn't catch. So he got a canister of naphtha gas from the fuel stoves and poured that in. He threw another match inside.

He backed up a hundred feet or so, in a hurry.

Fred Ritchie hurried out and looked at the flames licking the

Arctic sky. The fire seemed to have answered the wind. The storm was lifting; the weather was clearing; the winds were dying down.

Fred said to Jim Brown, "You're a crazy bugger. Know that?"

———————

The survivors were evacuated by Twin Huey. The pair of American Pavehawk helicopters arrived in time to take out the SARtechs and the bodies of the five dead. Alert became a busy place. The survivors were taken to the cafeteria, which had been partially given over to an infirmary.

Steven Cann and the other Go-Track drivers were working up something of a party at their barracks, the Monster House. Arnie and the SARtechs intended to go over; they figured they had earned a night of drinking beer and talking big. First they stopped at the warrants' and sergeants' mess for a bite to eat. The SARtechs had a boisterous table of their own. Jim Brown walked in carrying a fire extinguisher. He explained it away with some story about seeing a wolf outside. There were a lot of junior ranks around; no one was enforcing the rules.

One of the American para-rescue specialists walked over to the SARtech table. Arnie looked him up and down, admiring the man's equipment. He, too, was tall and well-built.

"You the guys that jumped in there?" the American asked.

"We are," said Arnie.

"You must be frigging crazy."

"No," said Arnie. "We're Canadians."

In the cafeteria, meanwhile, the survivors were receiving treatment and waiting for the Herkie birds to take them home. A full medical team was busily doing what they could when word came that the first evacuation flight to Thule was ready to go. For the first time since the crash, the survivors would be separated.

Wilma was laid out on her trestle in the cafeteria, thinking to

George. She was telling him the story, in her mind. She looked around and counted. Thirteen. There were thirteen survivors, and they were all in the same room, all together for the last time. Sue and Bob had finally come in from the cold.

Then she noticed Bill Vance. Sweet Bill, who had rested his head in her lap. He had always been eager to keep the roll call going, even after the spirits of the others had waned. They had him wrapped in an insulating blanket with an aluminum coating. He looked like he was wrapped in tin foil.

"Hey Bill, what are they doing? Getting you ready for the oven?"

"Not comblaining," he said with a smile.

The medical assistants stepped in. It was time for him to go.

"Wade a minute," he said, and they stopped. "Hey, Wilma. You going to start with me?"

Wilma didn't understand at first, but Paul West did: "Call roll, Wilma."

A few of the other attendants stopped what they were doing and waited. Wilma found she had to clear her throat. She ran through all the names in her mind – the first set of four, the second set of four, and then the flight crew, leaving off one name, poor John. Then adding the two who had been outside, Sue and Bob. Thirteen names. Precisely.

"Bill," she began, but her voice was unsteady and didn't carry over the background hubbub of the cafeteria. As she composed herself, people began shushing one another, raising fingers to lips. Word spread from one person to the next, rippling out across the room, until the whole cafeteria had fallen silent.

"Bill," said Wilma, in a clear, strong voice.

"Here," said Bill.

Epilogue

O N MARCH 19, 1992, the commander of the Canadian Forces Air Command, Lieutenant-General Dick Huddleston, told a news conference at Air Command in Winnipeg that a number of changes were planned as a result of the crash of Box Top 22. More survival gear kits would be placed on transport aircraft, and they would be clearly marked with reflective tape. The Air Command was considering the obvious expedient of placing the equipment in the tail, although there were concerns that this would affect the aircraft's weight and balance.

SARtechs would receive ten global positioning units. The first of the new square-canopy chutes, twelve years in the waiting, were due to arrive in May. They would be issued to SARtech parachute instructors first.

The military was also considering the purchase of new Arctic sleeping bags that could be opened, unlike the mummy-style bags. Testing is to start in the winter of 1992-93 at the Arctic survival school in Resolute, Northwest Territories.

The syllabus for the Hercules flight course was being revised, with greater emphasis on cockpit communications and teamwork. Aircrews were to receive more Arctic survival training. The military also committed itself to improving the experience level on Hercules flight decks.

The Air Force has started a search for a better parachute for dropping survival gear in high winds. Delivery of a parachute with a canopy release mechanism that actually works is expected to take about five years.

Many recommendations have been submitted, at the time of writing, for decorations for valour and bravery. It is expected that the rescue of Box Top 22 will be the most heavily decorated mission in Canadian peacetime history.

Mark Levesque's Labrador flew one hundred hours before it finally conked out. It's probably some kind of record. The directional gyro has now been fixed.

The SARtechs had their party at the Monster House. It was rare for so many to get together at once, rarer still for them to be in such high spirits. They drank and danced and told one another they were heroes. Then they returned to their unheralded jobs. Fred Ritchie was carried from the party in a Stokes litter. The next day, standing ramrod-straight in his dress blues, he gave a news conference in Edmonton.

The Honda marine pump hasn't yet been returned to the Coast Guard. Arnie Macauley had his hopes up for a pair of night vision goggles, but there won't be any under the tree this year.

Fred and Arnie were both promoted, whether because of the way they handled the rescue or in spite of it. Both are now master warrant officers. Both have been transferred: Fred to Air Command Headquarters in Winnipeg, and Arnie to Air Transport Group Headquarters in Trenton. They initially resisted the notion of accepting jobs of greater responsibility, because of the reduced fieldwork. Both bowed to the inevitable. In the spring of 1992, they celebrated their friendship with an assault on the 19,500-foot summit of Mount Logan in Yukon.

Marv Macauley and Jim Burger returned to their regular flying duties. Marv made it through the season without getting thrown off the Greenwood SARtech hockey team. At last sighting, he had just returned from a mid-Atlantic rescue operation. He was in the pilots' debriefing room, dressed in his hockey sweater.

Among the SARtechs, Arnie had the final word on the rescue. One night, shortly after their audacious work at the North Pole had earned its brief moment in the world's media spotlight, Arnie and Fred were being interviewed by a reporter at Fred's home. They sat over coffee at Fred's kitchen table. They spent many hours explaining what had happened.

Towards the end of the interview, the reporter asked what a SARtech does to relieve the tension after such a mission.

Drink beer, Arnie thought; but he decided that it wouldn't look good for the Canadian Forces. Fred thought of something that couldn't be printed in a family newspaper.

But what about the post-stress debriefings, the reporter insisted. Surely, SARtechs must have difficulty dealing with the traumas they face. Do they ever need professional help?

Arnie had, that same day, sent one of his men to the base counsellor because the man had taken the death of John Couch so badly. Arnie had recently lost another member of his team to suicide. But he didn't think he should mention either incident.

Well, the reporter finally asked, what about your dreams? Do SARtechs have nightmares after such an exploit? Arnie looked incredulously at the persistent reporter.

"SARtechs don't dream," he said.

All the survivors of Box Top 22 have recovered at least partially and returned to their lives. The severe cold they endured proved both a blessing and a curse. Most of their grotesque lacerations and burns healed rapidly and well, the result of an aseptic environment and excellent medical care. The eyesight of Private Bill Vance returned, once his facial burns were treated. Master

Seaman Douglas Montgomery fully regained his senses. And Michael Moore's burned face also healed well.

The cold injuries were another matter. Although the SARtechs were commended by base surgeons for their treatment of hypothermia and frostbite, the ravages of the cold had already registered. Frostbite injuries heal slowly, when they heal at all; and the patient suffers the same agonies as a burn victim. Months after the accident, some of the passengers were still in the long recovery from frostbite. Although some required surgery, all the military passengers expected to return to their old duties eventually. They were exempted from further service at Alert.

The surviving flight crew members of Box Top 22 returned to their former duties, except for Sergeant Paul West. He took a planned retirement from the military to work in commercial aviation.

A memorial service with full military honours for the deceased was held at the Kapyong drill hall at the Canadian Forces base in Edmonton, attended by the Chief of Defence Staff, General A.J.G.D. de Chastelain. The padre prayed for the Lord's keeping, "until that day comes when we shall no longer be alone, or in darkness, or in pain."

Wilma de Groot now practises medicine at the Canadian Forces base in Trenton. She spends long periods of time away from George, but he somehow manages to stay in touch. The night of the crash, he dreamed of her. When he reached out to her, she said, "I'm okay. Leave me alone. I have a lot of work to do." Although he did not communicate with her again until after the rescue, he had been alerted to her plight by her brother, Peter, who was in British Columbia at the time of the crash. He telephoned George, who was desperate at his inability to touch her mind, and said: "She's alive. She's broken her ankle and she's in pain. But she's alive." Peter had no way of knowing this by any scientifically valid means.

Shortly after that phone call, George felt Wilma's reassuring presence; a few hours after that, the padre telephoned to say that she had been rescued.

Bob Thomson's wife, Elaine, had a similar experience. She was speaking with the wife of Tom Jardine, who did not yet know she was a widow, but who told Elaine unequivocally: "Bob's alive. The two civilians are outside, in the snow. Either he can't walk or he can't feel his legs. But he's alive."

Bob spent six months in a rehabilitation centre in Ottawa following the confirmation of paralysis and the amputation of his right leg below the knee. He has regained partial muscle control in the amputated leg and, at the time of writing, had learned to crawl. His experience has robbed him neither of his indomitable spirit nor of his gentle nature. Elaine had already prepared their house for his homecoming. She rejected his suggestion that she leave him, and she is making plans for their continued enjoyment of the outdoors.

Sue Hillier's mother, Marg, also had an inexplicable experience. She had been sipping cold coffee in the kitchen, where she had resisted her temptation to tell Susan about an old woman's foolish dream, when Sue's sister, Sandra, dropped a cup, then said: "She's not dead. She's still alive." Sandra's children, who were five and three years old, came into the kitchen and, out of the blue, asked the adults why their Auntie Susan was sleeping in the snow.

Sue bounced back rapidly from her injuries and regained her spirits and vivaciousness. The lingering pain of frostbite, however, has prevented her from returning to her work as a hairdresser.

She thinks often of the wolf. Bob Thomson never actually saw it, and neither did he hear Sue screaming, but he was communing at the time with Buddy. There are many ways to consider the wolf. The Inuit have wise elders; perhaps a shaman paid a visit, although he would have had to have been very strong, to travel so far and to take the form of a wolf. Perhaps it was a dream. Perhaps it was death come calling, then deciding not to take her. Perhaps it was merely a wolf, drawn by curiosity or the scent of blood.

Sue was able to describe the wolf vividly; she recognized its markings instantly. She had a dog, a husky, whose coat was black with a white flash. The wolf was white with a black flash. Both animals had unusual eyes. Sue's husky had brown eyes, translucent as a wolf's; the wolf had the blue eyes of a husky. Sue's husky and the wolf were positive and negative images of each other.

Sue had no way of knowing it at the time, but her dog happened to experience great distress while she was away. It suffered kidney failure, and died at about the same time that she saw the wolf.

Her dog's name was Angel.

Appendix

People and Resources

Listed here are the names of some of the people who played a significant role in the flight, crash, and rescue of Box Top 22. It is only a partial list; the rescue involved hundreds of personnel at many air bases. The list of participating aircraft is complete.

SURVIVORS

Robert Thomson, CANEX manager
CFB Trenton

Susan Hillier, hair stylist
Trenton

Captain Richard Dumoulin, logistics officer
Canadian Forces Communications Command, Ottawa

Captain Wilma de Groot, physician
CFB Trenton

Lieutenant Joe Bales, first officer
435 Transport Squadron, CFB Edmonton

Lieutenant Michael Moore, navigator
435 Transport Squadron, CFB Edmonton

Master Warrant Officer Marc Tremblay, supply technician
Canadian Forces Communications Command, Ottawa

Sergeant Paul West, flight engineer
435 Transport Squadron, CFB Edmonton

Master Corporal Tony Cobden, communications researcher
770 Communications Research Squadron, CFB Gander

Master Corporal David Meace, radio technician
1 Canadian Division Headquarters and Signal Regiment,
CFB Kingston

Master Corporal Mario Ellefsen, communications researcher
CFS Leitrim

Master Seaman Douglas Montgomery,
communications researcher
CFS Leitrim

Private Bill Vance, communications researcher
CFS Leitrim

DECEASED

Captain John Couch, aircraft commander
435 Transport Squadron, CFB Edmonton

Captain Judy Trépanier, logistics officer
Canadian Forces Communications Command, Ottawa

Master Warrant Officer Tom Jardine,
CANEX regional services manager
CFB Trenton

Warrant Officer Robert Grimsley, supply technician
Canadian Forces Communications Command, Ottawa

Master Corporal Roland Pitre, loadmaster/traffic technician
435 Transport Squadron, CFB Edmonton

RESCUERS

405 Squadron Greenwood
Aircrew
Rescue 104
CP-140 Aurora
(Top cover for Rescue 315)
   Major William Norman Ricketts
   Captain Kevin Eric Anderson
   Captain Maurizio Braggio

Captain Nigel George Jackson
Captain Scott Cameron Latter
Captain Patrick Spiteri
Captain Kevin Stuart Thurston
Warrant Officer Joseph Guy Michel Richer-Lafleche
Sergeant Robert Alan Whitwell

408 Squadron Edmonton
Airframe crew
CH-135 Twin Huey
(Reassembled helicopter)
　　Sergeant Terry Sheppard
　　Private Jim Gilmour
　　Master Corporal Mary Smith
　　Master Corporal Dave Perrin
　　Corporal Tom Ortiz
　　Corporal Claude Dallaire
　　Corporal Dave Gunn

413 Squadron Greenwood
Flight crew
Rescue 305
CC-130 Hercules
(Top Cover/SARtech drop)
　　Major Marvin Macauley
　　Captain Marc Favre
　　Captain Randy Price
　　Sergeant William Sura
　　Master Corporal Chuck Coutts
　　Master Corporal James Norris

SARtechs
Warrant Officer Arnold Macauley, M.B.

Sergeant Gerry Dominie
Master Corporal Bruce Best
Master Corporal Alain Houle
Master Corporal Robert Mondeville
Master Corporal Jean Tremblay, M.B.
Master Corporal Robert Walker
Corporal Derek Curtis
Corporal Benjamin House
Corporal Eric Larouche
Corporal Marc Lessard
Corporal Keith McKellar
Corporal Ronald O'Reilly
Corporal Jean Roy

424 Squadron Trenton
Flight crew
Rescue 315
CH-113 Labrador
(Trenton-Alert)
   Aircraft Commanders:
   Captain Pierre Bolduc
   Captain Mark Levesque
   Captain Don Paul

   First Officers:
   Captain Steve Parry
   Captain Doug Roddick
   Lieutenant Chris Brown

   Flight Engineers:
   Sergeant Chuck Mearns
   Master Corporal Greg Forsyth
   Master Corporal Dan L'italien

SARtechs
  Sergeant John Carriere
  Master Corporal Paul Aitcheson
  Master Corporal Al Bevan
  Corporal Sid Drover
  Corporal Brian Weir

Flight crew
Rescue 342
CC-130 Hercules
(Top Cover/SARtech drop)
  First rotation:
  Major James Burger
  Major Daryl McBain
  Lieutenant Derek Stobbs
  Warrant Officer Wally Bélanger
  Master Corporal Bob Andrews

  Second rotation:
  Captain Duane Malone
  Captain Eric Volstad
  Lieutenant Darwin Ziprick
  Master Warrant Officer Frank MacNeil
  Master Warrant Officer Geoff Williams

440 Squadron Edmonton
SARtechs
  Warrant Officer Fred Ritchie
  Sergeant Ron Burke
  Sergeant Tom Elliott
  Master Corporal Jim Brown
  Master Corporal Yves Carignan
  Master Corporal Ron Condly

Master Corporal Tim Eagle
Master Corporal Mike Kobayashi
Corporal Darren Darbyson
Corporal Emilio Dechantal
Corporal Shawn MacDiarmid
Corporal Rick Peck

CFS *Alert*
Go-Track Drivers
   Master Corporal J.J. Dewolfe
   Master Corporal R.J. Fixter
   Master Corporal D.A. Getz
   Corporal S.L. Cann
   Corporal J.G.S. Grégoire

AIRCRAFT

Canadian (Military)

Unit	Squadron	Role	Hours
Rescue 104 CP-140 Aurora	415 Sqn Greenwood	Top cover for Labradors	23.3
Rescue 112 CP-140 Aurora	405 Sqn Greenwood	Top cover for Labradors	23.9
Rescue 113 CP-140 Aurora	415 Sqn Greenwood	Top cover for Labradors	22.1

Rescue 132 CH-135 Twin Huey (transported by Rescue 311)	408 Sqn Edmonton	Medevac Crash site–Alert	3.4
Rescue 301 CH-113 Labrador	103 RU Gander	SAR as far as Iqaluit	28.1
Rescue 304 CH-113 Labrador	413 Sqn Greenwood	SAR Turned back	1
Rescue 305 CC-130 Hercules	413 Sqn Greenwood	SAR Macauley SARtechs	30.7
Rescue 311 CC-130 Hercules	435 Sqn Edmonton	Transported Rescue 132 Edmonton–Alert	17.9
Rescue 315 CH-113 Labrador	424 Sqn Trenton	SAR Trenton–Alert	97.9
Rescue 321 CC-130 Hercules	429 Sqn Trenton	Medevac	5
Rescue 324 CC-130 Hercules	436 Sqn Trenton	SAR/Medevac	15.8
Rescue 327 CC-130 Hercules	429 Sqn Trenton	Airlift	17.3
Rescue 328 CC-130 Hercules	429 Sqn Trenton	Airlift	8.2

Rescue 338	435 Sqn Edmonton	MAJAID/	21.9
CC-130 Hercules		Paratroops	
Rescue 341	436 Sqn Trenton	Airlift	24.5
CC-130 Hercules			
Rescue 342	435 Sqn Edmonton	SAR	53
CC-130 Hercules		Ritchie SARtechs	
Rescue 452	442 Sqn Comox	Top cover/	14.5
CC-115 Buffalo		SAR standby	
Rescue 613	412 Sqn Ottawa	Medevac	9.8
CC-144 Challenger		from Thule	
Rescue 614	412 Sqn Ottawa	Medevac	24.2
CC-144 Challenger		from Thule	

Canadian Military Total: 19 aircraft 442.5 hours

Canadian (Civilian)

Bell 212	Greenland Charter	SAR	1.3
	Air Services	Turned back	
De Havilland	Bradley Air Services	RCMP/Coroner	9.3
DH-6			

Canadian Civilian Total: 2 aircraft 10.6 hours

United States Air Force

82102 KC-130 Hercules	11th Air Force Elmendorf	SAR Para-rescue	20.8
60024 C-5 Galaxy	22nd Air Force Travis AFB	Transported Pavehawks	9
105 H-60 Pavehawk	11th Air Force Elmendorf	Medevac	8.4
107 H-60 Pavehawk	11th Air Force Elmendorf	Medevac	8.4
95829 HC-130 Hercules	56th Air Rescue Keflavik	Air-to-air refuel	16.2

American Military Total: 5 aircraft   62.8 hours

All aircraft

Total aircraft: 26
Total flying time: 515.9 hours

Typeset in Minion, a contemporary digital type family created by Adobe designer Robert Slimbach. Minion incorporates many calligraphic elements derived from Slimbach's hand-lettering. The initial drawings were inspired by the rich variety of old-style typefaces from the fifteenth through seventeenth centuries. Named after one of the type sizes used in the early days of type-founding, Minion means "a beloved servant," which reflects the type's useful and unobtrusive qualities.

Book design: Gordon Robertson
Maps: James Loates